BESTSELLING BOOK SERIES

Senior Dogs For Dummies

Cheat Sheet

Adjusting to Seniorhood

As your dog ages, his needs change. You can help your dog adjust in the following ways:

- **Re-thinking the food regimen:** Your vet can suggest ways to tailor your dog's diet to his advancing age.

- **Easing up on eating:** If your pooch is porking out, work with your vet to devise a diet that will return his physique to its formerly svelte state.

- **Banishing bad breath:** Sweeten your senior's breath by brushing his teeth regularly — and, if necessary, scheduling a dental cleaning with your vet.

- **Padding your pad:** A creaky-boned senior appreciates having several comfy dog beds or pads spread throughout the house to catch some zzzs in.

- **Ramping it up:** If your senior has trouble hopping in and out of your car, get him a ramp to ease his entrances and exits.

What's Up, Doc?

Taking your senior to the vet's office can be stressful — especially when your visit is to find out what's causing his problem. Many owners remember what they wanted to ask the vet just after they return from an appointment. You can ask your vet everything you need to know by taking this list of questions with you:

- What does the test determine?

- When will the results of the test come back?

- Does my dog really need this shot?

- How much does the treatment cost?

- Can I get this medicine at my local pharmacy?

- Can I get this medicine as a generic?

- How often do I give my senior this medicine?

- Should I give him this medicine with food?

- When should I see some improvement?

- What are the possible side effects of this medicine?

- Will this new medicine interfere with the medicine I'm already giving him?

- When should we come back for a re-check?

For Dummies: Bestselling Book Series for Beginners

Senior Dogs For Dummies®

Cheat Sheet

Who Ya Gonna Call?

Life's too short to spend precious time routing through your address book for the phone numbers of the important people in your senior dog's life (besides you). If you record those phone numbers right here, right now, you'll have all the info you need right at your fingertips.

Contact	Name	Phone Number
Veterinarian		
Emergency clinic		
House call veterinarian		
Veterinary specialist		
Groomer		
Trainer		
Doggy day care/pet sitter		
Kennel		

Your Senior Dog's Health Record

Use this chart to record all health information about your senior — it'll come in handy the next time you and he visit your vet.

Date	Reason for Visit	Diagnosis	Treatment	Bloodwork Results	Heartworm/ Lyme Test Given	Vaccines Given

For Dummies: Bestselling Book Series for Beginners

Senior Dogs

FOR

DUMMIES®

by Susan McCullough

WILEY

Wiley Publishing, Inc.

Senior Dogs For Dummies®

Published by
Wiley Publishing, Inc.
111 River St.
Hoboken, NJ 07030-5774
www.wiley.com

Copyright © 2004 by Wiley Publishing, Inc., Indianapolis, Indiana

Published by Wiley Publishing, Inc., Indianapolis, Indiana

Published simultaneously in Canada

For general information on our other products and services or to obtain technical support, please contact
our Customer Care Department within the U.S. at 800-762-2974, outside the U.S. at 317-572-3993, or fax
317-572-4002.

Wiley also publishes its books in a variety of electronic formats. Some content that appears in print may
not be available in electronic books.

Library of Congress Control Number: 2004103141

ISBN: 0-7645-5818-8

Manufactured in the United States of America

10 9 8 7 6 5 4 3 2 1

1B/RU/QW/QU/IN

WILEY

About the Author

Susan McCullough writes about all things dog for media outlets all over the United States. Her credits include *Family Circle, The Washington Post, Modern Maturity, AKC Family Dog, AKC Gazette, ASPCA Animal Watch,* Cornell University's *DogWatch, Animal Fair, PetLife, Healthy Pet, The Dog Daily,* and *Popular Dogs.* She's also the author of *Housetraining For Dummies* (Wiley, 2002) and *Your New Dog* (Capital Books, 2003).

Susan belongs to the Dog Writers Association of America (DWAA), Association of Pet Dog Trainers, and the American Society of Journalists and Authors. She's a two-time winner of the DWAA Maxwell award for excellence in writing about dogs and won the 2001 Eukanuba Canine Health Award for outstanding writing about canine health.

When she's not writing or hanging out with friends and family (both two-legged and four-legged), Susan counsels puzzled people on how to deal with the quandaries that inevitably arise when dogs join human households. She lives in Vienna, Virginia, with her husband, Stan Chappell; their daughter, Julie Chappell; and their Golden Retriever, Allie.

Dedication

To Molly, the dog of my soul,
Cory, the dog of my heart,
and
Allie, the dog of my life.

Author's Acknowledgments

This book is a labor of love not only on my part, but also on the parts of many other individuals. I want to thank them all, including

- Kathy Cox, acquisitions editor at Wiley, who asked me to take on this project.

- Alissa Schwipps, senior project editor, who not only accommodated my writing process but also improved the results of that process.

- Lynn Whittaker, my agent, who once again did the tough stuff so that I could be free to write.

- Ron Spikloser, VMD, who made sure that the manuscript contained the best available info for those who love older dogs.

- Susan Lennon, Brette Sember, Laura Rubin, Liz Palika, Lynn Whittaker, Alissa Schwipps, Carole Dickerson Kauffman, Michael and Kimberly Smith, and Ron Spikloser for generously sharing the stories of their wonderful "Senior Super Dogs."

- Edie Galpin of Golden Retriever Rescue, Education and Training, Inc., who not only shared her story of Senior Super Dog Zack but also provided crucial last-minute assistance.

- Last but never least: Stan Chappell, my husband, who listened patiently to my end-of-the-day monologues about senior dogs and book writing; Julie Chappell, my daughter, who kept her promise to cut me lots of slack during Final Deadline Week; and Allie McChappell, resident pooch, who learned to be a good office dog between the day I started writing Chapter 16 and the day I finished the manuscript. I love you guys!

Publisher's Acknowledgments

We're proud of this book; please send us your comments through our Dummies online registration form located at www.dummies.com/register/.

Some of the people who helped bring this book to market include the following:

Acquisitions, Editorial, and Media Development

Senior Project Editor: Alissa D. Schwipps

Acquisitions Editor: Kathy Cox

Copy Editor: Michelle Dzurny

Technical Editor: Ron Spikloser, VMD

Editorial Manager: Jennifer Ehrlich

Editorial Assistants: Courtney Allen, Melissa Bennett, Elizabeth Rea

Cover Photo: AGE Fotostock

Cartoons: Rich Tennant, www.the5thwave.com

Production

Project Coordinator: Adrienne Martinez

Layout and Graphics: Amanda Carter, Denny Hager, Michael Kruzil, Brent Savage, Julie Trippetti

Illustrations: Lisa S. Reed

Proofreaders: John Greenough, Andy Hollandbeck, Carl William Pierce, Dwight Ramsey, Brian Walls, TECHBOOKS Production Services

Indexer: TECHBOOKS Production Services

Special Help

Kristin DeMint, Josh Dials, and Laura Miller

Publishing and Editorial for Consumer Dummies

Diane Graves Steele, Vice President and Publisher, Consumer Dummies

Joyce Pepple, Acquisitions Director, Consumer Dummies

Kristin A. Cocks, Product Development Director, Consumer Dummies

Michael Spring, Vice President and Publisher, Travel

Brice Gosnell, Associate Publisher, Travel

Kelly Regan, Editorial Director, Travel

Publishing for Technology Dummies

Andy Cummings, Vice President and Publisher, Dummies Technology/General User

Composition Services

Gerry Fahey, Vice President of Production Services

Debbie Stailey, Director of Composition Services

Contents at a Glance

Table of Contents

Introduction

*L*ying at my feet, in a rare moment of repose, is Allie, my 1-year-old Golden Retriever. In the ten months since she's joined my family, I've had my hands full coping with her puppy hijinks, which have included shredding a paycheck, destroying a new carpet, and attempting to sip vintage wine from a crystal goblet.

I have a hard time imagining that Allie will ever grow older. Her uninhibited *joie-de-vivre* and never-ending mischief-making are totally at odds with the idea that her muzzle will go gray, she'll sleep most of the day, or she'll acquire the stately dignity that typifies the older dog's demeanor.

But I know better. I've watched other dogs, including two of my own, evolve from puppyhood to seniorhood, and I know that Allie will undergo the same process. But reaching seniorhood shouldn't mean that Allie must feel any less joy in living than she apparently feels now. Her golden years, and those of any other dog, can be happy, active, and interesting — if owners know how to take care of their dogs after they achieve senior status.

I've written *Senior Dogs For Dummies* to help dog owners make the most of this uniquely sweet time in their relationships with their canine companions.

About This Book

Senior Dogs For Dummies can help you deal with the health, behavioral challenges, and other unique situations that face the older dog and enable you to savor the joys that come with living with an aging canine. Whether you have a chronologically older dog whose appearance and energy make it hard to believe that he's a senior or an older canine who spends most of his time slumbering by the fire, this book can help you and your canine companion take pleasure in his golden years.

I've divided each part of this book into chapters and each chapter into sections. Each section contains information about some aspect of living with a senior dog, like:

✔ What to expect when your dog crosses the threshold from middle age to seniorhood

✔ Symptoms of illness that your older dog may show, and determining when those symptoms indicate an emergency (and when they don't)

✔ How to save money caring for your senior dog without compromising the quality of that care

✔ How to know when it's time to give your senior dog a last gift of love: ending life with dignity and without suffering

The great thing about this book is that you can find the answers to those questions and any others in any way you want. If you want to know everything about living with an older dog, you may want to begin reading here and continue to the end. But if you have a specific concern, such as why your older dog wets her bed or why she's taking longer to get up from that bed, feel free to skip the preliminaries. Instead, just scan the table of contents and, from there, head to the pages that tell you exactly what you want to know.

Conventions Used in This Book

To help you navigate through this book and any other *For Dummies* book, all books in this series contain certain conventions:

✔ *Italic* is used for emphasis and to highlight new words or terms.

✔ **Boldfaced** text is used to indicate the action part of numbered steps and the main items in bulleted lists.

✔ Monofont is used for Web addresses.

In addition to the conventions that apply in all *For Dummies* books, this book has some of its own.

As a journalist who specializes in dog-related topics, I've always been told that references to a dog should be gender-neutral unless the writer is talking about a specific dog. In other words, rules for writers known as stylebooks decree that unless you're discussing a specific dog, such as King or Queenie, any members of the canine species should be referred to as "it."

Some rules are made to be broken, and I believe this rule is one. Any dog, even when altered, is clearly male or female and deserves to be designated as such. Consequently, I refer to any dog with the pronouns *he, she, her, him, his, her,* and *hers.* I alternate between using male and female pronouns, so any of those pronouns apply to both genders unless I say otherwise. I also use the word *who,* not *that,* to refer to our canine companions.

In addition, I'm not big into euphemisms. For example, when I refer to a dog's bodily wastes, I do so in the same way most of us talk about those wastes in real life. In other words, dogs *poop* and *pee;* they do not *tinkle* or make *number one* or *number two.* Similarly, when I discuss the decision to mercifully end a dog's life, I don't call it *putting a dog to sleep.* The correct term is *euthanasia,* and I use that word in the chapters that deal with that difficult passage.

Finally, despite the need to acknowledge that the owner of an older dog may face the sadness of losing that dog relatively soon, I want this book to show that many aging canines accomplish the same feats that younger dogs do. So, throughout the book, you find anecdotes that describe the exploits of real-life senior wonder dogs. You can find these anecdotes featured in sidebars (the shaded boxes) with the heading Senior Super Dogs. Their inspiring stories remind us that plenty of talent and potential may still reside within the bosom and brain of your own aging canine companion.

What You're Not to Read

I've written this book so that you can find information easily and easily understand what you find. I'd love to believe that you plan to read and savor every word I've written, but I know that you may not have time to do that. That's why I've made it easy for you to identify stuff that, although interesting and certainly related to the topic at hand, isn't essential for you to know:

- **Text in sidebars:** The sidebars are shaded boxes that appear here and there throughout the book.

- **The stuff on the copyright page:** No, I'm not kidding. You can't find anything here to interest you unless, for some strange reason, you think it's cool to read legalese or ISBN numbers (how many of us even know what an ISBN number is anyway?).

Foolish Assumptions

Every book is written with a particular reader in mind, and this book is no exception. Here's what I assume about you:

- You've never been responsible for taking care of an older dog before now, but you want to do everything possible to make the most of your own pooch's approaching senior years, or . . .

✔ You've cared for a senior dog in your distant past but don't really remember what it was like and want to prepare for your current dog's golden years, or . . .

✔ Your senior dog has a serious health problem, and you need to know the causes, treatment, and prognosis for that condition, or . . .

✔ You want the most current information available about senior dogs presented in terms that you or any other layperson can understand.

How This Book Is Organized

If you read any part of *Senior Dogs For Dummies*, no matter how small, you can add to your knowledge of how to meet the special needs of the aging canine. The following sections describe how I've organized the book to help you make the most of your dog's golden years and deal with any challenges that come your way.

Part 1: Loving and Living with Your Senior

This part describes what to expect as your dog ages and how to deal with basic age-related changes. You discover that not every dog attains senior status at the same age, and you also figure out how to determine when your own dog is likely to reach seniorhood, if she's not there already. I also discuss the care and feeding of the healthy aging canine, how to help her fulfill her social needs and, of course, how to teach your old dog some new tricks.

Part 11: Knowing What to Expect

Unfortunately, growing older inevitably means that your dog loses some energy. But Part II shows that losing a little pep doesn't mean that your senior pooch can't continue to have good health. This section opens with an explanation of how you and your vet can help keep your aging friend in tip-top condition for as long as possible. Following that opener, I explain exactly what happens to your best friend's body as he ages and how you can help him cope with such changes.

Part III: Dealing with Diseases

No matter how much you do to keep your aging dog well — or any dog, for that matter — you inevitably face times when she gets sick. Part III helps you determine when your dog's health is starting to take a nosedive and describes the symptoms, treatments, and prognoses of the more common illnesses among older dogs. A separate chapter addresses the big "C": cancer, which strikes fear into the heart of any caring dog owner but which offers more reason for hope than that owner may think.

Part IV: Bidding a Fond Farewell

Alas, dogs are mortal and, in the natural order of things, their life spans are shorter than ours. That fact requires most owners to face up to a sad part of living with dogs: saying goodbye. Part IV can't help you feel any less sad about your canine companion's departure from life, but it does help you know what to expect during this last life stage and how to cope with the aftermath of your four-legged friend's death.

Part V: The Part of Tens

Here's where you find lists that describe unique aspects of living with and loving a senior dog. One list describes ten reasons for people to appreciate their older canine companions. The other list points out ten ways to keep your senior dog happier and healthier for a longer period of time.

Icons Used in This Book

To make this book easier to read and simpler to use, I include some icons that can help you find and fathom key ideas and information.

This icon calls attention to ideas or items that are especially helpful in understanding and caring for your older dog, or that can save you time or money.

This icon tells you that the information that follows is so important that you should read it more than once — if not commit it to memory — just to make sure that you keep it in mind as you care for your older dog.

This icon flags dangers to your dog's health or well-being.

Where to Go from Here

If you've never lived with an older dog before or if your current canine companion has just reached seniorhood and you've forgotten what this life stage is like, you may want to start reading at this book's beginning and continue through to the end. But if you need information on a specific issue, such as how to live with a deaf dog, keep your dog's health-care costs within reasonable bounds, or adjust your canine's cuisine to the requirements of his advancing age, you don't have to read the whole book. Just consult the table of contents and the index, where you can find the topic that tells you what you need to know.

Finally, this book is a guide and a reference manual, but it doesn't replace the hands-on, tailored-to-your-dog advice that vets, trainers, and behaviorists can give in-person. If the suggestions here don't work for you or your dog, or if you can't find an answer to a particular question in this book, don't hesitate to consult any of these professionals.

Part I
Loving and Living with Your Senior

The 5th Wave
By Rich Tennant

"When we got him several years ago he was a Golden Retriever. Now, he's more of a Golden Recliner."

In this part . . .

You'll celebrate the joys of having a senior dog, even as you realize that defining canine seniorhood isn't a simple proposition. You'll also discover new ways to keep your dog healthy, both physically and mentally.

Chapter 1

Defining Seniorhood: To Each His Own

As a product of the Baby Boom, I've become acutely aware of the fact that I am aging. I'm not a senior citizen yet, but I will be all too soon. In the meantime, though, I'm getting a lot of reminders that time stops for no one. The AARP solicitations that regularly reach my mailbox are proof enough that I'm no longer part of a youthful demographic.

Even though time hasn't stopped for me, I still try to make it appear that it's at least slowed down. I spend way too much money highlighting my hair in order to cover the gray. I take excessive pleasure in still being able to wear size-2 jeans (they have to be stretch jeans, though). I've long since replaced the astringent designed to defeat my youthful zits with a moisturizer that's supposed to combat the not-so-fine lines on my mid-life face. And I take defiant pride in my ability to identify at least a few of the rock bands my teenage daughter listens to while I chauffeur her to one place or another.

Despite my desire to tell Father Time to go take a hike for another few years, he isn't listening to me. Sooner rather than later, I'll probably break down and get that AARP card. And I'll certainly pay more attention to political debates about the future of Social Security and Medicare because I'll be eligible for those benefits. Whether I want to or not, I'll eventually pass all those milestones that mark a person's passage from mid-life into senior citizenhood.

I'm all too aware that seniorhood will soon be upon me, but Allie, my youthful Golden Retriever, won't have a clue as to when she'll become a senior dog. Dogs don't get AARP cards, Social Security checks, Medicare payments, senior citizen discounts, or other societal signals of impending dotage. Only my knowledge and intuition will tell me when Allie's getting old.

I'm not alone in wondering when my pooch officially becomes a senior. The fact is, canine seniorhood doesn't occur at any specific age. Most vets, nutritionists, and other experts agree that, on average, a dog becomes a senior when he turns 7 years old, but that designation is only an average. Your own unique dog may actually reach seniorhood before or after his seventh birthday — depending on a number of factors.

In this chapter, I give you the real deal on canine aging. Instead of assigning seniorhood to your dog at some predetermined age, you discover how to determine whether your pooch actually is an elder states-dog or still just a mid-life canine. I also give you some basic information on what aging entails for your dog — and for you, as his loving human companion — emphasizing how you can make your dog's senior years the best they can possibly be.

Defining Senior Dog Status

The time when a dog crosses the threshold from mid-life to seniorhood is highly individual. Your 9-year-old dog could be a senior, but the 9-year-old pooch who lives down the street may not be. The 5-year-old dog who used to gallop around your local dog park may now be a canine elder, while another 5-year-old pooch may be as active as a 5-year-old human child.

 A good way to estimate when your dog will become a senior is to find out what his life expectancy is. The longer a dog is expected to live, the later the onset of seniorhood will occur. In the following sections, I discuss factors that affect a dog's life expectancy.

A matter of breeding

Breed plays an important role in determining how long a dog is likely to live. Some breeds simply live longer than others. For example, the average Toy Poodle is likely to pass his 14th birthday before mortality catches up with him; by contrast, a Bernese Mountain Dog isn't likely to live much past the age of 7. Scientists aren't exactly sure why breeding affects longevity, but they have a few ideas.

Research indicates that *inbreeding* (breeding close relatives to each other) may be a factor that affects a breed's longevity. Some dog breeders advocate inbreeding as a way to boost the odds that a particular trait or characteristic is passed on to future generations. For example, when a breeder wants to ensure that puppies have ears that fold over rather than ears that point upward, he may breed two half-siblings who both have the ears he desires.

The trouble with inbreeding is that it may not only increase the likelihood that the puppies will have a positive characteristic, but it may also increase the odds that they'll have an undesirable characteristic. For instance, if the two half-siblings with pretty ears also both have a gene that makes them vulnerable to a certain kind of cancer, their puppies are almost guaranteed to have that same gene.

Related to the inbreeding factor is the practice among some breeders of using the same male dog to father puppies from many different females. If the breeder uses the same male dog over and over again, other males aren't used and their genetic characteristics disappear. Meanwhile, the male dog who's getting all the action may be passing negative characteristics along with the positive to his progeny. If those negative characteristics affect life expectancy, eventually the breed's overall life expectancy decreases.

That's why many caring, reputable breeders have become geneticists-on-the-fly in their efforts to produce the best possible purebred dogs. They're careful to match their dogs with other dogs who are most likely to produce the heartiest, strongest dogs with the longest possible life expectancies for that breed. These breeders are looking for more than points and titles on their dogs; they're looking to better the breed.

Still, breeds vary widely in their life expectancies. Table 1-1 lists the 20 breeds that had the highest total number of American Kennel Club (AKC) registrations in 2002 and their average life spans.

Table 1-1	Breeds and Longevity
Breed	**Average Life Span (Years)**
Labrador Retrievers	11
Golden Retrievers	12
German Shepherds	11
Beagles	13

(continued)

Table 1-1 *(continued)*

Breed	Average Life Span (Years)
Dachshunds	12
Yorkshire Terriers	14
Boxers	10
Chihuahuas	15
Shih Tzu	13
Miniature Schnauzers	13
Pomeranians	14
Rottweilers	9
Pugs	13
Cocker Spaniels	12
Shetland Sheepdogs	13
Boston Terriers	12
Bulldogs	9
Miniature Pinschers	14
Maltese	13

If you want to know the average life expectancy of a breed that's not listed in Table 1-1, or if you want to know a lot more about any breed, check out *Choosing a Dog For Dummies* by Chris Walkowicz (Wiley). Walkowicz lists every one of the 160-plus breeds recognized by the AKC and their estimated life expectancies in that book.

Determining the life expectancy of a mixed-breed dog is a little trickier than determining the life expectancy of a purebred dog. On the one hand, a mixed-breed dog's life expectancy is affected by the life expectancies of each breed he's made up of — assuming you can figure out what those breeds are. On the other hand, a dog's unique mix means a unique gene pool, and the more unique the gene pool, the less chance the undesirable trait has of affecting the dog. And if you're looking for a precise figure for your particular dog's breed mix, research isn't a whole lot of help. If you're willing to take an average, though, a mixed-breed dog's life expectancy is about 13 years.

Size does matter

A good look at Table 1-1 reveals not only that breeding affects canine longevity but that size does, too. More specifically, smaller pooches typically live longer than larger dogs.

One theory why little guys live longer than big dogs is that small dogs' bodies don't need to work as hard as those of canine behemoths. Another theory is that large dogs are probably more prone to being overweight — and research shows that packing on too many pounds is likely to shorten a dog's life expectancy significantly. In Chapter 2, I suggest ways to pare some pounds off a portly pooch.

Individual factors

Understanding that size and breed affect a dog's average life expectancy is important, but other factors come into play, too. Many of those factors relate to the dog's overall health and the care that her people give her. Here are examples of some other factors that affect your dog's life expectancy:

- **Girth:** Research shows that a svelte dog is likely to live considerably longer than a portly pooch. Cutting calories and eating nutritious foods can help Fido slim down her physique, and exercise can get that physique into tip-top shape. In Chapter 2, I tell you how to put your pudgy pooch on a healthy reduced-fat diet, and in Chapter 3, I list exercises that keep your senior fit but do not push her beyond her endurance.

- **Nutrition:** "You are what you eat" applies to dogs as much as it does to people. If your dog's daily fare contains the nutrients she needs, delivered through high-quality food, she stands a better chance of living a long life than a dog whose diet consists of her people's dining leftovers. To find out what senior dogs need for optimum nutrition, flip to Chapter 2.

- **Dental health:** A dog whose canines get good care stands a better chance of living a long life than a dog whose choppers are in poor condition. To find out how to keep your dog's teeth healthy (and to keep her from having hoochy breath), check out Chapter 5.

- **Owner diligence:** An owner who makes sure her dog gets all the necessary checkups, consults a vet at the first sign of trouble, and gives her four-legged friend the best possible overall care is likely to have her dog with her longer than a laissez-faire owner. In Chapter 5, I outline ways that owners can keep their senior dogs in good health for as long as possible.

Is your dog a senior?

Are you still stumped as to whether your canine companion is an elder states-dog, a doggy dowager, or a middle-aged canine? The answers to these questions can help you determine whether your own very special dog is beyond her prime:

- ✔ **Has she slowed down?** Just like older people, older dogs don't move as fast as they did when they were younger. When your four-legged friend hits seniorhood, she's likely to take more time going up and down the stairs, getting up from a nap, and lying down.

- ✔ **Has she gotten grayer?** Gray hair, especially around the face and muzzle, can be a sign of seniorhood and so is a thinner, drier coat, compared to the one she sported in her youth.

- ✔ **Does she have accidents?** Some aging dogs, especially older spayed females, begin developing bathroom issues. If your one-time potty prodigy starts making puddles on the floor, she may have an old-age bladder or may be developing a condition called canine *cognitive dysfunction syndrome (CDS)*, which is common among senior dogs. In Chapters 6, 8, and 10, I address why a senior may have potty problems and how to solve them.

- ✔ **Does she get tired more quickly?** If your canine companion used to retrieve a Frisbee 20-some times without getting winded but now wants to quit after just 10 retrieves, she's probably approaching seniorhood, if she's not already there.

- ✔ **Is she getting lumpy?** Many older dogs develop soft, spongy lumps on their bodies, particularly on their trunks. These lumps usually aren't life threatening; I explain why in Chapters 9 and 10.

- ✔ **Does she seem to ignore you when you call her?** If so, she's probably not being rebellious; she may have lost some of her hearing, which is a common sign of aging. Go to Chapter 7 to find out why your senior dog may be going deaf and what you can do to help her.

- ✔ **Does she get lost in her own backyard?** If your four-legged friend can't seem to find her way back to the house after spending time in your backyard, she may be losing her vision or developing CDS. Flip to Chapters 7, 9, and 10 to find out why such dogs need to see their vets.

- ✔ **Does she get upset more easily than she used to?** Thunderstorms and other loud noises that never bothered her before may now cause her to whine, tremble, or otherwise show apprehension. Such behavioral changes occur quite often in senior pooches. For more info, see Chapter 4.

If you answered yes to most of these questions, your beloved pooch may well be entering the golden years of doggy seniorhood.

Although each question in this quiz describes a sign of seniorhood, it also depicts symptoms of illness. Don't automatically attribute any of these changes to old age. Play it safe and have your vet examine your dog.

Understanding the Effects of Aging on Your Senior Dog

The outward signs of canine aging are often readily apparent to the reasonably observant dog owner. But plenty is going on inside your senior as well.

The senior canine body

A lifetime of use eventually deteriorates a dog's body by the time he reaches seniorhood, but this deterioration isn't necessarily drastic. Just like with older people, older dogs' bodies simply don't function as efficiently as they did when they were younger. And your dog's loss of efficiency shows up in multiple ways:

- ✔ **Eyes:** Your dog's eyes change in several ways as he ages. He may experience nearsightedness and a diminished ability to see in either darkness or bright light. The lens of his eye may also become cloudy, although such cloudiness doesn't impede vision. However, several age-related conditions such as glaucoma, cataracts, and dry eye do affect a dog's ability to see (go to Chapter 10 to find out about common canine eye ailments and how they're treated, and see Chapter 7 to find out how you can help your dog deal with his loss of eyesight).

- ✔ **Ears:** As your dog acquires senior status, his hearing loses some of its edge. Some hearing loss is normal, but if your dog's ears also stink and sport a goopy discharge, he probably has an ear infection (in Chapter 7, I tell you how to deal with ear infections and how you can help your dog cope with his loss of hearing).

- ✔ **Mobility:** As dogs get older, their bones become more fragile, their cartilage becomes worn, and their muscles lose mass, all of which can make movement difficult or painful. The nerves, brain, and spinal column control a dog's movements, so deterioration of any or all of these tissues can mean diminished mobility. In Chapter 10, I discuss common conditions that affect senior mobility, and in Chapter 8, I describe the many adjustments you can make to offset your pooch's limited loco-motion. To find out how exercise can help keep your dog limber longer, see Chapter 3.

✔ **Metabolism:** An older dog's digestive system doesn't process food as efficiently as it used to, and the result can be extra inches on your senior's waistline. I discuss two common senior metabolic diseases, diabetes and Cushing's Disease, in Chapter 10. In Chapter 2, I describe how a dog's body utilizes various food sources, explain why sleek seniors do better than chubby ones, and tell you how you can slim down your aging canine companion.

✔ **Incontinence:** If your senior's ability to hold his water has diminished, you may wonder if he needs some remedial house-training. An older dog's bathroom lapses often have nothing to do with housetraining but instead may result from internal processes that have gone awry. For ideas on how to cope with a new influx of pooch potty accidents, turn to Chapter 6.

The senior canine mind

Just like with an older person, an older dog's ability to learn and retain information is likely to diminish as he progresses through seniorhood. This deterioration can result in all kinds of behavioral changes. For instance, a previously confident dog may become anxious, and a housetraining prodigy may start having accidents. One common reason for such changes is canine *cognitive dysfunction syndrome (CDS),* a canine version of human Alzheimer's Disease.

As an owner, you may need strategies so you can help your dog. Continued training and socialization can help keep your senior's mind sharper longer. Chapter 10 details the treatment and progno-sis for CDS.

The senior canine spirit

Being youthful is about much more than looks — it's also about attitude. The people who negotiate seniorhood best are the ones who remain interested in the world around them, appreciate their loved ones, interact with other individuals, want to have new expe-riences, and retain a zest for learning. Human beings act on their own to make sure their golden years are truly golden; however, dogs need help to make the most of seniorhood.

As an owner, you're responsible for keeping your dog engaged in the world around him. From teaching him new tricks to continuing social studies, you have plenty of ways to feed your senior dog's spirit and help him remain mentally active. For suggestions on how to deal with situations that may be tricky for senior dogs, such as meeting new people, meeting new dogs, coping with crankiness, and dealing with phobias, go to Chapter 4.

Maintaining Your Dog's Quality of Life

Once your dog enters seniorhood, expect her to become somewhat high-maintenance, as compared to her relatively untroubled youth and young adulthood. She needs some extra time, care, and consideration — but not necessarily a lot more. In any case, making an extra effort pays off big time because living with your dog during her seniorhood will produce some of the sweetest moments you'll ever experience.

Creating a senior-friendly environment

Have you ever noticed how all those ads for "active adult communities" mention that the houses are often on one floor, or, at the very least, that the master bedroom is on the main floor? Builders and architects have a good reason for creating such houses: They know that older people often have trouble climbing stairs as they age. These communities are marketed to active adults, but the houses are built to accommodate those adults when they're no longer able to be so active.

Senior dogs need to be accommodated, too. You don't have to move to a one-floor house, but you should look for ways to adjust your décor to meet the needs of your four-legged friend. For example, put a small set of steps near your bed, sofa, or any other elevated place that your senior now finds difficult to reach. You can also place doggy beds or cushions in several rooms of the house so your four-legged friend always has a soft spot to snuggle. I discuss such decorating adjustments in Chapters 7 and 8.

Of course, any dog's environment extends beyond the physical configuration of your home. The world in which your dog interacts may present new challenges for her. Some of those challenges take the form of real change, such as the addition of a new baby or pet to the family — and just like with older people, older pooches often have more trouble adjusting to change than younger ones do. Other challenges result from your dog's altered reactions to unchanged events: For example, she may suddenly become very afraid of thunderstorms. I explain in Chapter 4 how giving your dog a continuing education in social studies (and no, I'm not talking history here) can help her address challenges with poise and aplomb. She can even discover the satisfaction that results when an old dog learns new tricks.

Adjusting diet and exercise

Earlier in this chapter, I mention that even though I'm middle-aged, I can still fit into size-2 jeans. Well, I'm here to tell you that I haven't maintained my still-petite size without some effort. To avoid, or at least forestall, middle-age spread, I made changes to what I eat and when I get myself moving. Put simply, I eat less and exercise more.

Your senior or pre-senior dog probably requires similar adjustments to her diet and exercise. Like pre-senior people, mature pooches' metabolisms slow down a bit as they age, with predictable results: Their width is likely to expand. The resulting plumpness isn't pleasing; in fact, it can shorten your senior's life.

Conversely, keeping your dog trim can extend her life. A study conducted by Nestle Purina indicates that cutting a dog's daily food ration by 25 percent could extend the dog's life by more than 20 percent. In other words, giving your 10-year-old dog ¾ of a cup of food rather than a full cup at each meal could add at least two years to her life span.

If your objective is to prolong your time with your senior (and I assume it is, or you wouldn't be reading this book), adjust your dog's diet and exercise regimen. Both adjustments are easier said than done, though. Cutting back your dog's food intake involves not only adjusting quantity but also quality. Depending on the health issues she has, your senior may need to have a somewhat different diet than when she was younger (Chapter 2 describes dietary options for your unique older dog).

And just like people, seniors' exercise regimens need adjusting. My brother in his 50s can no longer run the marathons that he completed in his youth, so he's supplemented running with weight training to keep healthy. Similarly, you probably should restrain your senior from leaping up to catch a Frisbee; instead, show her the pleasures of swimming or brisk walking. In Chapter 3, I describe a number of senior-friendly exercises for your dog and tell you how to alleviate pain if she overexerts herself despite your efforts to moderate her workouts.

Keeping your senior dog healthy

No matter how self-sufficient and knowledgeable you are, you can't maintain your senior dog's health all by yourself. You need a partner who has the know-how needed to help you monitor your senior's health and, whenever possible, to catch any minor health problems before they become major.

That partner, of course, is your vet. In Chapter 5, I tell you how to work with your vet to optimize your senior's health and stay on top of any health issues or chronic conditions that your dog has. I also explain why regular checkups are as important for your dog as they are for you, and why once he reaches seniorhood, your dog needs those checkups more often than before.

Of course, you can do a lot at home to maintain your senior's health and good looks. To find out how to brush your dog's coat and teeth, give him a pedicure, and perform other grooming and health-maintenance tasks, go to — yes, you guessed it — Chapter 5.

Exploring treatment options

Sooner or later, your senior probably will develop some sort of illness or health issue. Even if she's never been sick a day in her life, the law of averages — not to mention a lifetime of wear and tear on her body — will almost certainly take its toll as she becomes an elder states-dog. Being an elder has a unique set of health issues because many diseases and conditions tend to strike senior dogs more often than younger ones.

Chapter 10 lists common senior-specific maladies and outlines the symptoms, diagnoses, treatments, prognoses, and prevention options (when possible) for each. You'll probably notice, though, that I didn't include one very common condition in that list: cancer. That's because I devote all of Chapter 11 to explaining why canine cancer is on the rise, describing some of the many forms cancer can take, and explaining what the treatments and prognoses are for each type. You'll also find out how clinical trials can offer hope to the canine cancer patient and her family if all other treatments aren't working.

Often, the key to successfully treating canine cancer and other senior doggy illnesses is to catch them early. However, because your vet sees your senior only a few times a year, he can't always detect the signs of trouble early. So that makes you the first line of defense for your dog's health. You're in the best possible position to know when something's amiss — if you know what to look for.

Senior Super Dogs: A senior dog hall of fame

When you see all those canine athletic prodigies on Animal Planet or heroic dogs performing remarkable feats, don't think that they're all young Turks or that youth is a prerequisite for canine notoriety and achievement. Plenty of pooches have captured the world's fancy during their seniorhoods. Here are just a few:

Pal: The original Lassie, Pal was a rescued Collie whom Hollywood animal trainer Rudd Weatherwax rehabilitated and trained to star in the Lassie movies of the 1930s and 1940s. When the movie gravy train ended, though, Pal didn't stop working. Television picked up the Lassie phenomenon in the early 1950s — and Pal starred in the pilot episode at the ripe old age of 14.

Moose: This Jack Russell Terrier portrayed Eddie, the cantankerous canine on TV's *Frasier*, well into seniorhood. Moose's other roles included the older Skip in the movie version of Willie Morris's book *My Dog Skip* (Eddie's son, Enzo, portrayed Skip in his prime). Moose is also credited with an autobiography, *My Life as a Dog* (HarperEntertainment, 2000), which was published when he was 9 years old.

Spot: Known more formally as Spot Fetcher Bush, this Springer Spaniel was a favorite companion of President George W. Bush. She's also the only dog to live in the White House during two administrations (she was born to the first President Bush's Springer, Milly, during his administration). Spot died in February 2004 when she was 14.

Bluey: An Australian cattle dog who reportedly worked Australian sheep flocks for more than 20 years, Bluey is believed to hold the all-time record for canine longevity. He died in 1939 at the age of 29 years, 5 months.

Missy: This mixed-breed dog was so beloved by her human dad, John Sperling, that he invested millions of dollars to determine whether she could be cloned. As word spread of his effort, dubbed the *Missyplicity Project*, other pet owners wanted to see whether their animals could be cloned as well. Those demands helped generate a company, Genetic Savings and Clone, which continues to research ways to clone beloved pets. Missy died in 2002 at the age of 15 before she could be cloned successfully. However, her DNA resides in the company's gene bank for possible cloning in the future.

Owney: In 1888, this mixed-breed dog was found abandoned outside a post office in Albany, New York. The postal workers took him in, warmed him up, and adopted him as an unofficial mascot. For the next nine years, Owney traveled wherever postal workers traveled. He died in 1897. Today his stuffed body is on display at the National Postal Museum in Washington, D.C.

Patsy Ann: Without fail, this deaf Bull Terrier greeted any ship that came into the port of Juneau, Alaska, during the 1930s. Between ship-greeting duties and visits to the wharf, she visited local businesses to receive the greetings of proprietors and score as many treats as possible. In 1934, the mayor named Patsy Ann the "Official

Greeter of Juneau." She died in 1942 at the age of 12. Fifty years later, the city commissioned a statue of Patsy Ann, which now greets Juneau visitors just as the real Patsy Ann did 60 years ago.

Strongheart: Before Lassie, Rin-Tin-Tin, Benji, and Air Bud, there was Strongheart — the first true canine movie star. Born in 1917, this imposing German Shepherd made his first movie, *The Silent Call,* in 1921 and continued to work well into his seniorhood. He died in 1929. The classic treatise on the human-animal bond, J. Allen Boone's *Kinship with all Life,* devotes many pages to describing writer and film producer Boone's friendship with Strongheart when the dog lived with Boone temporarily.

Rin-Tin-Tin: Although Strongheart was the first dog to star in the movies, Rin-Tin-Tin probably is the most famous. Rin-Tin-Tin was found as a puppy in 1918 as one of the few survivors of the destruction of a German dog kennel during World War I. His soldier-owner, who'd brought him to the United States from Germany, persistently tried to land him film roles and finally succeeded when Warner Brothers cast him in *Man From Hell's River.* The hit film gave the nearly bankrupt studio a much-needed financial boost. Rin-Tin-Tin's film career continued until his death in 1932 at the age of 13. A fifth-generation descendant starred in a television show, *The Adventures of Rin-Tin-Tin,* which ran for several seasons in the 1950s.

Man Ray: This Weimaraner was the first model for the world-famous photographs of his breed taken by photographer William Wegman. Man Ray died of cancer in 1992 when he was 11 years old. A few months after his death, the *Village Voice,* an alternative newspaper published in New York City, named Man Ray its "Man of the Year."

I list the symptoms that signal a possible health problem for your senior in Chapter 9. And to forestall any panic on your part, I group the symptoms into three categories: those symptoms that require an immediate trip to the vet, those that can wait until morning before calling your vet, and those that may not need a vet's attention at all.

Having this knowledge not only reduces stress for your dog, but it also saves you beaucoup bucks. Once your dog hits seniorhood, you'll probably need to spend more money on her care than when she was younger, so every little bit of savings helps. However, savvy dog owners know all kinds of tricks for getting the most out of their veterinary care dollars — and not necessarily by purchasing health insurance for their senior pets (in many instances, the dogs' ages preclude such purchases). To find tips on how to maximize your veterinary care dollars, see Chapter 12.

Letting go at the right time

The hardest part of loving and living with a dog is that, almost always, he dies before you do. The second-hardest part may be deciding when your beloved dog's death should occur.

There's no simple answer when you're trying to decide whether the time is right to give your senior dog a final gift of peace and freedom from pain. Your answer mainly depends on an assessment of your dog's condition but also on your condition — emotional, financial, and otherwise.

Still, you can do a lot to prepare for the time when your dog must leave you. In Chapter 13, I describe some of the decisions you need to make as your dog enters the evening of his life. Chief among those dilemmas is deciding when to end aggressive treatment for your senior in favor of simply keeping him comfortable. In Chapter 13, I also offer you some points to ponder while you make that decision.

While you keep your senior comfortable, you and your family can prepare for what's ahead. Part of that preparation involves dealing with the logistics of euthanizing a pet: when to book an appointment, when and how to pay the vet, and what to do with your dog's body afterward. In Chapter 13, I outline your options.

Letting go can be somewhat easier, and certainly less stressful, when you have some idea of how to determine the right time for euthanasia. Deciding when to euthanize your senior is as individual as you are. When you do decide to send your dog on that final journey, though, both you and he can approach the departure with less fear if you know what's going to happen. Chapter 14 describes what usually occurs when a dog is euthanized.

Giving your dog a compassionate final gift may be the right thing — but those who are left behind feel really lousy. Losing your dog may trigger a flood of grief as intense as any you've experienced previously. In Chapter 15, I offer ideas to help you and your family — humans and non-humans alike — work through your grief and come to terms with your loss.

Appreciating doggy seniorhood

My attention to dealing with the end of your senior's life may lead you to think that your dog's seniorhood is a time of sadness. Usually, though, that's not the case. A senior dog offers his people special joys that really don't occur at any other time in your lives together. In Chapter 16, I outline ten reasons to appreciate your senior (for example, he's already housetrained and has good manners), and Chapter 17 reminds you how to keep your older dog happy and healthy for as long as possible. Throughout this book, I emphasize what senior dogs can teach us in our portraits of "Senior Super Dogs" — starting with the ones I list in the "Senior Super Dogs: A senior dog hall of fame" sidebar in this chapter.

Chapter 2

Feeding for Health and Fitness

Not all that long ago, little girls were told that one way to enchant a man was to be a good cook. "The way to a man's heart is through his stomach" was a refrain that many Baby Boomer women heard countless times while growing up.

Of course, men aren't the only individuals who are suckers for good food. Women like having great meals prepared for them, too. And dogs also like good food, maybe even more than people do.

But for dogs, great grub means more than good nutrition or a tasty meal; doggy grub affects the dog's learning curve. Today's dog trainers recommend that dog owners offer tasty treats to motivate their dogs to respond to basic commands. The treat spurs the dog to learn what's expected of him. Clearly, the way to the canine heart and mind is via the tummy.

Reaching seniorhood probably won't alter your healthy dog's interest in food. However, the ingredients in that food may need to change somewhat when your dog achieves senior status. In this chapter, you find out about the nutritional needs of senior dogs and how their diet may affect or even stave off the many age-related problems dogs often face. I also compare home-prepared with store-bought chow.

Do Seniors Need Special Food?

No. And yes. But before you start thinking that I'm a timid fore-caster who hedges her bets, let me explain what I mean. Like any other dog, the aging canine needs four basic nutrients:

- **Proteins:** Proteins help transform food into energy. They're present in meats, grains, and vegetables, but meat proteins are easier to digest than those proteins from veggies and grains. The amount of protein a dog needs depends on her size and activity level: A Pug who's a couch potato needs less protein than a Doberman who trains for search-and-rescue work.

- **Carbohydrates:** Carbohydrates, which come from plants, are another energy source. Common sources of carbohydrates are wheat, rice, corn, and certain beans, such as soybeans. Less common sources include sweet potatoes and regular potatoes. However, proponents of feeding raw food to dogs (which is discussed later in this chapter) say that dogs don't need carbs at all and that they can cause digestive difficulties and food allergies.

- **Fats:** Fats keep a dog's hair and skin healthy, stabilize her body temperature, and encourage healthy digestion.

- **Vitamins and minerals:** Vitamins and minerals enable a dog's body to process the protein, carbs, and fats. They also help keep the dog's immune system healthy, maintain coat quality, and prevent many canine health problems ranging from uri-nary tract infections to anemia.

You find a senior-friendly level of these nutrients in most *premium* (in other words, not generic grocery-store stuff) dog foods. That's why most experts, no matter what their dietary philosophies are, believe that senior pooches can eat the same sorts of food as younger pooches. But you may need to change Fidette's food if she develops health problems. Certain unhealthy symptoms may respond to dietary adjustments, such as reducing the protein level and upping the carbohydrate levels in a dog's daily ration. Among the many canine health issues that can prompt dietary changes are

- **Aging organs:** Some diets can help slow down the aging of vital organs. For example, a diet that's relatively low in pro-tein, sodium, and phosphorus can ease the strain on a senior dog's heart and kidneys.

- **Cancer:** Researchers are making progress in their efforts to develop dog foods that slow down tumor growth and stimu-late the canine cancer patient's often-depressed appetite.

✔ **Dental disease:** Problems with the teeth and gums are very common among older dogs. One pet-food company, Hills, formulated a dry food called Prescription T/D that's designed to clean the teeth while the dog eats; however, it's available only from your vet. Another company, Iams, has a component for daily dental care in its products that's designed to reduce tartar buildup. You can find these products in most pet superstores.

Flip ahead to Chapters 11 and 12 for descriptions of health conditions that may cause more problems for older dogs than for younger ones.

If your senior develops a condition linked to her age, be sure to ask your vet whether you need to adjust her diet. He may suggest that you tailor your dog's diet by serving her foods potentially more suitable to the aging dog, such as products including antioxidants to strengthen the immune system, fatty acids to improve skin and coat quality, and fiber to prevent constipation and reduce obesity. Your vet also may recommend that you give your dog supplements to address a variety of other conditions. You can buy supplements from your vet, pet-supply stores, and sometimes your local pharmacy — but don't purchase any before consulting your vet first.

Deciding What's for Dinner

For owners, tailoring a dog's diet to address age-related needs or health issues is pretty easy. You have three ways to feed your senior dog: Serve store-bought food, cook the food yourself, or serve raw food.

If you change your senior's daily fare, do it gradually. Sudden switches can upset his stomach, resulting in diarrhea or vomiting. Mix progressively larger amounts of the new food with the old food over several days, until you're feeding the new food exclusively.

Store-bought and ready to go

People generally feed their dogs food bought from a retail outlet because they believe that pet-food companies make a better product than they could, or because commercial food is far more convenient than personally making the food. But for whatever reason an owner buys dog food from a store, she has many products to choose from. Usually, these products fall into one of three categories:

✔ **Dry food:** Also known as *kibble,* dry food consists of bite-sized baked pellets derived from grains and meats, with vitamins and other supplements added. A dry food meal is a snap to fix: Just rip open the bag, pour some kibble into your dog's dish, and let him have at it. Premium dry food also offers other advantages to the owner: It's usually nutritionally complete (in other words, you don't have to feed your dog anything else); produces easy-to-pick-up stools; helps clean the teeth; lasts longer than any other type of dog food; costs less than other types of food; and needs no refrigeration. However, a total-kibble diet may carry one big downer, at least from your dog's point of view: It may be boring.

Running warm water over dry kibble makes flavorful, aromatic gravy that may entice a bored canine gourmand. A turn in the microwave and adding a little garlic can also pique your pooch's interest.

✔ **Canned food:** Dogs usually love getting juicy meals from a can. However, canned foods carry several disadvantages: They're more expensive than dry food, they don't deliver as much nutrition as an equal amount of kibble, they're too soft to remove tartar from the teeth, and their shelf life is shorter. Also, dogs who eat canned food have bigger, wetter, harder-to-scoop stools than dogs who are on all-kibble diets.

✔ **Semi-moist food:** These foods may look like hamburger patties or come in a tube. Either way, semi-moist foods aren't as moist as canned foods but aren't as dry as kibble. When broken up and crumbled, semi-moist foods make delicious treats. Of course, such food also makes a complete meal. However, semi-moist foods may produce looser-than-normal stools; this effect, along with the preservatives included in such products, causes many vets to view them with disfavor.

The good news here is that you don't have to choose among these foods; you can feed all three types of commercial food to your dog in order to derive all the advantages of each and avoid at least some of their disadvantages. For example, your dog's regular meals could consist mainly of kibble but also include a little bit of canned food to add some flavor. Semi-moist food often makes wonderful treats, especially for training.

But no matter which food you choose, don't choose all by yourself. Your dog and your vet can provide valuable information as you decide what type of store-bought food to feed your Fido. For example, your vet has access to food that's specially designed to deal with specific conditions, such as food allergies, urinary tract difficulties, and a wide range of other health conditions. And your dog will provide valuable feedback regarding any food you choose: He'll scarf it down, pick at it, or completely ignore it.

WARNING!

A dog who suddenly turns up his nose at food he used to love may be seriously ill. If your four-legged friend goes on a hunger strike for more than a day or two, he needs to see a vet pronto.

After you choose your commercial food, you need to determine whether that choice benefits your pooch. Here's what to look for:

- ✔ **No runny stools:** A good food that's good for your senior canine is a product that he can digest easily — and the hallmark of easy digestion is reasonably compact poop. Stools that make you hold your nose and are too runny to clean up easily may signal that your dog is having trouble digesting the nutrients in his regimen. Switching to a different brand of food may solve the problem.

- ✔ **No dandruff:** Dry, flaky skin often means that a dog's food lacks fatty acids. Try switching to a food that has more fat or ask your vet whether your dog needs a fatty acid supplement.

- ✔ **No gas attacks:** If your dog frequently passes gas, his food may have too many carbohydrates. A higher protein/lower carbohydrate regimen may be in order.

- ✔ **No expanding waistline:** A dog food with too many calories and too much fat for your dog's metabolism probably will add some extra pounds to his physique. Look for a food that has more protein and less fat than what you're currently serving.

Home-cooked and mmm-mmm good

Although many dog owners head to the store to get their dog's grub, plenty of other owners fix their dog's meals from scratch. These do-it-yourselfers may want the complete control over their dog's food regimens that home-prepared meals offer. Such control is helpful if your dog has food allergies, and home-cooked meals often meet the needs of dogs with picky palates. In addition, do-it-yourself (DIY) cuisine may cost less than some commercial dog foods do.

However, the DIY option carries distinct disadvantages. Fixing Fido's meals yourself can be time-consuming and inconvenient, especially if Fido accompanies you on a road trip. Boarding him in a kennel is equally problematic. Most kennels don't duplicate your efforts; at best, you are able to make and send enough food to last the entire time that your dog is boarding.

But the biggest disadvantage to DIY feeding is that preparing a nutritionally balanced regimen for your senior dog can be quite complicated. Dog food, like human food, needs to contain adequate amounts of all nutrients — protein, carbohydrates, fats, vitamins, and minerals — to keep your dog in peak condition. That's especially true of senior dogs, who need the most nutritious food possible in order to offset age-related slowdowns of their immune systems and other bodily processes. Creating such food from scratch can be a real challenge, even if you get help from an expert such as a veterinarian or a veterinary nutritionist (which, incidentally, is a very good idea).

If you need more advice to get you started on cooking your dog's meals, check out *Dog Health and Nutrition For Dummies* by M. Christine Zink, D.V.M., Ph.D., (Wiley).

Eating in the raw and wild

A third feeding option either comes from a manufacturer or from your own kitchen: feeding your dog uncooked food. But before you choose this route, it's important to understand that going raw — what some people call a biologically appropriate-raw-food (BARF) diet — has equally passionate supporters and opponents.

Those who feed BARF to their dogs feel that a regimen based on uncooked meats, vegetables, and bones is not only the closest equivalent to what animals eat in the wild, but also lets pets live longer, healthier lives. Cleaner teeth, glossier coats, infection-free ears, and an end to food allergies are just some of the results that BARF proponents say raw feeding gives to pets.

However, many vets, not to mention pet-food companies, take a different view. They're concerned that raw bones can cause internal injuries or choking, and that any raw food heightens the risk of salmonella and other bacterial poisoning (just like in people). Some people also find that feeding uncooked food causes dogs to develop chronic vomiting and diarrhea.

Anti-BARFers also note that preparing a raw food regimen for a dog is time-consuming and inconvenient. However, some enterprising companies have begun to counter that contention by selling pre-made raw food. Two such companies are Aunt Jeni's Natural Pet Food (www.auntjeni.com) and Bravo (www.bravofood.com). Both companies, among others, sell prepackaged raw food in tubs of various sizes through selected commercial outlets, by mail, or through online order. Depending on your dog's current regimen and the product you switch to, these pre-made raw foods may cost the same or even less than what you're currently paying for more traditional Fido fare.

If you want to feed BARF to your senior dog, talk to other people who feed this diet to their pooches and do plenty of research beforehand. A good place to start is Wendy Volhard and Gerry Brown's *Holistic Guide to a Healthy Dog,* 2nd Edition (Howell Book House). Another option is Dr. Ian Billinghurst's *Give Your Dog a Bone,* a self-published book sold from the author's Web site (www. drianbillinghurst.com).

Come and Get It! Enjoying Mealtime

No matter what your dog's dining preferences are, or whether she's skinny or not (I discuss both topics later in this chapter), some parts of the mealtime experience should be consistent for all senior dogs. Here are some points to keep in mind:

- ✔ **Dish it out.** The best dishes with which to feed your senior are healthy for her and convenient for you. Stainless steel is dishwasher-safe and poses no threat to your dog's health. Ceramic dishes are iffy: They're microwave-safe and dishwasher-safe, but imported dishes may contain lead; for that reason, it's best to stick with American-made dishes. Plastic is a no-no, because it causes some dogs to lose their nose pigment or have discolored chins. No matter what kind of dishes you use, make sure that they're clean and sparkling every time you serve food to your dog.

- ✔ **Stay on the floor.** For a long time, experts thought that raising a food bowl off the floor would make dining more comfortable for arthritic senior dogs and giant breeds such as Great Danes. However, researchers have found that a raised food bowl increases a dog's chances of being felled by a deadly condition known as *bloat,* a gassy swelling of the abdomen (find out more about bloat in Chapter 10). For that reason, dishes should stay on the floor when your dog eats.

- ✔ **Spread out the servings.** Although it's possible to feed a dog only once a day, most dogs do better with two daily meals. A morning meal can help a dog feel more content if she's alone during the day; an evening meal may help her sleep better at night (don't you sleep better with a nice, full tummy?). Just divide your dog's regular meal in half, feeding her one half in the morning and the other half in the evening.

- ✔ **Abolish anxiety.** Dogs who dine while stressed don't get as much nutritional value out of their food and may eat less of it than their more relaxed compatriots do. Think about it: When you're nervous or upset, don't you have trouble eating? Can you even eat at all? Your dog is no different. Common causes of canine-dining anxiety include younger dogs who go after the older dog's grub, loudly blaring TVs, the presence of people (especially noisy or inquisitive children), or loneliness for people. If you know that these or other elements in your dog's mealtime environment give her the jitters, just eliminate the jitter-causing elements.

✔ **Go easy on table scraps.** Although vets and other experts strongly suggest otherwise, most people can't resist giving their dogs a taste of that juicy turkey or a bite of that succulent roast beef. But if you choose to indulge your dog's taste for people food, at least go easy on the indulging. Too much fatty, spicy food may send a dog's tummy into a tizzy. Consider, too, whether you really want to feed your dog directly from the table. A begging dog is obnoxious, even if she's a senior.

✔ **No free feeding.** Sure, leaving a brimming bowl of food out all day and letting your dog eat whenever she wants to is more convenient for you. But that practice, which experts call *free feeding,* makes it tough for you to spot potential health problems because you can't tell exactly how much food your dog eats or when she eats it. Free feeding also makes it difficult for your senior dog to maintain her bathroom manners, which age may already have made a little shaky (find a detailed discussion about senior dogs' bathroom issues in Chapter 7). That's because what goes into a dog's tummy must eventually come out — and if you don't know when she's eaten, you may find it difficult to anticipate when she needs to do her business.

Encouraging Picky Princess (or Prince) to Eat

Pooches who pick at their food may be objecting to *how* they're being fed rather than *what* they're being fed. The care you take in finding just the right fare for your gourmand is all for naught if his surroundings aren't conducive to eating that good stuff.

Wouldn't you be grossed out if your filet mignon were served to you on a plate that clearly contained residue from the scrambled eggs that were served on that plate earlier? Wouldn't you lose your appetite for that wonderfully creamy mushroom bisque if you had to eat it with a dirty spoon? And doesn't a great meal somehow taste better when you eat with a friend than when you eat it by yourself? By the same token (and I don't mean to offend parents here; I'm a mom, too), wouldn't you find it tough to enjoy a five-star meal in a chi-chi restaurant if the other guests include screaming toddlers who are running around the dining room?

The answers to these questions should help you see that ambience is an important component of both the human and canine dining experience. If dogs could talk, they'd probably tell us that they prefer a certain atmosphere when they eat. Actually, though, when you stop to think about it, dogs already do send such messages to their people. The dogs in my life — senior and otherwise — won't drink the water I serve them if there happens to be a crumb of food in that water. Two dogs in my past would go on hunger strikes if they had to eat in solitude. Other dogs find it tough to chow down if the humans in their families create a racket in close proximity to where they're eating.

Unless you've just adopted a senior dog, chances are you already know some of his eating preferences. The key at this point in his life is for you to be even more sensitive to his dining desires.

Although most seniors don't enjoy change, exceptions are plentiful in the kingdom of canines. If you sense, for example, that your long-time social diner is now making like Greta Garbo and "vants to eat alone," respect that change of preference. If, on the other hand, a previously solitary diner refuses to eat without the presence of human company, stick around for a few minutes after you plunk down his dog dish. Either way, you minimize dining-induced stress, which all too often can upset your dog's tummy, make him toss his cookies, or diminish his appetite.

A dog who suddenly starts picking at his food, and whose pickiness doesn't respond to simple solutions within a day or two may well be sick. Have your vet check him out.

Helping the Portly Pooch

Repeat after me: There's no such thing as a pleasantly plump dog, especially if that dog is a senior.

A round (notice that I didn't say "well-rounded") dog may appear healthy. Actually, though, the dog who's on the skinny side is probably in much better health than her portly counterpart. That's because the dog who's overweight has a greater chance of having to deal with a variety of ailments: arthritis, diabetes, and heart disease, to name just a few (head to Chapter 10 for more on these conditions). Coincidentally, these conditions also tend to be more prevalent among senior dogs than among more youthful pooches. The bottom line: The overweight older dog carries a higher risk of acquiring conditions that at best cause discomfort, and at worst can be life-threatening.

Dealing with snack attacks

Should you allow your aging dog to snack? Sure — don't you enjoy between-meal treats on occasion? Your dog's no different.

But just like with yourself, your dog's treats shouldn't only taste good, but they should also be healthy for him — at least most of the time. Human or canine junk food contains few, if any, nutrients. And when consumed too often, these calorie-laden treats pile unneeded pounds onto the human or canine physique.

Take heart, though. You can serve your dog snacks that he finds delicious and that also satisfy your concerns about his health. Some possibilities are bits of frozen or fresh fruits and vegetables; canned dog food broken up into small pieces and microwaved until it's almost dried out (make sure it's cooled to room temp before serving to your dog); whole-grain cereal; rice cakes (I think they're tasteless, but many dogs adore them); ice cubes; and lean pieces of meat (for example, white-meat turkey). Of course, if you give in to your dog's snack cravings, adjust his regular meal portions accordingly.

Commercial dog treats are okay *if* your canine companion isn't fighting the battle of the bulge. Often these treats are high in calories, so feeding them to the dieting dog probably will work against the results you're trying to achieve.

Understanding why pooches pork out

Generally, dogs pork out for the same reasons people do: They eat too much and exercise too little. To make matters worse, older dogs and older people both experience metabolic slowdowns, which means senior members of either species can't convert food into energy as quickly as they did when they were younger. All too often, the results of this metabolic slowdown are spare tires or love handles for pooch or person.

Senior Super Dogs: Two dogs, two diets

Harley and Ivanhoe are both senior retrievers who needed to lose 10 pounds a few years ago. Both succeeded in paring back their overly large waistlines — but their owners took two very different approaches to getting their dogs trim.

Ivy's owner, Brette Sember of Clarence, New York, used a commercial dog food and low-calorie snacks to help her 10-year-old Golden Retriever slim down from his all-time high of 95 pounds. The snacks consisted mainly of fruits and veggies that

Sember fed Ivy regularly and an occasional dog biscuit. In addition, Sember made sure Ivy got extra exercise such as walks, running, and playing catch in the yard. The result: A newly svelte Ivy who lost more than 10 pounds in just 6 months.

Courtesy of Brette Sember

Harley's owner, Susan Lennon of Rocky Hill, Connecticut, decided to help her 9-year-old Labrador Retriever slim down by switching him to a vegetable-heavy diet. The dog had been on a BARF diet that helped him lose weight, "but he was still bulky," Lennon recalls. "He was having a harder time running and exercising. One day, I decided to cut his ration in half and add more fresh vegetables to make up for the lost 'bulk' [in his diet]. To my surprise, he did not act any hungrier, nor beg for any more food than usual."

Harley lost 12 pounds in 12 months, and Lennon couldn't be happier. She enthuses, "At 83 pounds, Harley is noticeably leaner, has more stamina, and is very buff!"

Courtesy of Susan Lennon

Sometimes, though, a health condition causes your senior dog to pick up extra poundage. Two examples are *hypothyroidism*, which occurs when the thyroid gland doesn't produce sufficient hormones, and *Cushing's Disease*, which results when too much adrenal hormone is produced. You can find out more about hypothyroidism in Chapter 9 and get details about Cushing's Disease in Chapter 10.

Determining whether your dog is fat

How do you know that your dog is packing on too many pounds? Sometimes it's tough to tell just by looking: Very furry breeds, such as Rough Collies, Shetland Sheepdogs, or Keeshonden, may conceal their spare tires underneath their glorious coats. But if a dog's looks don't tell, her ribs will. Run your hands firmly along your dog's sides. If you can't feel her ribs easily, she's probably overweight. Another way to check a furry dog's physique is to give her a bath. After her wet fur is matted against her body, it's easier to see if your four-legged friend is as sleek as she should be.

If you want a more precise assessment of what sort of shape your senior dog is in, check out Nestle Purina's Body Condition System at www.purina.com/dogs/nutrition.asp?article=292. There you find nine ratings that not only tell you whether your dog is fat, they also tell you just how fat she is — and without either of you having to step onto a scale.

Slimming down your senior

Unless your dog's excess poundage results from a medical problem, you can help her regain the trim physique she sported when she was younger. Here's how to help your senior regain the svelte shape of her youth:

- ✔ **Visit your vet.** Your dog's doctor not only can help you develop a diet and exercise program that helps your canine companion lose weight safely, but your vet can also rule out conditions that prompt weight gain and sabotage any weight-reducing diet.

- ✔ **Ban free-feeding.** No dog should be free-fed, but for the dumpy senior dog, free-feeding is an even more definite no-no. Many dogs don't know when to stop eating, so a continually full food bowl just makes it more likely that your friend will turn rolypoly, if she isn't already.

- ✔ **Limit intake.** This is a no-brainer: Dogs who eat too much and weigh too much need to eat less. With your vet's guidance, gradually reduce the food portions that you dole out to your senior dog. Make sure the reduction is significant enough to help take off weight, but not so significant that she continually begs for more food.

- ✔ **Feed more often.** Yes, you *can* feed your dog more often without giving her more to feed on — and by doing so, you help her tummy stay fuller for a longer period of time. Just divide the reduced rations suggested in the previous bullet by the number of meals you feed your dog each day. If you're feeding your four-legged friend only once a day, feed her twice a day. If you're feeding her twice a day, consider feeding her three times a day. You don't need to give her more than three meals per day, though, unless your vet specifies otherwise.

✔ **Add some fiber.** If your dog scarfs her reduced rations and begs for more, add some fiber to her daily fare — either by switching to a low-calorie dog food or by adding fruits and vegetables to her current regimen. Either way, the fiber fills your dog's tummy without adding calories. Fruit and veggie options to try include apples, carrots, frozen green beans, and frozen Brussels sprouts. Go easy on the fruits, though, in order to avoid giving your senior too much sugar, and avoid giving your senior other less-than-tummy-friendly veggies such as peas and corn.

✔ **Get moving.** Exercise is as important for pooches as it is for people, especially if that pooch is on a diet. Extra walks help your dog burn more calories than she otherwise does without overtaxing her already strained joints and ligaments. Swimming is great because it gives your dog a good aerobic workout without her having to bear any weight. Get the low-down on doggy workouts in Chapter 3.

✔ **Go slow.** A 30-pound dog should lose 1 pound per month, max. Smaller dogs should lose more slowly, and larger dogs can lose a little faster.

Chapter 3

Staying on the Move: Exercising Your Senior Dog

The fact that your dog reaches seniorhood doesn't mean that she has to spend the rest of her life as a couch potato. In fact, if she can possibly avoid doing so, she shouldn't.

Active human seniors set a great example for the senior canine. Advertisements for gated communities targeted to people over 55 invariably feature good-looking men and women whose only concession to seniorhood is perfectly coiffed silver hair. Senior professional tennis and golf tours reportedly draw as much interest as the regular pro tours. And some musicians are becoming Rocks of Age: at the time I wrote this book, Rolling Stones frontman Mick Jagger was several months beyond his 60th birthday, and former Beatle Paul McCartney was a full year past the big 6-0.

Of course, no one is suggesting that your senior dog prance about on a stage at a breakneck pace or try to serve an ace to John McEnroe. But Mick, Paul, and other humans exemplify the value of staying active well into seniorhood. You can help your senior dog follow those examples. In this chapter, I tell you how.

Why Seniors Should Be Fit and Feisty

In pre-Baby Boom generations, turning 65 or even 55 years old seemed like a remarkable accomplishment. Those lucky few who managed that feat often felt entitled to take up permanent residence in a rocking chair. Unfortunately, exercising (pun fully intended!) such an entitlement often diminished both the quality and length of the rest of a person's life.

Today, of course, seniors know better. Not only is today's human life expectancy way beyond 65, but more dogs are also reaching comparable senior status. Those dogs — and their younger counterparts — reap many benefits from getting and staying fit, including

- **Greater mobility:** When it comes to physical fitness, the operative maxim is "use it or lose it." Staying fit prevents your dog's muscles from wasting away due to lack of use and ensures that his joints don't get creaky.

- **Less fat:** Because exercise uses calories, a dog who stays on the move is less likely to be overweight than his more sedentary counterparts.

- **Healthier hearts and lungs:** Exercises that increase a dog's pulse and respiration can help both the heart and lungs function more efficiently.

- **Less boredom:** The exercise that a dog needs to stay fit also can make a dog tired — and a tired dog is much less likely to be bored and indulge in boredom-behavior, such as chewing, counter-surfing, and raiding the household trash can.

Modifying Your Senior's Workout

Just because dogs of any age derive similar benefits from regular exercise doesn't mean that senior dogs should work out the same way that younger pooches do. For one thing, some conditions that you find more often among senior dogs, such as arthritis, affect the older dog's endurance when she performs any exercise and may entirely rule out some activities, such as running or even jogging. Chapters 11 and 12 offer detailed information about conditions that senior dogs suffer from more often than younger animals.

Even if your aging friend doesn't have special health issues, though, you still need to adjust her exercise routine to fit the physical limitations that getting older often imposes. Here are some ways that you can alter your canine companion's fitness program:

✔ **Soften the surface.** If you and your dog have always jogged on sidewalks, streets, or other hard surfaces, now's the time to move to terrain that's easier on her hips and joints. Grass is a good alternative, as long as it's not slippery, and a roadside or trailside shoulder is an option, too.

✔ **Warm up first.** Any exercise routine should begin with a warm-up, but for senior canine fitness fanatics, the warm-up is crucial. For example, if you and your pooch like to power-walk, precede your workout with a few minutes of strolling at a more leisurely pace. A dog who's already limber and loose performs better and is less likely to get injured.

✔ **Have water on hand.** No matter what exercise your dog is doing, she needs to have water on hand to prevent dehydration. If your senior has kidney problems, keeping her hydrated is especially important.

✔ **Exercise daily.** Being a weekend warrior causes just as much pain for your dog as it does for you — and, in either case, you can't gain much for such pain. To minimize strain on your dog's muscles, bones, and joints, exercise daily or, at least, three times per week.

✔ **Heed the weather.** Senior dogs feel the elements more keenly than younger pooches do, so take special care not to exercise your older friend during very hot or very cold weather. Such caution helps prevent heatstroke, heat exhaustion, and frostbite.

✔ **Heed your dog.** Watch your dog for signs that she's had enough exercise for today. If she's lagging behind, slowing her pace, and panting heavily, it's time for her to quit.

Before beginning any fitness program, have your vet take a look at your senior dog. A veterinary examination can uncover hidden conditions that may affect your dog's ability to exercise. Make sure your senior's exam includes a blood profile to ensure that she doesn't have any underlying conditions that would preclude her starting a fitness program. For more on why a senior needs to have her blood profiled, analyzed, and otherwise looked at, see Chapter 5.

Exercises for the Aging Athlete

Certain physical activities lend themselves more easily than others to an older dog's relatively mellow pace. The following sections provide some examples.

Sauntering with your senior

Even for a senior canine, going for a walk can mean much more than a trip to the doggy bathroom. A slow saunter around the block gives aging joints some needed exercise, and it also gets the housebound older dog into a new, more stimulating environment. Walking at a faster pace for about 20 minutes can give him aerobic benefits as well.

Although walking is an ideal exercise for almost any senior dog, owners still need to take some precautions. Stay on cool pavement or grass, stop and rest if your dog seems to be getting tired, lay off long-distance walking if your dog starts limping, and avoid long walks in very hot or very cold weather. And of course, keep your dog on a leash unless you're in an enclosed area from which he can't run out into the street.

Getting aerobic

Jogging can give your dog even more of an aerobic benefit than walking can — if your senior canine companion's bones and joints can withstand the impact that jogging inflicts on them. If your dog is arthritic or has other mobility issues, jogging may not be the greatest exercise for him. The same guidelines that apply to walking also apply to jogging, with one additional warning: Don't let your dog jog at all if he's limping.

Stretching for yoga

Although you're not likely to see any dog — senior or otherwise — assume the lotus position or otherwise twist into a canine pretzel, yoga is catching on as an exercise alternative for both pooches and people. Also known as "doga" or "ruff yoga," yoga for dogs involves owners placing their dogs in traditional yoga positions and stretches. Adherents say that a yoga routine not only relieves stress for pooch and person alike, but also enhances the bond between the two. Moreover, yoga may come easier to canines than to humans because many typical pooch postures lend themselves to yoga poses — as Figure 3-1 demonstrates. You may want to check out *Bow Wow Yoga: 10,000 Years of Posturing* by Gerry Olin Greengrass (J.P. Tarcher) and *Doga: Yoga for Dogs* by Jennifer Brilliant and William Berloni (Chronicle Books).

Figure 3-1: A normal doggy stretch can be part of a canine yoga program.

Working your dog's mind and body

An aging dog's mind needs exercise, too. You can provide that mental exercise with some common activities while giving your four-legged friend a mild to moderate physical workout. Best of all, you can do these exercises from the comfort of your own home. These workouts include fetching and hide-and-seek of either an object or a person. Either game forces the dog to use his senses of smell, hearing, and sight to find something and bring it back to the owner.

The mental challenge of these activities can be a tonic to any dog, but especially to a senior canine. As usual, though, don't overdo either activity — and don't make either activity so challenging that your dog has no chance of success. Whenever he does find what you've hidden, uncovers the concealed object, or brings back the ball you tossed, reward him with praise, a play session, or a low-calorie treat such as a piece of raw veggie (see Chapter 2 for suggestions on good vegetables for dogs).

Be careful, too, about throwing a ball or object in such a way that your older friend may try to leap from the ground or twist quickly to catch what you're throwing. Such strenuous efforts can wreak havoc on aging bones, muscles, and ligaments.

Diving into swimming

Few exercises are better for a senior dog (or any dog . . . or any person!) than swimming. Dog paddling provides an excellent aerobic workout for your senior pooch's muscles, joints, and ligaments without placing undue strain on any or all of those body parts. The dog in the swim doesn't have to bear any weight because the water does it for him. Swimming is also an excellent form of physical therapy for dogs who are recovering from surgery, suffering from a spinal injury, dealing with arthritis, or needing to lose some weight. You can find plenty of doggy pools to take your senior swimming — and in some cases, you don't even need a pool.

Not every dog needs a pool to benefit from swimming. If your senior dog is a short-legged breed, such as a Miniature Dachshund, or a toy breed, like a Shih Tzu, you can probably let him take a dip in your own bathtub. Just make sure that you've made the water warm enough and don't let him swim unsupervised.

No matter where your dog takes a dip, keep the following suggestions in mind:

- ✔ **Check out the facility.** Make sure that the place you take your senior swimmer is clean and that the personnel are knowledgeable. Ideally, a veterinarian or a physical therapist should manage a swimming facility for dogs.

- ✔ **Check the temperature.** If your dog swims for therapeutic purposes, the water temperature should be about 90 degrees Fahrenheit.

  To find a heated pool for your dog to paddle around in, try doing a search on the Internet. Type "dog hydrotherapy" and "U.S." into your search engine. Such a search serves up quite a few possibilities.

- ✔ **Don't force the issue.** Although swimming is a great activity for just about any dog, not every dog thinks that hitting the pool is such a terrific idea. Let the skittish swimmer get used to a pool slowly, and be sure to put a doggy life jacket on him to help him float better in the water. Throwing floatable treats, such as oyster crackers, into a pool can give the reluctant swimmer an incentive to test the waters.

The thrill of victory: Dog sports

The senior-canine couch potato probably can't aspire to the glory of the canine lure course-runners, ball catchers, and other athletes who show up on Animal Planet. But a moderately active, healthy senior may well enjoy both the mental and physical challenge of dog sports, such as the following:

✔ **Agility:** This canine sport is growing fast. Human handlers guide their dogs through an obstacle course of tunnels, teeter-totters, hurdles, weave poles, A-frames, and balance beams. Almost any breed can participate in this sport. However, if you want to start your senior, let your vet check him out first and slowly start your dog. You can find more info on agility competitions from the American Kennel Club (www.akc.org), the North American Dog Agility Council (www.nadac.com), and the United States Dog Agility Association (www.usdaa.com). Figure 3-2 shows a senior dog who excels at agility. (Flip to the sidebar at the end of this chapter for an in-depth look at Jason.)

Photo by Mary Jo Sminkey, courtesy of Laura Rubin

Figure 3-2: Jason, a 9-year-old Shetland Sheepdog, is still winning titles in the exciting canine sport of agility.

✔ **Flyball:** This sport involves a relay race that requires teams of dogs to catch tennis balls released from a spring-powered ball launcher. The dogs then race back over hurdles to the starting point. Your dog (and you!) can have a lot of fun with this sport, but you have to be careful with the senior flyball enthusiast — he's no spring chicken! You can find out more about this exciting sport by logging on to the North American Flyball Association's Web site at www.flyball.com.

✔ **Obedience:** This activity tests — you guessed it — a dog's ability to obey commands under challenging circumstances and the pressure of competition. This activity isn't nearly as physically strenuous as agility or flyball. However, obedience does require concentration on the part of both dog and handler, and it helps keep both of you mentally sharp. You can find info on obedience from the American Kennel Club (AKC) at www.akc.org.

✔ **Field trials:** These activities give your dog the opportunity to track, point, and retrieve quarry in environments that resemble the hunting conditions for which people originally bred dogs. A physically fit senior — particularly a retriever, pointer, or spaniel — may well enjoy such competition. However, as with any vigorous sport, make sure that your senior dog gets the green light from his vet first. Hunt up some info about field trials by logging on to the AKC's Web site at www.akc.org.

Helping Your Dog Unwind After a Workout

One of the best parts of any exercise program is the way that you feel after you've finished working out. All those bliss-producing endorphins that result from sustained physical activity are still circulating through your tired body, helping you feel happy and proud that you made it to the gym.

But those endorphins don't work as well if you rush into a stressful activity immediately after your sessions. The full benefit of getting physical occurs when you give your body a chance to relax, unwind, and recoup after you've finished your regimen. For that reason, many health clubs feature services such as massages and other types of hands-on therapy.

The senior dog who's gotten physical has as great a need to unwind and relax as her human companion does. Tired canine muscles, joints, and ligaments respond just as well to some post-exercise TLC as their human counterparts do. For that reason, no chapter on exercising a senior dog can be considered complete unless it also discusses what to do after the exercise session.

Fortunately, the same massages and other tactile therapies that bliss you out can have the same effect on your senior dog. Even better, these hands-on treatments can enhance the bond you already have with your aging canine companion. In some cases, though, foregoing tactile therapies in favor of more conventional meds may be the way to go. Either way, the following sections provide some handy-dandy ways to soothe a senior dog's movable parts after she's worked them out.

Giving your dog a massage

Massage is probably the most common form of tactile therapy that people can give to their pooches (or to each other). Generally, massage requires the person to use her hands to rub and knead her dog's muscle tissue. When done properly, massage loosens muscle fibers that have become tense or sore during exercise and increases the circulation of blood to those muscles.

In fact, even your daily petting sessions (you do pet your dog several times a day, right?) may constitute a form of massage. You can simply extend the long, slow strokes that you bestow on your dog's head and neck to the entire body. These body-length, even-pressured strokes are what massage pros call *effluerage,* and they can be the precursor to a more extended massage session or constitute a mini-massage in and of themselves.

Most experts suggest that after the opening effluerage, you should apply your fingertips in circular patterns all over your dog's body. You want to use firm pressure so that you can move the dog's muscle underneath the skin, but don't be so firm that the dog winces, moves away, or shows any other signs of discomfort. Finish with a closing effluerage, and savor the look of sleepy contentment on your four-legged friend's face.

Massage isn't for every dog. Professional practitioners caution against massaging a dog with an obvious injury, such as a broken bone or broken skin. Sick dogs aren't good candidates for massages either — especially if they have cancer. The increased circulation that results from a massage may help the cancerous tumor grow.

Good books on dog massage include *How to Massage Your Dog* by Jane Buckle (Wiley) and *Dog Massage: A Whiskers-to-Tails Approach to Your Dog's Ultimate Petting Experience* by Mary Jean Ballner (Griffin Trade Paperback).

Using other hands-on treatments

Massage isn't the only hands-on therapy available to the senior canine athlete and her people. Other touch treatments provide older dogs — and their younger canine counterparts — with benefits that range from less pain to better behavior.

Acupressure and acupuncture

Acupressure is kind of like acupuncture with the hands. Where *acupuncture* uses specially placed needles to achieve their therapeutic benefit, *acupressure* requires the practitioner to place her fingers on the places where acupuncture needles would go.

Both acupressure and acupuncture are ancient Chinese medical practices that attempt to influence the body's energy flow. According to traditional Chinese medicine, such energy — or *chi* — flows along unseen pathways called *meridians*. Practitioners believe that each meridian in the body influences another part of the body. In a healthy dog or person, the chi flows smoothly; when either individual is ill, something disrupts the flow of the chi. Both acupressure and acupuncture aim to restore the smooth flow of the chi by stimulating points on the meridians that influence the part of the body that needs healing.

Only a qualified veterinarian should administer acupuncture, but you can perform acupressure yourself. However, you can't absorb acupressure from a book; if you want to try this form of therapy, you need to find a massage therapist or other practitioner who has advanced training in traditional Chinese medicine. The therapist can either perform the treatment himself or show you some of the basics.

Some acupuncturists specialize in treating animals. To find such specialists in your area, log on to the American Holistic Veterinary Medical Association's directory at www.ahvma.org/referral/index.html.

Two good books that deal with acupressure and acupuncture are *The Holistic Dog Book: Canine Care for the 21st Century* by Denise Flaim (Wiley) and *Four Paws, Five Directions* by Cheryl Schwartz, D.V.M. (Celestial Arts).

Tellington T-Touch

Back in the 1970s, equestrian Linda Tellington-Jones was looking for more humane, less domineering ways to train horses. Eventually, she found that moving the fingers and hands in circular patterns all over the horse's body was a very effective way to remedy chronic irregularities in the animal's gait. Somehow, she theorized, the circular motions and related exercises affect the nervous system in a profound way. Soon, Tellington-Jones was expanding her T-Touch therapy to include cats, dogs, and other animals.

Today, many people believe that the Tellington T-Touch helps relieve dogs' problems, ranging from aggressive behavior to arthritis. In fact, people who've tried this therapy for their pooches report that it improves both behavioral and physical problems.

Tellington-Jones has written a book that explains how to practice and use T-Touch, and she teaches the technique at seminars for pet owners. However, to perform the T-Touch on other people's pets for business purposes, a person needs to be certified as a practitioner by Tellington-Jones's organization. You can find more

about becoming certified and finding a certified practitioner at
www.lindatellington-jones.com. The book *The Tellington
T-Touch: A Revolutionary Natural Method to Care for and Train
Your Favorite Animal* by Linda Tellington-Jones (Penguin Books)
explains more about the technique itself.

Helping without hands

The road to fitness isn't always totally paved with endorphins and
other triggers of all-over well-being. Any human who's started an
exercise program knows that he's bound to be a little bit achy to
start with. Those aches and pains are by no means confined to
canine or human seniors: My 14-year-old daughter always com-
plains about feeling sore when the soccer season starts and she's
forced to replace a few months of being a couch-potato with thrice-
weekly wind sprints.

Your senior dog is no different. After his first few workouts, he's
very likely going to feel a little bit stiff and sore. And if he's the typical canine stoic, his signs of soreness are very subtle — a little bit
of slowness in getting up from a reclining position may be the only
signal you see.

Although some post-exercise soreness is probably inevitable, you
can limit the achiness of your not-yet-fit Fido by adjusting his exercises for his age, as I describe in the section "Modifying Your
Senior's Workout" earlier in this chapter. You can also perform the
hands-on maneuvers featured in the previous section. You may
wonder, though, whether you can do the same thing for your hurt-
ing hound that you do for yourself — pop in a couple of painkillers
and let them work their magic.

The answer is that yes, you can — but you need to proceed with
caution. Buffered aspirin can help ease the aches in any athlete —
aging or youthful, canine or human. The standard dose is about one
tablet per 30 pounds of body weight, no more than twice a day; consult your vet to determine the right dosage for your dog. But the
okay on aspirin doesn't apply to other pain relievers for people,
such as naproxen sodium (Aleve), ibuprofen (Advil), or acetaminophen (Tylenol). All three are poisonous to pets and can be fatal.

If you give your dog aspirin, watch for signs of gastric ulcers, such
as appetite loss, depression, vomiting, and darkening of the stool.
Should you spot any such signs, discontinue use and consult your
vet immediately. You can also pack some heat: Warm compresses
or a heating pad can help relieve sore muscles. For the arthritic
dog or other pooch who needs consistent pain relief, a heated
doggie bed can be a source of significant comfort.

Senior Super Dogs: Jason the Versatile

Human athletes typically retire when they're in their 20s or 30s — but one canine athlete is still racing around the agility course at an age that's the human equivalent of his mid-60s.

This seemingly ageless athlete is officially known as Ch. Royl Marchwind Just Lookin' CD, MX, NAP, MXJ, NJP, AAD, OAC, NJC — but to most people, he's just Jason. That long name isn't an affectation, though. The acronyms that appear before and after Jason's official name show that this 9-year-old Shetland Sheepdog not only is a champion show dog, but also excels in obedience competition and has won titles from three U.S. canine agility associations.

Photo by J. Kay Kernan, courtesy of J. Kay Kernan and Laura Rubin

According to his owner, Laura Rubin of Potomac, Maryland, Jason didn't rack up all those agility titles solely in his youth. In fact, the spirited Sheltie was competing in agility trials only a few months after undergoing major surgery to repair a damaged hip in November 2002. "Age does not seem to have affected his performance at all," says Rubin.

What's Rubin's secret to keeping Jason active and strong? "We are having fun together on a regular basis," she says. Such fun includes walking, trotting, and practicing on agility equipment.

Despite his relatively advanced age, Jason will continue to compete in agility competitions according to Rubin's plans. "If he keeps his eyesight, he could have two or three more years," Rubin explains. "I know of 11-year-olds that still participate."

Although Jason has racked up a boatload of accomplishments, this supremely versatile senior Sheltie is no prima donna. "He has a wonderful temperament," Rubin enthuses. "He's happy and confident, friendly and outgoing. Nothing seems to bother him, and he only shows signs of worry if he thinks he's getting his nails trimmed or he's having a bath."

Chapter 4

Boosting Your Senior's Social Savvy

My late Shetland Sheepdog, Cory, was the perfect puppy: cooperative, a quick study (especially with housetraining!), and almost unfailingly obedient after he understood what I wanted him to do. He worked hard to be the dog I wanted him to be — and I worked hard, too.

I tried to do everything that experts suggested in order to help him grow up to become a happy, well-adjusted dog. I trained him to be a model citizen and took him to extra obedience classes just to reinforce what I was teaching him. And I heeded the warning that all training pros give their human students: I socialized him to the max. In other words, I took Cory out and about to public places where he could encounter new people, new pooches and new situations. The idea, of course, was to raise a pup with poise; a pup who could deal with any new situation with complete aplomb.

But by the time Cory reached his seventh birthday and showed clear signs of approaching seniorhood, most of his social skills had gone down the toilet. He avoided other dogs if possible — and when that wasn't possible, he'd curl his lip and snap at the smallest perceived provocation. He wouldn't let people pet him until he decided it was okay — and he'd take a long time before he made that decision, if ever. In short, my beloved canine companion was pretty much a social failure, despite my efforts to socialize him during puppyhood. What had I done wrong?

After talking with trainers, I got my answer. I didn't realize that when it comes to socializing a dog, the doctrine to follow is "use it or lose it." You have to expose your four-legged friend to new and novel situations and people throughout his life, including his senior years. Otherwise, he becomes a social washout, even if he was a social butterfly during puppyhood.

Even if your senior dog is a social ace, some situations may be a little dicier for him than for younger dogs. This chapter describes some of those situations and suggests how an owner can help his aging friend deal with them.

Introducing Your Dog to Strangers

Like seniors of other species, older dogs like predictability. They take comfort in knowing — or, at least, believing — that their lives will unfold the same ways every day. They have more difficulty adjusting to change than their younger peers do. But humans know something that dogs don't: The only aspect of life that doesn't change is that it does change (how's that for a paradox?). One set of changes facing a senior dog is meeting individuals whom the dog has never seen before. The canine who clings to the comfort of the old may feel considerable discomfort when encountering a new person, dog, or other animal. However, you can help your aging four-legged friend meet new pooches, people, or other beings with confidence — whether out on the street, in the home, or when welcoming such individuals into the family pack.

Bringing home baby

It happens to many aging dogs: A happy pack of three that consists of a loving human couple and a doted-upon dog suddenly (to the dog, not to the humans) becomes a pack of four. The fourth member is, of course, a new human baby.

The arrival of a squalling, smelly infant can be disconcerting to any dog who's never encountered one before — and for the senior dog who's had years to bond with her people, the new arrival may not only be disconcerting but distinctly unwelcome. And when you look at the situation from the dog's point of view, can you really blame her? For years she's had the undivided attention of her human mom and dad, who have considered her their four-legged child. But when a human child arrives, everything changes.

I know that all too well — I've been there, along with a much loved, now departed senior dog named Molly. At the age of 10, Molly was confronted with the arrival of a new family member: my husband's and my infant daughter, Julie. We worried about how Molly would adjust to the arrival of her new "sibling." Would she be jealous? Would she feel hurt or left out? And if so, how would she deal with those feelings?

But after Julie arrived, truth be told, I didn't have time to think about my fears regarding Molly. I didn't have time to think about anything, period. I was learning Baby Care 101 on the spot and, in the process, was losing sleep — lots of sleep. But I didn't worry about Molly. I knew that I had no reason to worry because my husband and I had prepared Molly for Julie's arrival for weeks before the arrival actually occurred.

The following items tell you what you can do to prepare your senior dog for the stork's delivery.

✔ **Practice ahead of time:** A month or so before the due date, start giving your dog an idea of what's to come. Get hold of an infant-sized doll and pretend to feed it, dress it, and change its diaper when your four-legged friend is around. Let your dog hear what a baby sounds like, too. Find or make an audio tape of a baby crying and play it in your dog's presence. If your dog exhibits any distress, like barking, growling, or hyperactivity, have her perform a down-stay or a sit-stay. (If your dog doesn't know how to sit or lie down on command, check out the "Lifetime Learning for the Senior Canine" section in this chapter.) When she complies, pet her and talk to her while you hold the baby stand-in and play the audiotape. Keep doing this once or twice a day until after the baby comes home.

✔ **Bring home some scent:** You can't mimic the baby's scent before she's born, but you certainly can introduce your dog to that scent before mother and child arrive home from the hospital. While Mom and baby are still in the hospital, Dad or another person should bring home a T-shirt that the baby has worn for a couple of hours and offer the shirt to the dog to sniff. That pre-arrival encounter with the baby's scent makes the baby's arrival home less of a surprise to your four-legged friend.

✔ **Reunite right away:** The way the parents bring the baby home can make a world of difference to your canine companion. It's a good idea for the new mom to greet the dog privately in another part of the house away from the baby while Dad or another person holds the baby. That way, the dog gets undivided attention from the returning family member and a chance to calm down before being introduced to the newest member of the family.

✔ **Introduce with care:** After mother and pooch greet each other, Mom should leash the dog and lead her out to meet the baby. Dad should sit on the floor with the baby, who you should cover loosely with a blanket over every part of the body except for the eyes. Let your leashed dog sniff the baby — but be prepared to pull her back away from the baby if she tries to do anything but sniff or lick the child.

✔ **Include the dog in baby care:** Your senior can be welcome company during those middle-of-the-night feedings and other less-than-terrific aspects of baby care (think smelly diapers and sour-milk spitups). Have your canine companion join you when you feed, change, or clean up after the baby, and make sure that you talk to and pet the dog at least a little bit while she's there.

✔ **Be vigilant:** When it comes to human babies, no dog is totally trustworthy. A crying infant can turn on your pooch's instinctive prey drive — and when that happens, the results can be tragic for every family member.

Never, ever leave your dog alone with your baby until that baby has grown into a school-aged child. Figure 4-1 exemplifies how babies and dogs should interact with each other: under a parent's close supervision.

If you and your aging dog encounter an infant at someone else's home or out on the street, caution is key. You may be sure that your faithful friend will behave well, but those who care for the baby don't have that knowledge — and may even define good behavior differently than you do (some parents don't want a dog to even sniff their child). Keep your dog under your control and ask the parents' permission before allowing the dog to meet the infant.

The ABCs of meeting a child

The way that you introduce your senior dog to a child who's beyond infancy depends, in large measure, on that child's age. You can't expect a toddler to know how to conduct himself around a dog; to him, the dog simply looks like a walking, barking stuffed animal. In fact, many dog breeders and rescue groups don't permit a family with very young children to adopt a dog, senior or otherwise. However, a child older than 6 can understand that your aging pooch is a living being with feelings and needs, and that he should treat your senior accordingly.

No matter what a child's age, however, your senior dog needs to know how to behave around that child — and you need to be ready to protect both individuals. Here's how to do just that:

Courtesy of Susan McCullough

Figure 4-1: Any dog — including your senior — may prove unpredictable around an infant; so don't leave your baby alone with any dog.

✓ **Prepare your dog.** Your senior dog should know basic commands, like sit, down, come, and stay — and he should execute them reliably. If your four-legged friend is a little rusty in that area, now's the time to give him a remedial course in basic doggy manners. The "Lifetime Learning for the Senior Canine" section that appears later in this chapter provides guidelines for remedial and other training.

✓ **Prepare the child.** Any dog, senior or otherwise, can't be expected to have sole responsibility for keeping encounters with children safe and happy for all concerned. If you have children, it's never too early (or too late) to teach them how to behave around dogs:

- They need to know that they should never tease a dog, never touch the dog without the owner's permission, never reach to pat a strange dog's head (instead, they should extend a hand for the dog to sniff), and never touch the dog in any way other than a gentle pat or stroking.

- They should also understand that shouting, screaming, or running around when in canine company is a bad idea.

- They should never run away from a dog who they don't know. Instead, they should back away to prevent a dog's prey drive from kicking in.

- And with senior dogs, in particular, you need to teach children not to roughhouse, take away food or toys, or surprise the dog. Such behavior may provoke your dog to snarl, snap, growl, or even a bite.

If the children who meet your dog aren't your own, you can still prepare them for meeting your four-legged friend. Ideally, the parents will tell their little darlings how to behave around dogs; unfortunately, many parents don't impart any such instructions. Such parental failures put the ball squarely in your court. You're the person who must teach uninformed children the basic rules listed in the preceding bullets. If the parents object — well, that's their problem. Just walk your dog and yourself away.

✔ **Protect both parties.** A dog of any age can bite or otherwise menace a child, so it's important for you to make sure that neither pooch nor person gets hurt when encountering each other. Keep your dog on a leash when you meet children while outdoors, and be ready to pull your dog away from the kids if you feel the least bit uneasy. In fact, if you don't know the children, you may want to avoid them altogether; crossing with your dog to the opposite sidewalk isn't a bad idea. If the children are visiting your home, watch canine and kid carefully and be ready to remove your dog if you don't like the way they're interacting. (I didn't leave my daughter and her friends alone with any of my dogs until they hit their teens.) Such caution ensures the safety of all concerned.

Getting used to grown-ups

Your senior dog may not have any problem meeting humans whom she doesn't know. But if she does, she may have a good reason. Maybe guys in hats treated her badly when she was a puppy, or women of a particular ethnicity yelled at her. Maybe just the smell of a particular person or group of people bothers her. Whatever the reason, your senior pooch may be nervous or upset around certain individuals or groups of individuals (yes, dogs can be racist and/or sexist). Sure, you can ignore her negativity — but life will be more pleasant for both of you if you give her a chance to change her mind about the people who bug her. A little bit of bribery can help your dog do just that. Here's how:

1. **Teach a goodie word.**

    Whether it's "cookie," "treat," or some other word that tells your dog that she's going to eat something delicious, teach her that word now, if she doesn't know one already. Just offer your dog the goodie several times every day, and say exactly the same thing each time immediately before you offer it. Sample phrases are "Do you want a cookie?" or "How about a treat?" Then, assume that your dog wants to answer in the affirmative and give her the goodie.

Dogs are sooooooo easy to bribe. Whether you want them to change their minds about a person, persuade them to drop an unauthorized object, or lure them into leaving the dog park before they're ready, just hold out their favorite treat. One sniff of that treat, and they gladly do whatever you want them to do. For more information on what makes a good training treat for a senior pooch, check out Chapter 2.

2. **Do it in company.**

   After your aging pooch connects hearing the goodie word with actually getting the goodie (and believe me, it won't take her very long to make that connection), perform the same maneuver when she's around the people who make her jittery. After this happens a few times, she associates getting a treat with meeting the people who once made her nervous.

3. **Let someone else do it.**

   Another way to help your dog get over her fear of certain individuals is to have one of those individuals give her the goodie. Brief the person beforehand on what you'd like him to do, give him the goodie, and make sure that he uses the same word or phrase that you do.

The preceding suggestions apply only to dogs who exhibit no more than benign discomfort at meeting adult human strangers. If your senior canine companion's discomfort manifests itself as stiff tail wagging, prolonged staring, growling, snapping, or (heaven forbid) biting, your dog isn't just having issues. She's being aggressive and needs to see a vet pronto. The vet can determine whether the behavior has a physical cause. If that's the case, medication often can clear up the problem. If the vet can't find any physical cause, he can refer you to a dog trainer or animal behaviorist who may be able to help you deal successfully with your dog's problem.

Close encounters of the same kind

The experienced senior probably doesn't have much of a problem meeting other pooches when the two of you are out on the street, unless he's had dog-to-dog issues to begin with. If that's the case — or if you encounter another dog who you know doesn't like other canines — you have a simple solution: Walk away. Cross the street or do an about-face — just get on the move, and avoid the situation entirely.

Sometimes, though, you can't get away, particularly if you and your dog are walking on a leash but the other dog is untethered and headed your way. In that case, you need to stand your ground and protect your dog. An effective way to do just that is to look directly at the other canine and say, loudly, that you want him to leave you alone. A firm, near-shouting-level warning to "Go away!" stops most dogs dead in their tracks, and you can continue on your jaunt. If you can, pick up your dog — and back away as you do so.

However, when the other dog is a new canine family member, your senior may not be as laid back. And, when you stop to consider the matter, your pooch's angst is completely understandable. Here he is, perfectly happy to have you and the other humans in your family all to himself. Then, in comes this interloper who threatens his place in the household hierarchy.

If the interloper is a puppy, your senior may be even less enthusiastic. Not only is a pup way younger and more energetic than your long-time canine companion, but also the puppy may be totally ignorant in the ways of canine etiquette, much to your dog's annoyance.

Although your senior dog may hate the very idea of another pooch in the house, you may have very good reasons for wanting a second dog. Perhaps another dog in your family recently died, and you're looking to fill an empty space in your canine pack. Maybe you're thinking that your old dog may not be around much longer, and you want to make sure that you're not totally dog-less when that sad day arrives. Maybe, too, you think that a lively puppy can give your less-than-vibrant senior dog a new lease on life.

You may be right. But then again, you may be very wrong. And if you are wrong, everyone in the family loses: the new pooch, the old one, and all the humans. You can end up with a situation in which you're forced to choose between your older dog spending the rest of his life feeling disgruntled and unhappy or having to relinquish your new canine companion for the sake of your older dog's well-being.

If your dog is an easygoing, socially adept individual who relishes the company of other canines — or who clearly is bereft at the loss of another dog in the family — a second dog can be a great idea. But if your dog sticks with you like a Post-It sticks to paper, a second dog may mean disaster. You may get the same disastrous results if your older dog is very old; in that case, the arrival of a younger pooch is, at the very least, likely to be stressful to your elderly friend. At worst, the younger dog's rougher, more energetic play could injure your older canine companion.

Say that you've weighed the pros and cons and decide that a second dog is really in the best interests of your first dog, not to mention the human members of the family. Here's how to get the relationship between the two canine siblings off to the best possible start:

 ✔ **Let your old dog choose the new one.** Yes, really. It's worth taking the time to see whether your old dog and prospective new dog are compatible before you bring the new dog home. Bring your dog to the animal shelter, the breed rescue foster home, or breeder (with permission from these places, of course) to see whether your senior can get along with the new junior.

 ✔ **Set boundaries.** A new puppy needs the protection of confinement when meeting and getting to know an older dog. Keep the little one in his crate or behind a baby gate when you can't supervise (see Figure 4-2). When you are around, be ready to remove either dog from a stressful situation.

Figure 4-2: A baby gate can help your senior dog and your new puppy get used to each other.

 ✔ **Let them work out the pecking order.** Initially, a puppy usually defers to an older dog, but as that puppy grows up, he may challenge the senior canine for top-dog position. To a dog, being the Big Kahuna means getting first dibs on food, toys, playtime, and other perks of pooch-dom. As long as your younger pooch isn't keeping your older dog away from food, her bed, or you — and if no fights ensue — let the two animals work out their relationship on their own.

If your younger dog is consistently beating up on the senior dog, get help from an expert, such as a professional dog trainer.

✔ **Reassure your older dog.** Make sure that no matter what happens, your older dog knows that you still love her. Carve out some one-on-one time for the two of you, and maintain shared rituals as much as possible.

Dog-park dynamics

Fenced areas that are dedicated to allowing dogs to frolic together off leash are appearing all over the United States, and your senior dog may be one of the many members of the canine kingdom who enjoys a daily or weekly trip to the local dog park. The emphasis here is on "may."

Why am I being cautious here? Because not every dog enjoys mixing it up with his own kind, and that's particularly true of senior dogs. The pro-wrestling-style body slams and takedowns that younger dog-park denizens see as standard operating procedure are often too rough for an older dog to handle. If your dog's days of rough-housing are history, a visit to a dog park should probably be history, too.

Keep in mind, too, that a senior's immune system may not be as strong as it was when he was younger. He may find it harder to withstand the concentrations of fleas, worms, and unvaccinated dogs' diseases that may abound at a dog park. At the very least, make sure your dog's immunizations are up-to-date. If you've chosen not to vaccinate your senior, consider foregoing trips to the dog park. Instead, treat your senior to one-on-one romps with dogs you both know.

But if your senior pooch does enjoy regular trips to your local canine meet market, more power to him. Make sure, though, that you retain some power; specifically, you need to ensure that visits to the dog park stay as fun for your Fido now as they did when he was younger. Here are some tips for dealing with dog parks:

✔ **Remove the leash.** It's an off-leash park, right? That means dogs can and should frolic without being tethered to their human companions. Keeping your dog on leash while you're among unleashed canines can prove dangerous for all concerned. Pulling on a leash creates stress for your dog — and if he's stressed, he's more likely to react fearfully or aggressively to other dogs' overtures.

✔ **Bypass the crowd.** The most recent canine to arrive at any dog park is almost always met at the entrance gate by the dogs who arrived earlier. The result may be a canine mob scene that turns ugly quickly. To forestall such new-dog-in-the-park fights, move yourself and your dog away from the gate quickly — and keep moving after you've cleared the immediate gate area.

✔ **Control your dog.** A dog who obeys his owner is less likely to bully other pooches or be bullied himself. Teaching your dog to come on command — and to come every time — goes a long way toward helping you maintain such control. However, many dogs may have a shaky grasp of this command, at best. If your senior's one such dog, bring some tasty treats with you to the park. Those treats can entice your dog away from potentially sticky situations, or even just bring him over to you when it's time to go home.

✔ **Monitor behavior.** You need to keep a close eye on your dog so that he stays out of trouble and so you can intervene before things get out of hand. If the dogs show signs of getting ready to fight, such as deep growls, bared teeth, or stiff postures, intervene by luring your dog away with a treat, grabbing his collar and pulling him away, and asking the other owner to get his dog. If you're too late and a fight already has started, yell loudly or throw a non-harmful object at the group to break up the combatants.

✔ **Listen to your dog.** If your four-legged friend is standing by the gate, gluing himself to you, or lying down under a bench, it's time to leave. Don't force him or yourself to stay; do as he asks and head on home.

Close encounters of the non-canine kind

The senior dog probably deals better with meeting non-canine pets than the curious puppy or exuberant young adult dog does. In many cases, the older pooch's reaction to meeting another type of animal may be the human equivalent of been-there-done-that. Still, it's important to safeguard all the animal members of a family, no matter how experienced the canine member is at dealing with other species. Because cats grace even more American homes than dogs do, this section focuses on canine-feline relations. Here's what to consider when introducing your senior dog to a new feline family member:

✔ **Make sure that your dog's ready.** Before bringing a cat home, consider whether your senior dog is really suited to living with a feline family member. A dog who doesn't respond to commands or who exhibits other unpredictable behavior may be an animal that you can live with — but you shouldn't expect a cat to.

✔ **Let her get used to the idea.** A dog who's lived in your home for awhile may be less than thrilled at having to share her domain with anyone, including a kitty. To give her a chance to adjust to this possibly unwelcome development, put up a baby gate that confines your new cat to one room but allows your dog access to the rest of the house. This way, the two can see, smell, and hear each other without either coming to harm.

✔ **Manage the first meeting.** After your dog exhibits no more than mild curiosity about the feline interloper (and the interloper appears unafraid of the barking beast on the other side of the gate), take the gate down and let the two animals get up close and personal. Make sure, though, that your dog is on a leash and that your cat has a high shelf or other area where she can escape if the first tete-a-tete doesn't go well.

✔ **Think short and sweet.** Keep the first several canine-feline encounters no longer than a few minutes. At each meeting, praise both animals, if all goes well, and give them treats to underscore your approval. Then, put the cat back in her single room until she and Fido have their next date.

✔ **Be ready to backtrack.** After the animals consistently exhibit either total disinterest in each other or apparent enjoyment of each other's company, you may be able to retire the gate. But stay vigilant for a little while longer — and be ready to put the gate back up if tempers flare or other problems ensue.

As for meeting other animals, such as rabbits, guinea pigs, gerbils, and hamsters, the safest policy is to make sure that they don't meet your senior dog at all. Such animals will probably jump-start your dog's instinctive drive to chase prey — and kill it.

Addressing Other Behavioral Issues

Sometimes, the challenges facing the aging canine arise from special situations, not special individuals. Although dogs of any age can face such circumstantial challenges, some experts believe that older dogs deal with these difficulties more often than their younger counterparts do.

Many factors contribute to a senior's tendency to have issues. For some seniors, especially those who've come from rescue groups, shelters, or have experienced physical or psychological trauma, these behavioral difficulties may reflect emotional baggage from the past. However, even a senior who had an idyllic puppyhood and happy adulthood may react in a less-than-ideal manner to certain situations after he achieves senior status. In the following sections, I discuss some senior-style trauma-ramas and provide suggestions on how to ease such difficulties.

Helping your freaked-out Fidette

Some experts have observed that situations that prompt a bit of nervousness in a younger dog trigger total terror when that dog gets older. For example, the thunderstorm that caused your puppy to show mild concern may prompt outright panic when that puppy hits seniorhood. She may tremble, pant severely, or run wildly through the house. And even if your aging friend doesn't totally freak out, she may hide, drool, whine or howl anxiously, or exhibit Velcro-like behavior (in other words, she glues herself to your side).

The fearful dog isn't having any fun — and if you're her person, you're not having any fun, either. Here are some ways to ease your four-legged friend's fears and phobias:

✔ **See your vet.** A vet can examine your dog to make sure that no physical factors are behind her fearful or panicky behavior. And if her problem appears to be all in her head, he can pre-scribe medication such as antidepressants or other drugs that can relieve her anxiety and put a stop to her fearful behavior.

If you think your dog needs an antidepressant, don't whip out your own bottle of Prozac and pop your dog a pill or two. Only your vet has the technical knowledge and training to pre-scribe the type and amount of medication that's right for your individual dog.

✔ **Don't overreact; distract instead.** If your aging canine com-panion is getting upset over something like repeated rumbles of thunder, the worst thing you can do is try to comfort her. As tempted as you are to do so, refrain from crooning softly to her, telling her "It's okay," petting her excessively, pulling her onto your lap, or otherwise comforting her the way you would comfort a human child. Why? Because such actions, however well-intentioned, reinforce your dog's fearful behavior. In other words, comforting your canine may give her the idea that she's supposed to react in a fearful or phobic manner — exactly the opposite of what you want to achieve.

An approaching storm or other fear-inducing event may be the perfect time to play a game, put her through her training paces, give her a massage, or otherwise redirect her attention away from the oncoming event.

✔ **Desensitize her.** Some trainers suggest helping a dog combat her fear by gradually exposing her to the cause of that fear. Taking the thunderstorm example, find a recording of a storm and play it for your dog to hear. Start by playing the tape softly for just a minute or so. If your dog doesn't show any dis-tress, give her a treat or other reward. Next time, play the same recording a little bit louder and for a slightly longer period of time — and again, reward your dog for staying calm. If she becomes nervous, reduce the volume of the recording. Eventually, you may be able to play the tape for 15 or 20 minutes at the volume of a real storm, and your dog may not react at all. If you reach that goal, you've successfully desensitized your dog — in other words, you've diminished her hypersensitive reaction to thunderstorms by getting her accustomed to the racket they make.

✔ **Give her some flowers.** No, I'm not saying that a bouquet of roses can turn your fearful Fidette into a happy camper. But many holistic veterinarians and other devotees of alternative veterinary medicine recommend giving dogs flower essences — either from single flowers or from combinations such as Bach's Rescue Remedy — to calm the fears of a phobic canine. Squirt a dropperful of a flower essence (or, in the case of Rescue Remedy, the essence combo) into your dog's water once a day, whether you think a storm or other fearful event is coming or not. You can find flower essences at health food stores and more info about them at www.bachflower.com and in the section "Soothing separation anxiety" in this chapter.

Curbing crankiness

The older dog may be more likely to grumble, growl, or snap when touched or even approached than a younger pooch.

Often, such reactions have physical roots. For example, pain often triggers cranky or even aggressive reactions from older pets. The infected ear that a clueless toddler pulls can prompt the unhappy canine to growl, snap, or even bite the human offender. Similarly, an arthritic dog's inability or unwillingness to move away from a situation from which she may have skedaddled when she was younger can trigger a snarl or a show of teeth purely for self-defense.

Other senior dogs may react badly when being startled — usually because they've lost some or all of their eyesight or hearing. Many a veterinarian or behaviorist has dealt with a deaf or blind dog who doesn't expect to be touched and reacts with a fearful show of teeth. Chapter 7 gives you advice on how to cope if your senior loses her eyesight or hearing.

If your canine companion shows signs of crankiness — or worse — you need to act quickly, both for your dog's sake and the sake of the people she encounters. Here's what to do:

✔ **See your vet.** The senior dog who's suddenly acting cranky or aggressive may be a dog in pain. Get your four-legged friend to the vet as soon as possible for a checkup. The vet will look closely for signs of arthritis, ear infections, and dental problems. Other problems that your vet will check for include loss of eyesight, loss of hearing, and decreased hormone production.

✔ **Change your approach.** Even after your vet addresses any underlying physical problem that your dog has, you still want to avoid any action on your part that triggers a negative reaction from your dog. Don't sneak up from behind or otherwise startle her and try to avoid handling sensitive bodily areas.

✔ **Protect your pooch.** Often, the best thing you can do for a cranky canine is to keep her away from what's causing the crankiness in the first place. If you're having a dinner party with guests who are likely to stress out your dog, confine her in an area of your home that's safe and quiet. If you're playing host to babies, toddlers, or preschoolers, don't leave the dog alone with them — not even for a second.

Soothing separation anxiety

Ideally, every dog should love her person. Sometimes, though, that canine love morphs into apparent terror at being separated from that person. The pooch who trashes the house when the owner's not home, or who moans, yelps, or bays when left by herself may well be suffering from *separation anxiety:* a debilitating fear of being away from a beloved human.

Separation anxiety besets dogs of any age, but senior dogs seem to be especially vulnerable to this condition. In fact, some experts say that aging canines who destroy their homes are more likely to be suffering from separation anxiety than from any other condition (such as boredom) that can prompt such behavior.

If your senior pooch turns into a demolition dog when you're not home, or if you hear a heart-rending canine aria when you leave the house, she may suffer from separation anxiety. Experts suggest trying the following tactics:

✔ **Vary your routine.** Many dogs with separation anxiety start feeling that anxiety long before their owner departs. If the owner's pre-departure routine doesn't vary, the dog starts to anticipate the farewell that follows. To forestall such anticipatory anxiety, try changing what you do before you head out the door. If, for example, you always pick up your keys and then put on your coat, try putting on your coat and then picking up your keys. If you put on your lipstick before picking up your keys, wait until you're in the car before applying the lipstick (and the dog can't see you). Bottom line: Do what you can to lessen the likelihood that she anticipates your departure.

✔ **Low-key your leave-taking.** Efforts to comfort your anxious canine by giving her a lot of hugs and soothing words before you depart will probably backfire. Such efforts serve as cues that — horrors! — you're leaving again. Try being non-committal, instead. A casual "Bye now; watch the house" may be easier on your four-legged friend's emotions than an impassioned "Goodbye, my poor sweetums, everything will be fine!" accompanied by multiple hugs and kisses. The emotional goodbye from you may cause your canine companion to rev up her own emotions — and leave her with a huge letdown when you're gone. A no-big-deal goodbye from you may help her realize that your departures are nothing for her to get upset about.

✔ **Turn on the telly.** A little bit of background noise, such as a classical music station or a low-key TV program, may soothe your nervous Nellie more than total silence. It can also fill the void left by your departure and the resulting silence in the house.

✔ **Pick some flowers.** Well, not literally. However, some owners, trainers, and vets have found that certain flower essences may help calm your anxious four-legged friend. A commonly used collection of flower essences for the anxious or otherwise stressed dog is Bach's Rescue Remedy, which combines Cherry Plum, Clematis, Impatiens, Rock Rose, and Star of Bethlehem into a liquid tincture that you drop into your pooch's water with a medicine dropper. Other individual essences, such as gentian, honeysuckle, and walnut, also may be helpful. You can find flower essences at health food stores.

✔ **Reconsider long stays at the kennel.** If your elderly canine companion doesn't deal well with being away from you, reconsider long vacations or other trips that involve your being away from your senior pooch for more than a day or three.

✔ **Go visiting.** Or, take your dog visiting. Spending time at the home of a person who's around when you can't be can help soothe your senior's anxiety.

✔ **Consider meds.** If you can't avoid those long trips or if other measures don't work, think about seeing your vet for your pooch's problem. Your vet can prescribe anti-anxiety medications that can help relieve at least some of your dog's anxiety.

When senior dogs develop new behavior issues — or if small behavior problems suddenly become big ones — the underlying reasons are often physical. A thorough checkup by your vet can uncover the source of your aging friend's behavioral difficulty and help solve it.

Lifetime Learning for the Senior Canine

Unless you've just come from another planet, you've undoubtedly heard the saying about being unable to teach old dogs new tricks. I'm stating here, that for now and for all time, that saying is absolute bunk.

If a dog is physically capable of performing the maneuver in question — and if he's not brain-damaged in some way — he can learn anything in later life that you could have taught him in puppyhood. I once taught a 9-year-old dog how to catch a Frisbee. It didn't take that dog long to learn the art of disc retrieval, and she enjoyed playing that game for several years thereafter. Only after the fact did I figure out that Frisbee-catching is a less-than-ideal pursuit for an older dog (see the section "Retiring old tricks" in this chapter for further information).

But even without the opportunity to become a disc-catching whiz, your senior dog can acquire plenty of new skills that rejuvenate him and help you see just how much he still can learn.

Getting down to basics

Training any dog, not just a senior dog, shouldn't be a haphazard affair. Like many undertakings, a systematic approach works better than seat-of-the-pants tactics. Here are some basic principles to keep in mind when you're tapping your older pooch's inner genius:

- ✔ **Think positive.** Teaching your senior needs to be a happy, upbeat experience for both him and you. The quickest route to such an experience is to think in terms of catching your dog doing something right — and giving him positive feedback when you do. That feedback can take one or more forms: Lavish verbal praise, a short play session, or a tasty treat.

- ✔ **Keep sessions short..** Don't overestimate your senior dog's attention span. Several short sessions in one day are far more productive than one marathon affair. A lesson for your senior Fido should be no more than ten minutes long.

Being a good citizen

If you want to be able to brag about a title your heretofore-untitled senior dog has earned, consider teaching him what it takes to be a Canine Good Citizen (CGC).

The American Kennel Club (AKC) created the CGC program in 1989 to reward dogs who exhibit good manners in their homes and communities. Dogs who pass the ten-part test receive a certificate from the AKC; owners may place the initials "CGC" after their dogs' names. The test requires no athletic ability from the dog (a good thing for seniors!); your dog just has to conduct himself in a mannerly fashion, no matter where he is.

Only certified AKC evaluators may give the CGC test. To obtain a list of evaluators and test dates, log on to the AKC's Web site at www.akc.org/love/cgc/index.cfm.

To pass the test and earn the CGC certification, a dog must

- **Accept a friendly stranger:** While standing in place, the dog lets the evaluator pet him on the head without showing any shyness or resentment.

- **Sit politely for petting:** The dog lets a friendly stranger touch him while he sits alongside his handler.

- **Accept an examination:** The dog lets his evaluator inspect him to determine that he's clean and well groomed, gently comb or brush him, examine his ears, and pick up each front foot.

- **Walk nicely on a loose lead:** The dog and handler walk together with the leash held loosely while the evaluator tells the two where to stop and turn.

- **Walk through a crowd:** The dog and handler walk around and pass closely by at least three people without straining the leash, being rambunctious, or exhibiting any signs of aggression or fear.

- **Sit, lie down, and stay in place:** The dog sits and lies down when told, and then he remains in place while the handler walks 20 feet away.

- **Come when called:** The handler walks 10 feet away from the dog and then calls the animal, who must come when called.

- **Behave politely around other dogs:** Two handlers and their dogs approach each other, stop, shake hands, speak briefly, and continue on. Both dogs should show only a passing interest in each other.

- **Keep cool when distracted:** The evaluator presents two distractions, such as dropping a saucepan onto the floor or running in front of the dog. The dog may react mildly but shouldn't panic, bark, or try to run away.

- **Deal with separation:** The evaluator takes the dog's leash while the owner goes out of sight for three minutes. The dog should show only minimal concern or nervousness.

✔ **Be realistic.** If your dog has a gray muzzle and is about to celebrate his first double-digit birthday, don't expect him to master an agility course.

A better bet may be to see whether your four-legged friend can master some of the elements of a Canine Good Citizen (CGC) test, such as sitting politely for petting or coming when called from the opposite end of a room (see the "Being a good citizen" sidebar in this chapter for more info about the CGC test).

✔ **Have happy endings.** Don't you feel better at the end of a class when you realize that you've succeeded in learning something? Your dog is no different. No matter what happens — and especially if the session isn't going as well as you want — end the lesson asking your dog to do something that you know he can do. When he executes the maneuver and earns your positive feedback, you both feel good, despite any challenges you encountered earlier.

Retiring old tricks

Although I once successfully taught my 9-year-old pooch how to catch a Frisbee, I now know that helping her master that maneuver wasn't as good for her body as it may have been for her mind. Disc retrieval and other tricks that require sudden, strenuous movement may place too much stress on a dog's aging bones, muscles, tendons, and ligaments. Any trick that requires a dog to jump up high from the ground, twist his body in the air, or sit up in a traditional begging position probably should be retired if the dog has already mastered the maneuver. And if he hasn't discovered those tricks already, now is not the time to teach him.

Senior Super Dogs: Dax, the four-legged therapist

A little boy's home had been leveled by one of the wildfires that ravaged southern California in the fall of 2003. Now, in his first day back at school since the blazes had started, he needed to tell someone what had happened to him and what he feared. "My house burnt up," he explained. "All my toys burnt up. My Mommy and Daddy are sad, and they don't know what we're gonna do for Christmas."

The little boy's confidante wasn't a psychologist, social worker, or other mental health pro. In fact, the confidante wasn't even human. She was an Australian Shepherd named Dax, who was well past her ninth birthday.

(continued)

(continued)

Dax's owner is Liz Palika, an author and dog trainer who lives in Oceanside, California. Palika founded "Love on a Leash," an organization that certifies and deploys canine therapists and their human partners to wherever they're needed.

Palika started training Dax for therapy work when she was just a puppy. Basic obedience was part of that training but so was "lots and lots of socialization" so that Dax would feel comfortable around people of all ages, sizes, and backgrounds, not to mention other novelties such as slick floors and elevators. Since then, Dax and Palika have been offering comfort to special needs children and Alzheimer's Disease patients, and also have dealt with emergencies such as the aftermath of the California wildfires. According to Palika, Dax brings some very special talents to her work.

"Dax is very, very serious about her work," Palika says. "She learns quickly, retains what she has learned, and is a wonderful problem solver. When all those qualities are combined with a wonderful empathy for people, she makes an awesome therapy dog. She just seems to know what people need from her."

The little boy who confided his troubles to Dax may well agree. But in any case, his encounter with the Aussie prompted Palika and her friends to start a special Christmas project: raising enough money to give a Christmas stocking and some toys to every child in the two area schools hardest hit by the fires.

"The toys are not expensive or fancy, but every single kid — 650 total — will get something," Palika says proudly. "It's a big project for us, but it all started because a little boy confided in Dax. "

Dax (left) with Riker, courtesy of Liz Palika

Part II
Knowing What to Expect

The 5th Wave   By Rich Tennant

"Well, someone's starting to show his age.
Look at how Rusty has to hold his
chew-toy at arm's length now to see
which one he's got."

In this part . . .

To help your dog make the most of his senior years, you need to know what to expect as he grows older and how you can help keep him in top condition as he ages. In Part II, I describe some common effects of aging on dogs, suggest how you can offset some of those effects, and recommend ways you can work with your vet to ensure that your canine's seniorhood remains golden for as long as possible.

Chapter 5

Staying Healthy

· ·

In This Chapter

▶ Taking your senior dog for a wellness exam

▶ Deciding for or against vaccinations

▶ Keeping your senior looking good

▶ Maintaining your senior's health

· ·

Among the countless commercials that bombard my eyes and ears whenever I watch television, one has the voiceover intone, "If you think good health just happens, you're fooling yourself." The voiceover then urges me to buy whatever health product it's hawking. Clearly, the commercial doesn't do its job because I can't remember the name of the product in question. But the commercial's hook — that people can't just sit back and expect to be healthy — has glued itself to my memory, even now as I write about senior dogs.

People can choose whether or not to listen to that commercial. They can decide whether to sit back and hope good health stays with them or get out and do whatever they can to remain in tip-top condition. They can resolve to go to the gym today or make the appointment for that mammogram tomorrow. And they can say no to scarfing a bag of potato chips and opt instead to snack on fresh fruit or veggies so that they feel virtuous later.

Senior dogs don't have such choices. Although good health doesn't just happen to them either, they can't decide whether or not to work at staying healthy. Owners must make that decision for them and — assuming you opt for good health — do what's necessary to keep them in mint condition. Before you start the doing, though, you need to know exactly what you have to do. That's what this chapter is for: describing ways to keep the older dog healthy for as long as possible.

The Senior Wellness Exam

Keeping your senior dog healthy is much more than a matter of getting her to the vet's office when she's sick. A crucial component of achieving and maintaining good health, for pooch and person alike, is to take a proactive approach. In other words, don't wait until your aging dog has an obvious health problem before taking her to your vet. Instead, take steps to prevent and contain such problems, starting with regular checkups — or, in 21st-century jargon, regular *wellness exams*.

The wellness exam is exactly what it sounds like. Your senior dog gets a thorough going-over by a vet to make sure that your pooch is as healthy as she appears to be. The vet measures your dog's vital signs; peers into her eyes and ears to look for redness, discharge, or other signs of eye and ear disease; runs his hands over the dog's body to check for lumps, bumps, and any tender areas; looks at the teeth and gums for redness, puffiness, and plaque; and checks her skin for flakiness, rashes, or other abnormalities.

In addition, the vet may draw some of your dog's blood and ask you to bring in a urine sample. These samples, when analyzed at a lab, can reveal a lot of information about your dog's state of health. Table 5-1 outlines some common canine geriatric screening tests and what those tests are designed to do.

Table 5-1	Testing, Testing — Why's and What-For's	
Test	**What It's For**	**What It Reveals**
CBC (complete blood count)	Tabulates components of blood, such as white cells, red cells, and platelets	Possible presence of many diseases and conditions, such as infections, anemia, and clotting problems
Blood chemistry profile	Evaluates how well individual organs are functioning	Possible presence of systemic profile diseases, such as diabetes, liver disease, and kidney disease
Urinalysis	Evaluates color, specific gravity, and chemical makeup of urine	Possible presence of urinary tract disease and impaired kidney function
Thyroid panel	Evaluates thyroid gland functioning through a blood test	Possible presence of *hypothyroidism* (insufficient thyroid gland production of thyroid hormone)

To better understand what the results of any tests mean, the vet looks for earlier test results to compare with the new measurements. That's why you should take your dog in for a *baseline exam* as soon as she crosses the threshold between canine middle age and canine seniorhood (If you're not sure when that crossing occurs — or even whether it's happened already — check out Chapter 1.)

The baseline exam consists of the same tests included in regular wellness exams, but because it's the first assessment performed after your dog reaches senior status, the results of the exams and tests are especially important. Those results provide the standard, or baseline, against which the vet measures future tests. Information on common older-dog disease symptoms and what they may mean appears in Chapters 10 and 11.

Uncovering potential problems before they become obvious often greatly increases the likelihood that the problem can be solved or at least managed. The same early detection principles that work for you and your human family members also work for your senior dog.

Of course, a cornerstone of this proactive approach is regular checkups. Most adult dogs do fine with an annual wellness exam, but seniors need more frequent attention. Generally, vets like to see healthy older dogs every six months or so, just to give any potential problems less time to develop.

 A baseline exam can easily cost a couple hundred dollars or more — and that's if the vet doesn't find any problems. To get at least a small break on the cost, check to see whether your vet offers a "Geriatric Pet Month" or "Senior Pet Month" promotion. Such promotions usually feature price reductions on individual features of the baseline exam, such as the blood screening or an entire package of older pet exam services for a reduced price. Another option may be to see if your vet reduces senior well-pet costs during "Adopt A Senior Dog Month," which the American Society for the Prevention of Cruelty to Animals (ASPCA) observes each November.

To Vaccinate or Not to Vaccinate?

Should you vaccinate your dog or not? This is the question, especially for people who own senior dogs.

Once upon a time, not very long ago, the answer to that question was simple: Yes, you should vaccinate your dog — and you should do it every year. The idea was that by being vigilant and prompt in vaccinating their dogs, owners protected them from dreaded canine scourges such as rabies, distemper, parvovirus, hepatitis, and leptospirosis.

Recently, though, many experts have speculated that traditional yearly shots may be too much of a good thing. They suspect that immunizations may protect a dog for much longer than a year. Experts' concern is also growing over the possibility that yearly immunizations may be dangerous to some dogs. Such dangers include the (remote) possibility of the dog developing a tumor called a *sarcoma* at the immunization site — although such tumors are far more common in cats than in dogs. Another concern is that too-frequent immunizations may send a dog's immune system into overdrive, triggering chronic autoimmune diseases, such as lupus.

For those reasons, many vets are now immunizing their canine patients once every three years rather than once a year. Other experts suggest that you ask your vet to perform antibody tests for specific diseases to determine whether your dog needs immunizations for those diseases. However, these tests, which are called *titers,* are more expensive than shots, and some vets don't believe that they're very reliable.

In addition, many vets and other experts question whether senior dogs should be immunized at all. They believe that because vaccines may be effective for much longer than was previously thought, regular vaccinations may not be worth the risk of triggering autoimmune reactions. Even basic math brings the practice of immunizing seniors into question. For example, if a dog is vaccinated at the age of 8, and the vaccination lasts several years, the dog may die before he needs another shot.

The American Animal Hospital Association (AAHA) suggests that owners work with veterinarians to develop individualized immunization plans for their dogs, depending on the age, overall health, and specific needs of the individual animal. No matter how often you decide to immunize, though, it's vitally important to continue taking your dog to the vet for regular wellness exams.

Senior Grooming 101

Your vet has oodles of tools and a noggin full of knowledge that help keep your senior dog healthy and happy. But despite such advantages, the vet can't maintain your dog's well-being single-handedly. When it comes to your dog's health, the first line of defense against disease has to be you.

Grooming your senior regularly helps you succeed in that role. A good grooming session means that you're touching many parts of your dog's body, parting the hair, squirting stuff into his ears, and brushing his teeth (yes, really), among other tasks. Such activities give you ample opportunity to check him for skin changes, ear discharge, bad breath, hair loss, and countless other signs of trouble. At the same time, grooming your senior helps keep him looking good. Even better, this one-on-one time spent with your four-legged friend can't help but deepen the bond between the two of you.

But before you treat your senior dog to the delights of home grooming, you need to make sure that you have the equipment needed to do the job right. Here's a list of the grooming gear that most dogs need:

- ✔ **Brush and comb:** A regular session with a brush and a comb goes a long way toward keeping your senior looking his best. Brushing stimulates the oils in the skin (and with dry-skinned seniors, every bit of oil helps), aerates the coat, removes dead hair, and untangles knots. Combs can put the finishing touches on certain breeds with silky edges to their double coats, such as Collies. Dogs with long, flowing coats, like Salukis, fare well with a comb and a wooden pin brush. Short-coated dogs, such as Boxers, need regular sessions with a currycomb and natural bristle brush.

- ✔ **Spray bottle:** For double-coated and long-coated dogs, a pre-brushing spritz with water eases brushing and prevents hair breakage.

- ✔ **Warm water:** To properly bathe a dog, you need to have warm water at hand — in other words, don't think that bathing a senior outdoors in a water-filled bucket or dousing him with water from the garden hose gets the job done. Most dogs need to bathe in bathtubs; toy dogs and small puppies can use the kitchen sink.

- ✔ **Bath mat or towel:** A senior dog's often less steady on his feet than his younger counterpart, and he may find the bathtub or sink to be frighteningly slippery. A bath mat for the tub or a towel for the sink eases his fear and keeps him on his feet.

- ✔ **Big, fluffy towels:** You can speed up the time needed to dry your dog's coat by wrapping one or more big, fluffy towels around him after his bath.

- ✔ **Dog-friendly shampoo:** Shampoos designed for people are too harsh for a senior dog's thinner coat and more sensitive skin. Use a high-quality dog shampoo instead. Depending on your dog's needs, your vet can prescribe a special shampoo or recommend a brand for you to buy at a pet store.

- ✔ **Cotton balls:** These little mounds of fluff help you protect a dog's ears from soap and water, wash and rinse the face so that soap doesn't get in the dog's eyes, and clean a dog's bottom.

- ✔ **Hand-held shower attachment:** These devices, available in department and bath stores, attach to the faucet and create a shower stream that you can direct onto your dog. They make rinsing much easier, especially for big dogs.

✔ **Waterproof duds:** During dog baths, both the canine bathee and human bather get soaked. The wise human bather dons a swimsuit or waterproof apron to keep her regular clothes dry.

✔ **Small scissors:** You need these scissors to cut stubborn mats and for minor trims, such as the hair between the paw pads.

When you wield those scissors, be careful not to cut too close to your dog's skin.

✔ **Nail gear:** Either regular nail clippers or small scissors keep your canine companion's claws from becoming too long.

Boning up on bath basics

A generation ago, dog owners were told to bathe their dogs as little as possible because experts thought that too many dunkings dried out the canine coat and skin. Today, though, gentler shampoos and additional knowledge have experts recommending at least a monthly bathing — and even more frequent sudsings if the dog has a close encounter with mud or another equally icky substance. Whenever you give a bath, here's what to do:

1. **Brush your long-haired dog before her bath to get rid of tangles.**

   If you don't, the tangles clump like dreadlocks during the bath and are next to impossible to untangle when dry.

2. **Place a cotton ball in each ear to protect it from water.**

   For dogs, water in the ear is very uncomfortable.

3. **Put her in the tub.**

   If your dog won't enter the tub by herself, lift her carefully and put her in the tub atop the bath mat.

4. **Apply some restraint.**

   Keep one hand on your dog to prevent her from making a break for it. Just in case she does, though, keep the bathroom door closed so that she can't run all over the place before you've finished bathing her.

5. **Pour warm water all over your dog, making sure that the water goes all the way down to the skin.**

   Start at the top of her head and neck and then wet the length of her backbone. After that, water the sides, chest, legs, and tail.

6. **Lather up.**

   Apply enough shampoo to work up a lather all over your dog's body, but avoid generating clouds of suds. If you do see such clouds, you're using too much shampoo.

7. **Clean the face.**

   Gently apply a damp cotton ball to your dog's face and wipe.

8. **Rinse for five minutes.**

   Use the hand-held showerhead to rinse your dog from front to back and top to bottom for at least five minutes. By then, the rinse water should be clear, and there should be no itch-producing, flake-making soap residue on your dog's skin.

9. **Wrap one or more towels around your dog's body to soak up excess water.**

   Blot instead of rubbing (rubbing can cause tangles). Then, let her perform that standard canine after-bath ritual: running crazily around the house. After that, towel her some more or wield a blow dryer (if your dog tolerates it).

10. **Do her hair.**

    Most dogs need a post-bath brushing to style their coats, but when to brush depends on your dog's coat. Long-haired, kinky-coated, or double-coated dogs fare better with damp brushing; curly coated canines, such as Portuguese Water Dogs, do fine with dry.

Giving the brush-off

Generally, a weekly brushing date keeps most dogs looking well-groomed. But for brushing to do more than make your dog look good, the brush needs to reach not only the hair but also the skin. Doing so removes accumulated oil and dandruff and stimulates the skin surface. Reaching the skin is easy when grooming a short-haired breed, such as a Dachshund, but it's tougher when brushing a long-haired Afghan Hound or a double-coated Shetland Sheepdog.

Giving a mini-bath

If you don't have time to give your senior a full bath but need to clean her up, try using a rinseless shampoo. Cherrybrook (www.cherrybrook.com), a dog-supply company, manufactures several such products. Simply lather up your senior and wipe off the suds with a damp cloth. Her tresses will be bright and sparkling again!

Professional groomers employ special techniques to give double-coated and long-coated dogs the gentle but down-to-the-roots brushing they need. For them, the brushing method of choice is called *line brushing*. To line-brush your dog, here's what to do:

1. **Place your senior on his side.**

   Senior dogs may find standing during an entire brushing session difficult. A better option is to have your aging friend lie down on his side. That position is easier on his joints, helps him relax, and makes it easier for you to brush hard-to-reach places, such as above his tummy and inside his hind legs. You can see in Figure 5-1 that placing your hand on your dog's side gives you an extra second or two to grab him if he decides to bag the grooming ritual and bolt.

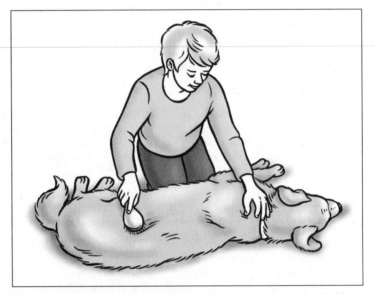

Figure 5-1: Placing your dog on his side makes grooming easier for him and for you.

2. **Fill your spray bottle with semi-warm water and mist the coat along the backbone.**

   Don't soak the hair, though; you're aiming for a damp coat here.

3. **Starting at the neck and working toward the tail, gently brush small sections of the coat along your dog's backbone from the skin out to the hair tip.**

   Brush opposite the hair's direction. After you complete this step, your dog may look like he has a Mohawk along his back.

4. **Mist the row of the coat that's just below the Mohawk and brush as before.**

   Repeat this process, line by line, until you've brushed the entire side.

5. **Then, turn your dog over and repeat the process on his other side.**

   Make sure that you also do his inner flanks, chest hair, and tail.

6. **Tame the tangles.**

   Tightly tangled clumps of fur look unsightly, cause discomfort to your dog, and may lead to skin infections. To tame these tangles, pay special attention to prime matting areas: the backs of all four legs, the front armpits, and behind the ears.

   To remove a mat, start by moistening it and gently working it free with your fingers, a comb, or a brush. If that doesn't work, use small scissors to cut the mat.

7. **After you've brushed the entire coat against the grain, you're ready for the final step: Brush the hair back in the direction it grows.**

   A double-coated dog's hair falls down on its own except perhaps at the area just above the base of the tail; gently comb the hair there to help it lie down. A comb can also help style long hair around the face and feathery hair on the legs. Long-haired, silky-coated dogs benefit from all-over combing.

Short-haired dogs don't need such thorough brushing, but they still need the skin stimulation, hair removal, and overall attention of a regular session with a brush. Just go over the coat once a week with a natural bristle or rubber currycomb.

Be very careful if you move the brush or comb over a lump or tumor on the dog's skin. Tumors are easily broken by either grooming implement, which could result in your senior needing surgery.

Banishing bad breath

The phrase "dog breath" isn't a slam on the canine species; it simply states a truism that's backed by the American Veterinary Dental College (AVDC). The AVDC reports that more than 8 of 10 dogs and cats show signs of dental disease by the age of 3. Clearly, senior dogs have had more than twice as much time to accumulate damage to their untended teeth. That damage includes not only hoochy breath but also separation of the tooth from the gum, tooth loss, and bacterial infections that can be fatal if the infections spread from the teeth to organs elsewhere in the body.

But you can prevent all those problems. You just need to brush your canine's canines and other teeth every day or at least a few times a week. Frequent brushings help your dog's teeth the way they help yours: They remove the food particles, saliva, minerals, and bacteria that form a coating of plaque on the teeth and create a nursery for the bacteria that cause life-threatening infections.

Brushing your dog's teeth doesn't have to be complicated. Here's how to make it routine:

- ✔ **Get the right stuff.** Pet-supply stores sell toothbrushes for dogs, but a human child's toothbrush can do the job just as well. Human toothpaste doesn't cut it, though, because it upsets a dog's stomach if swallowed. Toothpastes made just for dogs clean the teeth and gums, won't upset your dog's tummy if she swallows some, and usually come in dog-friendly flavors. (Alas, mint isn't one of those flavors. Your dog's teeth are clean after brushing with doggy toothpaste, but her breath isn't minty-fresh.)

- ✔ **Give her the finger.** If your four-legged friend has never dealt with a toothbrush before, now's not the time to rush the process. Instead, try rubbing a gauze-wrapped finger on your dog's gums so that she gets used to having her mouth worked with. After she accepts the finger readily, you can gradually introduce her to the toothbrush for a few seconds at a time.

- ✔ **Be consistent.** You're more likely to remember to brush every day if you brush at the same time each day.

- ✔ **Keep her close-mouthed.** Dogs don't need to open their mouths to have their teeth brushed. Simply lift your dog's lips gently and brush the outer surfaces of the teeth. The dog's tongue keeps the inner surfaces clean.

- ✔ **Bribe her.** If your dog can count on having something nice happen right after a tooth brushing, she's more likely to put up with the procedure. Good rewards include a walk or play session. Don't give her a treat, though. Doing so defeats the purpose of brushing.

If for some reason your dog simply won't tolerate a daily brushing (or even if she does), you can try giving her special dog foods designed to reduce plaque and plaque-fighting treats. But don't lose heart. Some dogs actually enjoy getting their teeth brushed.

My Golden Retriever, Allie, is one of them. If I say, "Time to brush your teeth," she comes running into the bathroom and sits down, ready to have her choppers tended to.

Lending an ear

Keeping your dog's ears clean helps keep him more comfortable, not to mention smelling nicer (if you've ever smelled an infected canine ear, you already know what I mean). More importantly, regular cleanings help prevent ear infections. Such infections, if left untreated, not only cause your pooch a lot of pain, but they can also result in a loss of hearing in the affected ear.

Generally, a dog's ears need cleaning once a month or so — although, if your dog has floppy ears (such as a Cocker Spaniel, Golden Retriever, or Basset Hound), you may want to do the job once a week. The floppy part, or flap, covers the rest of the ear, which limits airflow and prevents the ear canal from drying out. A moist ear canal is a welcome mat for bacteria, mites, and other undesirables.

To do the job, you need some cotton balls, soft cotton cloths, or cotton swabs, as well as some ear cleanser made especially for pets. You can get such cleansers from your vet. After you have your ear gear,

1. **Have your four-legged friend either sit or lie down.**

2. **Squirt a little bit of the cleanser into the ear.**

3. **Fold the ear flap over the rest of the ear and gently massage for about 60 seconds.**

4. **Let your dog shake his head.**

5. **With your cotton ball, square, or swab, gently clean the visible parts of the ear.**

   Don't go into the ear canal (especially with a cotton swab) — if you do, you risk driving organisms deeper into the ear and even puncturing the eardrum.

If your dog shakes his head a lot, runs his ears along the ground, has a foul odor coming from the ears, or sports any dark, smelly discharge from the ear, he probably has an ear infection. Take him to your vet for evaluation and treatment. Ear infections are nothing to mess with; left untreated, they become extremely painful for your dog and cause hearing loss.

Giving your pooch a pedicure

Experts recommend keeping your dog's toenails short enough to be off the ground when she's standing still. You should keep the *dewclaws* (the nails that you find higher up on the leg, near the ankle) sufficiently short to prevent them from curving back into the skin of the leg. Here's how to give your pooch a pedicure:

1. **Put your four-legged friend in either a sitting or reclining position — whichever is more relaxing for her while also being reasonably easy for you to reach.**

2. **Wield the scissors.**

   If your dog has hair growing between her paw pads, trim it as short as possible without nicking the pad itself. Small scissors or clipppers do the job nicely.

3. **Look for the *quick* (the blood vessel in your dog's toenails).**

   A dog's toenail has a blood vessel inside it that runs almost to the end of the nail. If your dog's nails are light in color, you can see the quick; it's the pink area inside the nail. Dark nails are more problematic because you can't see the quick; you need to estimate where it is.

4. **Slowly pick up the clippers, gently squeeze the paw to extend the nails a bit, and place the clippers around the very end of one nail.**

5. **Squeeze the clippers quickly to trim off the nail tip.**

6. **Continue trimming a little at a time until you see the black dot in the center of the trimmed nail.**

   The black dot signals the start of the quick. Avoid cutting into it.

If you goof, stay calm. Despite your best efforts, you may trim off too much nail and hit the quick — and when that happens, the nail bleeds. To stop the bleeding, just apply some styptic powder (available in pharmacies) or ordinary baking flour to the nail. These compounds help the bleeding stop very quickly.

If your dog hates getting a pedicure, a little bribery and a lot of patience can get the job done, though at a much slower pace than with a dog who tolerates this procedure. Wait until your dog's relaxed. (Most dogs are relaxed when they're watching television with their people. TV time often makes for a good pedicure time.) Have some treats on hand and then pick up one of your dog's paws. Trim just one nail — and then end the session for the day. Give your dog a treat. After your dog tolerates getting one nail trimmed per day, start adding a second nail to the daily regimen — again, using a treat to sweeten the process. Taken slowly, even a clipper-phobic dog may learn to tolerate a session with the hated instrument.

A more comfortable alternative to nail clippers is a grinder. Grinders are designed to drill, sand, shape, and detail wood. You can find them at home improvement stores and department stores. Introduce your senior slowly, though; start off by turning it on and giving your dog a treat when she looks at it. Keep doing this until your dog pays no attention to the grinder. When the grinder elicits a ho-hum reaction from your senior, start working on the nails — but grind only one nail per day and give a treat afterward. After your senior is cool with the one-nail treatment, you can proceed to doing more nails until you trim them all.

Maintaining Health from Home

Cutting-edge veterinary medicine can do a lot to prolong the life of your senior canine companion — but you can make your vet's job a lot easier by being your dog's one-person health maintenance organization. From monitoring your dog's vital signs to medicating him when he's sick, here's how to perform some basic health-related chores for your older four-legged friend.

Getting your dog's vital signs

They're not called "vital signs" for nothing. Your dog's *TPR* — temperature, pulse, and respiration — is a crucial health indicator. A dog whose temperature is above or below normal, whose heart rate is way faster than usual, or whose breathing is quicker than it should be is a dog who clearly needs veterinary attention. But for you to pick up on the clues that your dog's TPR provides, you need to know normal TPR rates and how to measure your own particular pooch's TPR.

Table 5-2 provides a one-glance answer to the normal-rate question.

Table 5-2	What's Normal TPR?
Vital Sign	*Normal Range*
Temperature	100.5° Fahrenheit to 102.0° Fahrenheit
Pulse	60 to 140 beats per minute at rest
Respiration	10 to 30 breaths per minute at rest

Taking your dog's temperature

To find out how hot (or how cold) your pooch is, you need three items: a clean, shaken-down rectal thermometer, some petroleum jelly, and another person. After you have your equipment, you need to

1. **Have the other person hold your dog still.**

2. **Put some petroleum jelly on the bulb of the thermometer.**

3. **Carefully slide the thermometer about 1 inch into the dog's rectum.**

4. **Wait for two minutes.**

5. **Remove the thermometer slowly and read it.**

Measuring your dog's pulse

To take your pooch's pulse, you just need yourself and your dog — and perhaps, a look at Figure 5-2.

1. **Have your dog lie down on her side.**

2. **While sitting behind your dog, place your hand on top of her hind leg.**

3. **Move your hand forward until your fingers are curled around the front of the leg.**

4. **Slide your hand upward until your hand is touching the wall of your dog's abdomen.**

   At this point, you should be able to feel a pulse beating beneath your fingers.

5. **Count the beats for 15 seconds.**

6. **Multiply that number by four, and you have your dog's heart rate per minute.**

Measuring your dog's respiration

To determine how many breaths your dog takes per minute, do the following:

1. **Have him lie down on his side.**

2. **Place your hand lightly over his rib cage and count the number of times your hand rises in 15 seconds.**

3. **Multiply that number by four for your dog's respiration rate.**

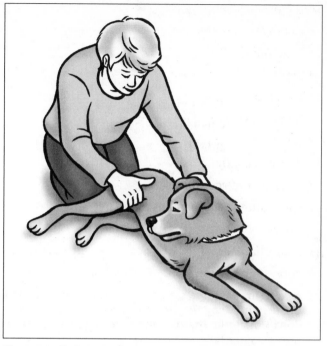

Figure 5-2: To find your dog's pulse, move your hand to the top of his inner hind leg.

Setting up a doggy first-aid kit

To prepare for any illness or injury that may befall your senior dog, assign a portion of your bathroom medicine cabinet for storing first-aid gear and medications. A tackle box, a toolbox, or a shelf in one of your kitchen cabinets does the trick if your medicine cabinet's too full. Here's what to stock the box or shelf with:

- Adhesive bandages (for small wounds)
- Antibiotic ointment
- Benadryl (25 mg)
- Buffered baby aspirin (*not* acetaminophen, also known as Tylenol, or ibuprofen, which is better known as Advil or Motrin, because both are poisonous to dogs)
- Cortisone cream or ointment
- Cotton swabs or balls
- Flexible plastic digital rectal thermometer
- Gauze sponges

- ✔ Hand wipes
- ✔ Hydrogen peroxide
- ✔ Immodium
- ✔ Latex gloves
- ✔ Muzzle and leash
- ✔ Non-adhesive bandages
- ✔ 1-inch adhesive tape
- ✔ Petroleum jelly
- ✔ Small pair of scissors
- ✔ Soft padded gauze bandage on a roll
- ✔ Tweezers
- ✔ Phone number for vet and nearest emergency veterinary clinic
- ✔ Phone number for ASPCA Poison Control Center: 888-426-4435
- ✔ A good first-aid book, such as *First Aid for Dogs: An Owner's Guide to a Happy Healthy Pet* by Stefanie Schwartz (Howell Book House) or *The First Aid Companion for Dogs and Cats* by Amy D. Shojai (Rodale Press)

Many American Red Cross chapters offer courses in first aid for dogs and other pets. To find such a course, log on to the home page of the American Red Cross (www.redcross.org), type in your zip code where the site allows you to find your local chapter, and check out the local chapter's schedule of first-aid classes.

Giving your dog meds

Most dog owners don't relish giving either pills or liquid medications to their four-legged friends, and for good reason: The dog usually makes the job very difficult. The typical pooch either fakes out the owner by appearing to take the pill and later spitting it out in some out-of-the-way place, or struggles so much that you may think you've both signed up for a wrestling tournament.

The trouble is, dogs need their meds — and senior dogs generally need more meds than their younger counterparts do. However, the job doesn't have to be difficult.

With pills, you have basically two methods of giving them to your dog: the Easy Method and the Even Easier Method. To use the Even Easier Method, you just have to fake out your dog rather than vice versa. Just bury the pill in some cream cheese, peanut butter, or moist dog food. Most dogs fall for this ploy and are none the wiser.

However, a few canine geniuses don't fall for the Even Easier Method. They eat around the offending pill and leave it in the dish. For these individuals, the Easy Method — also known as the Down-the-Hatch Method — does the trick:

1. **Place your dog in a sitting position (or ask her to sit).**

   If you opt for the latter and she complies, give her a quick treat before proceeding further.

2. **Tilt her head back about 45 degrees.**

3. **Gently run your fingers along her upper lips until your fingers are about halfway back along the lip line.**

4. **Place a slight bit of pressure on both sides of her lips to open her mouth.**

5. **Place the pill as far back as possible on the tongue.**

6. **Close the mouth and hold it.**

7. **Keeping her head tilted upward, gently rub her throat until you feel her swallow the tablet.**

Liquid medicines are a little trickier. You generally can't mix them into food because the smell of the meds interferes with the aroma of the food, causing your senior dog to turn up her nose and walk away from the concoction. Not to worry: A variation of the Down-the-Hatch Method works here, too. Find a clean eyedropper and proceed as follows:

1. **Have your dog sit down.**

2. **Tilt her head upward and open her mouth.**

3. **Inject the liquid.**

4. **Close her mouth, hold it shut, and stroke the throat until you feel her swallow the liquid.**

Purging parasites

Parasites, such as worms, mosquitoes, fleas, and ticks, are never any fun and often are dangerous for a dog of any age. But for senior dogs, who may not have the robust constitutions of younger pooches, unwanted critters are even more, well, unwanted.

Common freeloaders, such as fleas, cause most dogs to itch. Many victims scratch those itches so intensely that they develop large, oozing sores known as *hot spots.* The little bloodsuckers can also cause your dog to become anemic. Worms, such as roundworm, hookworm, and tapeworm, can also cause anemia. Heartworms lodge in the heart (surprise!). If left untreated, a heartworm infestation kills the dog. Mites tend to cluster in a dog's ears, causing intense itching and discomfort.

Dealing with fleas and worms is largely a matter of prevention. Your vet can offer a variety of products in either pill or topical form that can prevent those parasites from plaguing your pooch in the first place. Don't use over-the-counter stuff, though; most of it is ineffective and can cause serious side effects or even death. You also need to get your dog a yearly stool sampling for roundworms, hookworms, whipworms, and tapeworms, and a yearly blood test for heartworm.

Make sure that the heartworm preventive your vet prescribes is appropriate for your dog's breed. Any medication that contains ivermectin can be poisonous to Collies, Shetland Sheepdogs, and their mixes. If your dog falls into one of those breed categories, ask for a different heartworm medication.

Ticks can cause serious problems, too. They transmit a variety of serious diseases, like Lyme Disease, erlichiosis, and Rocky Mountain spotted fever — all of which ticks also can transmit to people. Symptoms include loss of appetite, loss of weight, fever, lethargy, and stiffness. You can often treat such diseases with antibiotics, but experts agree that prevention is crucial to combating these maladies. Prevention starts with checking your dog often to see if she has any ticks on her body — and removing any ticks properly. To do this,

1. **Put on gloves and use tweezers.**

2. **With the tweezers, grab the tick's body and pull it straight off the dog.**

   Don't twist or jerk while you pull.

3. **If it looks like the tick's head stayed behind in your dog, remove the head with an alcohol-sterilized needle.**

4. **Put the tick in a bowl of rubbing alcohol to kill it.**

5. **Clean the wound with soap, water, and alcohol.**

6. **Note the date that you removed the tick.**

7. **Watch for signs or symptoms of tick-borne disease.**

   Symptoms such as stiff joints, limping, and fatigue may appear as early as four to ten days after you remove the tick, but also can take months to show up. Either way, if your dog exhibits such symptoms after you know a tick's bitten her, take her to your vet.

Chapter 6

Having Accidents

. . . .

In This Chapter

▶ Understanding why older dogs develop potty problems

▶ Discovering that accidents aren't always what they seem

▶ Dealing with your dog's bathroom issues

▶ Helping the incontinent senior

. . . .

I used to think that television commercials about incontinence were silly. I wondered why in the world anyone would want to talk about such problems on TV, much less buy some sort of adult potty product. But now that I've gotten older, I understand why those commercials remain on the air.

Just as older humans develop bathroom management challenges, so do older dogs. An older female dog who hasn't needed middle-of-the-night walks since early puppyhood may start wetting her bed at night. An older male dog may have trouble peeing or pooping. Dogs of either gender can develop housetraining amnesia — they forget to ask to go out to do their duties.

None of these dogs means to be incontinent. Their potty problems are beyond their control; they don't want to leave unauthorized puddles or piles around the house. However, such accidents don't necessarily mean that an aging dog's bathroom equipment has broken down. Instead, a senior dog's bathroom issues may reflect problems going on elsewhere in his body. This chapter explains what that something else may be and what you can do about it.

Do Senior Dogs Need Diapers?

If your senior dog dribbles throughout your house, you may be tempted to head to your nearest pet-supply store and look for a set of doggy diapers. And you can find some, too. Over the short-term — or if you can't find or successfully treat an underlying cause — diapers can well provide a solution to your dog's potty problem (see the "When Housetraining Doesn't Help" section at the end of this chapter). Over the long-term, though, you should try to deal with doggy bathroom boo-boos by searching for the underlying cause of those boo-boos.

Many dogs' kidneys weaken as they age, or they may lose muscle tone in their bladders. Still, normal age-related changes don't always account for an individual dog's inability to hold her water.

For example, if a dog's extra pee-pee output comes from drinking extra water — and if she's also losing some hair on her trunk and has a drooping abdomen (also known as a *potbelly*) — she may well have *Cushing's Disease* (see Chapter 10 for more on this condition). Conversely, a dog's failure to drink much water can cause a problem that often troubles older humans: Constipation. Seniors of any species can acquire this condition, but in most cases, you can prevent and correct it.

Accidents May Mean Something Else

The bodily systems of the aging dog — like those of any species of any age, humans included — interact with each other. When one system goes awry, at least a few others are probably affected. This interdependence is particularly true with respect to senior pooches' potty problems. More often than not, an older dog's bathroom accident results from a problem that has nothing to do with either the urinary system or the digestive system. The following sections give you some examples of apparent pooch potty problems that really aren't potty problems at all.

Housetraining amnesia

A dog who suddenly seems to forget the very idea that he needs to conduct his bathroom business outdoors may be suffering from a condition that has nothing to do with housetraining. Such dogs often exhibit a variety of additional symptoms, such as appearing to be lost in their own homes, failing to recognize family members, losing interest in eating, barking for no apparent reason, and pacing throughout the night instead of sleeping.

If you think that such dogs sound senile, you're absolutely right. The condition that triggers this behavior is called canine *cognitive dysfunction syndrome (CDS),* and the cause is very similar to that of human Alzheimer's Disease. In both dogs and humans, the syndrome develops when a certain type of protein begins to coat the brain. Eventually, the coating causes the brain to shrink while pockets of fluid inside the brain become larger.

CDS has no cure, but you can ease your dog's symptoms. The U.S. Food and Drug Administration (FDA) has approved the use of a drug called *Anipryl* to treat the condition. This drug can bring back at least some of a dog's normal functioning — if only temporarily.

To save money, ask your vet if the generic version of Anipryl, *selegiline*, would be appropriate for your senior.

Another option comes from a major pet-food company, Hills Pet Nutrition, which has developed a diet for dogs called Hill's Prescription Diet b/d. The company says that this diet, which you can get only through veterinarians, contains extra antioxidants and other nutrients that can help fight the brain damage that CDS causes. For more information about CDS, check out Chapters 9 and 10.

Wetting the bed

A dowager doggy who wakes up with a puddle underneath her tush hasn't suddenly forgotten what she learned in Housetraining 101. Instead, she probably lacks estrogen, a hormone that's crucial to helping her maintain bladder control. Just as human females do, canine females lose estrogen as they age. Although all species normally lose this hormone as they age, for the older lady dog, too little estrogen can lead to way too many morning puddles.

Prescription meds can help senior female dogs regain their bathroom aplomb. The two treatments of choice are *phenyl-propanolamine* (PPA) and *diethylstilbestrol* (DES). Both these drugs may be somewhat problematic, however. The FDA banned PPA for human use in 2000 because people who used diet medications that contained the drug risked developing strokes. However, vets can prescribe chewable PPA just for dogs.

As for DES, doctors haven't used that compound for human beings in many years because young women whose mothers had taken the compound while pregnant developed cancer and other health problems. But vets can still prescribe this medication, too.

If you are pregnant or plan to become pregnant, and your dog is taking DES, don't administer the drug yourself. Have another person do it. A pregnant woman who exposes herself to DES — even by touching one of the pills — risks giving her child one or more serious health problems.

Perpetual peeing

Even if your senior dog isn't having any accidents, he still may be having potty problems. A very common older dog bathroom issue is the need to pee more often. This development signals the onset of any one of several potentially serious conditions.

Among those conditions is *kidney disease,* which is one of the most common afflictions in older dogs. Problems occur when the kidneys fail to function efficiently and can't retain enough water for the dog's body. Consequently, the dog tries to offset his water deficit by drinking more often, which in turn triggers more peeing and more fluid loss. Some kidney troubles are simple infections that you can treat with antibiotics; others are much more serious and can result in permanent damage to the affected organ. Other symptoms of kidney problems include clear (or almost clear) urine, an ammonia-like smell to the dog's breath, loss of appetite, weight loss, and lethargy.

However, kidney problems aren't the only conditions that frequent drinking and peeing may signal. Another illness is *diabetes,* which occurs when the pancreas produces either poorly functioning insulin or not enough of it. Either way, though, the sugar level in the dog's bloodstream rises, and the dog drinks more water to dilute the sugar. More water, of course, means more trips outside to pee. You can find more information about diabetes in Chapter 10.

Still another condition that leads to frequent drinking and peeing is *Cushing's Disease,* a condition in which the dog's body produces too much cortisone. A dog with Cushing's also may experience hair loss, increased appetite, increased panting, muscle weakness, and a potbelly.

For more information about diagnosing and treating kidney disease, diabetes, and Cushing's Disease, check out Chapter 10.

Not all instances of frequent peeing mean that a dog is seriously ill. A dog who needs to pee all the time may have a simple urinary tract infection (UTI). Dogs with this condition often have very dark urine, which reflects the presence of blood. And for a dog with UTI, during those trips to the outdoor potty, he may release very little urine, causing the uninformed owner to wonder why the dog bothers to go at all.

You can cure UTIs with antibiotics available from your vet, but you should deal with UTIs promptly. Failure to do so can, at the very least, result in extreme discomfort for your dog. And after your senior starts his antibiotics, you should be sure to finish the entire prescription, even if his symptoms disappear. Your dog may still have the infection, even though he no longer shows signs of having a UTI. Stopping the meds prematurely allows the infection to worsen, which soon results in your dog feeling worse than ever. Worse still, a second course of the same antibiotic may not work because the bacteria causing the UTI may have developed the ability to resist the medicine.

Also, be patient with your dog's frequent requests for potty breaks and encourage him to drink a lot of water. That way, he flushes the infection out of his body sooner.

If your senior dog is peeing more often — and especially if he's also drinking more water — seek veterinary attention as soon as possible. The sooner your dog gets help, the better he'll feel, and the better his prognosis will be.

Getting the runs

Diarrhea — or, as it's commonly called, the runs — is a condition that may or may not be a big deal. If your dog's stool turns to water, or is just very soft, here's what to do:

- ✔ **Make her fast.** A 12- to 24-hour fast can help your four-legged friend's overworked digestive system get some much-needed rest.

- ✔ **Turn on the water.** A dog with diarrhea is a dog in danger of dehydration because her near-liquid poop leaches precious fluids from her body. Encourage your dog to drink a lot of water to combat this danger.

- ✔ **Start a bland diet.** After the 24-hour fast ends, start giving your senior some tummy-friendly food. A mixture of boiled hamburger or white-meat chicken (make sure to skim the fat off) and rice is a good choice. Keep her on this diet for a few days and gradually reintroduce her regular fare.

- ✔ **Don't wait too long to get help.** If these measures don't end or at least diminish the diarrhea, take your dog to the vet. If your pooch also vomits, go sooner. Prolonged diarrhea can signal conditions such as worms, a food allergy, or cancer — and only a vet can treat those conditions.

Getting all stopped up

Unlike the senior dog with diarrhea, the little-or-no-flow oldster tries to pee with little or no success or doesn't bother trying to poop for days on end. Both conditions are potentially serious.

The dog who strains to pee needs to see a vet right away. Such blockages may result from stones blocking the urinary tract — a condition that can be fatal if you don't treat it.

The constipated canine may be suffering from one of several conditions: A lack of fiber in his diet, a blockage in the intestinal tract caused by your canine friend eating something he shouldn't have (wonder where that sock went?), inflammatory bowel disease, or cancer. You need to take an immediate trip to the vet to diagnose the problem and treat it. But if the vet can't find an underlying cause, some extra fiber can get things moving. Try adding one or two teaspoons of canned pumpkin to a dog's food. A little bran cereal or non-flavored Metamucil can help, too.

To keep your Rover regular, try adding some fruit or vegetables to his food every day. Good veggies include broccoli and carrots; equally good fruits are apples and bananas.

Reinforcing Housetraining

If you've taken your dog to the vet and her potty problems don't have a physical cause, your four-legged friend may not have been housetrained properly in the first place. The senior dogs most likely to have flunked Housetraining 101 during puppyhood include very small or toy dogs whose owners may not have noticed their teeny-tiny dribbles or newly adopted seniors who never had the opportunity to learn proper potty protocol when they were younger.

But don't fret. Healthy older dogs can acquire good bathroom manners just like younger pooches do. You just need to tap into your dog's instinct to keep her den clean and teach her how to hold her you-know-what for increasingly longer periods of time.

Crate training revisited

If your senior hasn't seen his crate for a while, now's the time to bring it out of storage. The crate is crucial to effective housetraining because it serves as the den that no self-respecting dog would dream of contaminating with bodily waste. This disdain for dirty dens is hard-wired into almost every dog's brain, and you can capitalize on this trait when retraining your lapsed housetrainee. Put the crate in a place that's important to your senior, such as your bedroom or the family room. Then, perform the following tasks:

 Create and follow a schedule. Take your senior-in-potty-training out to do his business at the same times every day.

For the recently lapsed housetrainee, consider giving him bathroom breaks four times a day: Morning, mid-day, early evening, and late evening. If your senior can't hold it that long, plan additional trips outside — but again, take those trips at the same times each day. The schedule helps your dog retrain his bathroom equipment to stay shut until the appropriate time.

✔ **Be vigilant.** When you can't supervise your senior, put him in his crate. While he sits in the crate, he does everything he can to hold his water (or the other stuff). When you let him out of his crate, watch carefully for signs that he needs to do the doo. Typical pre-potty maneuvers include sniffing, circling, pacing, going to the door, and whining. If your senior engages in any such behavior, get him outside before he unloads.

✔ **Be patient.** It may take your dog a week or so to refresh his memory about proper potty protocol. Don't be upset in the meantime, just clean up the accidents without comment (see the "Dealing with Potty Output" section later in this chapter).

✔ **Be ready to re-evaluate.** If more than a couple of weeks go by and your senior's bathroom manners are still in the toilet (yes, that pun was fully intended), take him back to the vet for a recheck. Your vet may be able to find a cause to your canine's incontinence that didn't show up during earlier checkups.

Making the outhouse in-house

Sometimes, an older dog who does her bathroom business outdoors can no longer make the trip to an outdoor potty. Perhaps the distance to the backyard bathroom has become too long for the senior to negotiate — either because she can't hold her you-know-what that long or because she has difficulty walking. Perhaps the dog's owners have moved to a place like a high-rise apartment, where whisking the pooch outdoors to potty is no longer practical. Or maybe the owners have aged along with their dog, find movement difficult, and thus can't get their animals outside. In any case, teaching the dog to do her business indoors rather than outdoors can be a good solution.

You can make indoor potties out of newspapers spread on the floor or from a special doggy litter box. The following sections tell you how to help your dog make the transition from outdoor potty to either type of indoor commode.

Newspapers: Not just for reading anymore

Relocating the canine bathroom from out in the backyard to on top of yesterday's front page isn't hard to do, but it does take time and patience:

1. **Begin by bringing a piece of toilet paper along when you take your aging Fido out to do his bathroom biz.**

2. **After he poops or pees, wipe his abdomen and bottom with the toilet paper.**

3. **When you're back inside, wipe the soiled toilet paper on top of a sheet of newspaper.**

   Chuck the toilet paper, but save the newspaper for the next jaunt outside.

4. **The next time Fido needs to do the doo, take the wiped newspaper and some fresh sheets of newspaper with you.**

5. **When you reach the potty place, put the wiped newspaper on the ground and the fresh newspapers on top.**

   Hold them in place with a rock. At this point, Fido should be sniffing the papers curiously and proceeding to anoint or make a deposit on top of them. Praise him lavishly when he does.

6. **Continue this ritual until Fido consistently does his business on top of the newspapers.**

   When he does, you can move the papers indoors.

7. **Place a pre-scented newspaper beneath a sheet of fresh newspapers spread out on the floor of the designated indoor potty area.**

8. **At Fido's next potty break, take him to the papers, and give him a few minutes to do the doo.**

   If he does, heap on the praise; if he doesn't, try again in about 15 minutes.

After he consistently uses the indoor paper, you can consider him to be indoor-trained.

Be very patient during this process. You're asking your dog to make a huge change after years of using an outdoor potty spot. He may be less than thrilled with switching to an indoor potty, but your enthusiasm and encouragement can help him overcome his reluctance. If, despite all your efforts, your four-legged friend just can't move his bathroom inside, take him back to your vet for a recheck.

Litter boxes: Not just for cats anymore

A litter box can be a great alternative to newspapers for the pooch who needs to potty inside. Litter boxes make less messy toilets than newspapers, and commercially manufactured litter boxes blend in far better with home décor than sheets of newspapers do. Figure 6-1 shows a dog inside his litter box.

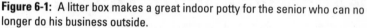

Figure 6-1: A litter box makes a great indoor potty for the senior who can no longer do his business outside.

Moving a canine potty from an outdoor spot to an indoor litter box is similar to the process of moving the outdoor potty to indoor newspapers:

1. **Start by placing some dog litter on the outdoor potty place.**

2. **At potty time, bring your dog outdoors and encourage her to do her duty on the litter.**

   Lure her there with a treat, and/or use your usual language to suggest that now is the time to do the doo. For example, if you tell your dog "Go potty" to induce her to unload, use that term to give her the idea that she should do that unloading on the litter.

3. **Praise her when she does.**

4. **When Fidette consistently uses the litter-covered potty spot, introduce her to the litter box by placing the litter-filled box next to the litter-covered outdoor potty area.**

5. **Encourage her to investigate the litter box and praise her to the skies if she does.**

6. **After your dog is accustomed to seeing the litter box, encourage her to do her duty inside the box (no thinking outside the box at this point).**

Just put some used litter or pre-scented newspaper in the box.

7. **When Fidette poops or pees inside the box, go crazy with praise for her accomplishment.**

8. **After she uses the litter box consistently, stop placing the litter on the ground and start to move the box toward your house.**

Do this shift slowly, by only a few feet each day. Eventually, you can install the litter box inside your house.

If your dog balks at any point in this process, she's telling you that you need to ease up. Slow down and be sure that she's comfortable with the current step in the process before moving on to the next one.

Dealing with Potty Output

No matter why your senior pooch has bathroom issues, you need to deal directly with his poop or pee in two ways:

- ✔ Make sure that you thoroughly clean up any and all accidents.
- ✔ Bring stool or urine samples to the vet so that she can diagnose the cause of the problem.

The following sections explain how to perform each of those tasks.

Cleaning up right

A senior pooch with potty problems means more work for you, mainly because you need to clean up her accidents. But you can minimize that work by performing clean up the right way every time you're forced to do it.

Why? Because your dog's doo-doo is like a magnet to her. If your senior Fidette takes an unauthorized pee on your good carpet and you fail to clean up the resulting puddle promptly and thoroughly, Fidette will come back and do an encore on the very same spot — I guarantee it. To prevent such encores, you need to get rid of not only the stuff that you can see, but also the stuff that your dog can smell.

Some cleaning products get rid of both kinds of stuff. Others don't do so well. Here's how to find the right product and avoid the wrong one:

✔ **Look at the label.** An effective cleaner's label specifies that the product is designed to clean up canine bathroom indiscretions. Such cleaners contain enzymes that break down the dog's waste and neutralize its odor. If there's no odor, the dog doesn't have a reason to repeat her earlier performance.

You can find commercial pet-stain removal products at any good pet-supply store, in pet-product catalogs, or at most pet-supply Web sites. Look for brands such as Petastic (formerly Nature's Miracle), Simple Solution, or the wonderfully named Anti-Icky-Poo. Then, be sure to follow the manufacturers' directions.

✔ **Forget about ammonia.** To dogs, ammonia smells just like their own urine. So, if you use an ammonia-based cleaner to mop up your pooch's puddle, you can count on her to come back and re-anoint the spot that you cleaned.

✔ **Don't even think about club soda.** Club soda may be cheaper than a commercial pet-stain cleaner, but you have just one problem: It doesn't work. The soda may remove the stain of a dog's bathroom boo-boo, but it does nothing to get rid of the odor. The result? Yup, a re-christening of the spot that you cleaned up earlier.

If you think that you've cleaned up all your dog's doo but she performs encores on the same spots, get a black light. You can find these handy little devices at pet superstores for $20 or less. *Black lights* (sometimes called black-and-white lights) use ultraviolet rays to highlight areas where old pee or poop stains reside and beckon your pooch to do repeat potty performances. After you and your black light find all the spots that previously eluded detection, treat them with a commercial pet-stain cleaner and all should be well.

Gathering the evidence

To diagnose a pooch potty problem, your vet will probably ask you to bring in either a stool sample or a urine sample. If you haven't had to obtain such samples yet — well, it's never too late to learn. Here's how to get your dog's doo without getting any doo on you:

1. **Find a long plastic bag, such as bread loaf bag or the bag that covers a newspaper.**

2. **While your dog does his business, place your hand inside the fully extended bag so that the bag comes over your hand like a glove.**

3. **Pick up the poop with your bagged hand; then, grasp the open end of the bag with your other hand, and pull it inside out.**

   Now the poop is inside the bag — and neither of your hands has touched the offending material.

4. **Knot the bag and place it in an airtight container (a clean, empty yogurt container that has an airtight lid, rather than foil, works great).**

A stool sample should be no more than 12 hours old. An older sample may not yield accurate results.

To obtain a urine sample,

1. **Get a bag (the same sort of plastic bag used for bread or newspapers) and a plastic container (an airtight plastic container, such as a margarine container and lid works perfectly for this task).**

2. **While you and your senior walk together, watch him for signs of an impending pee, such as intense sniffing, circling, and pacing.**

3. **While your dog finds a spot to pee, place the bag over your hand like a glove, and hold the open plastic container with your bagged hand.**

4. **As your dog begins to pee, push the container under your dog's urethra or penis and catch the pee.**

   Let only a little bit of urine accumulate in the container; you don't need more than about a tablespoonful.

5. **Remove the container and cover with the lid.**

6. **Find a dry part of the bag, remove it from your hand, and put in the trash.**

7. **Ignore your neighbors' snickers, giggles, or other signs that they find your task entertaining. Better yet, ask them to help.**

8. **Bring the sample to your vet as soon as possible.**

   Urine samples should be no more than 8 hours old if you want them to yield valid results.

When Housetraining Doesn't Help

Sometimes, an elderly dog has a condition that makes bladder control an unreachable goal. A condition that affects hind-leg mobility can also affect a dog's ability to hold his water. Even just plain age can reduce the effectiveness of a dog's once iron-cast bladder.

In days of yore, such incontinence prompted many owners to euthanize their senior dogs. Now, though, most people view their dogs as members of the family, and euthanizing a potty-challenged pooch is just about unthinkable. Instead, the compassionate owner finds ways to keep his older dog more comfortable and also minimize any damage to carpets, furniture, and other areas of his abode. Here are some suggestions on how to manage your incontinent pooch:

- ✔ **Get some doggy diapers.** The pooch with perpetual potty problems does a lot better (and so do you) if you get him some special diapers made for dogs. You can find such products at pet stores.

  Bear in mind, however, that doggy diapers are gender-specific; some are made for males and others are made for females. Make sure that you're buying the right diapers for your dog's gender.

- ✔ **Keep it clean.** As long as you diaper your dog, you can count on having an accident-free house. However, your dog's skin may not fare so well — and his social acceptability becomes less than zero as odor builds up. The obvious solutions are to change his diapers reasonably often and to clean his diaper area every time you change him. Baby wipes are good cleaning options — they're just as gentle to canine skin as they are to human skin.

- ✔ **Put him to bed.** No one likes sleeping in a wet bed, your dog included. If your dog tinkles a little bit during the night, consider investing in a SleePee-Time bed. The bed is made of a polyester mesh stretched on a frame. If your senior leaks some urine, the leakage flows through the mesh to a tray underneath. The price per bed ranges from $89 to $125, depending on the dog's size. For more information, log on to www.sleepeetime.com or call 888-824-7705.

- ✔ **Rout the rash.** Your dog can get diaper rash just like a human baby can. The rash or general redness results when the acid in the dog's urine burns his skin. Products such as A & D ointment or Desitin — both of which you can find in just about any pharmacy's baby-care or first-aid sections — can soothe the burn, heal the rash, and protect your senior from infection. Such ointments can also keep the rash from coming back and protect against recurrent urinary burns.

Water works

It's a simple fact: When it comes to eating and drinking, what goes in must come out — or, conversely, nothing comes out if nothing goes in. For poop and pee to emerge from your pooch, she needs to have eaten and drunk first.

Any dog — senior or otherwise — can't exist on food alone. Every living being also needs to drink water, and dogs are no exception. Dogs can pass on food for a few days, but they can only last a day or so without water. Just like for people, water regulates a dog's body temperature and is a crucial component of both the blood and lymph that carries nutrients throughout the body and moves waste products on out.

The healthy senior dog can regulate her own water intake: She drinks when she needs to and refrains when she quenches her thirst. However, different dogs need different amounts of water each day. The active adult generally needs more water than a couch potato does. Even within the same dog, water requirements vary; for example, during a summer heat wave, your canine companion probably needs more water than she does in the dead of winter.

For the healthy senior, what's important is not how much she drinks, but whether that level is consistent. Give your dog the same amount of water each day: If her water intake increases or decreases significantly for no apparent reason, she may be sick. You should make a call to your vet.

Until you know just how much water your dog normally drinks each day, measure the water that you give her. For a 50-pound dog, try giving her 2 cups of water in the morning, 2 cups at mid-day, and 2 cups in the evening. Before each refill, pour any leftover water back into the measuring cup.

Just as important as water quantity is water quality: At the very least, the water should be clean and fresh. Wash your dog's water dish daily with a mild detergent (better yet, put it in the dishwasher) and change the water several times per day. Above all, make sure that your dog has access to water at all times.

And if you don't like water from the tap or if you worry that it may not be as healthful as it should be, consider that your dog probably could benefit from higher-quality water, too. Getting your dog her own six-packs of bottled water may be very expensive, but installing a water purifier for a one-time cost or coughing up a couple of extra dollars each week for jugs of distilled water can be as good for your dog as it would be for you.

Chapter 7

Going Blind or Deaf

*M*ax, a spirited 8-year-old Dalmatian, used to hurry to his owner's side whenever he heard his name, but now he appears to ignore his owner's summons. Molly, a 10-year-old Cocker Spaniel, started walking smack into her owner's sofa after her owner moved it to an empty space on the other side of the living room. Max's owner wonders whether his dog is experiencing some late-life rebellious urges, and Molly's owner can't figure out why her dog has suddenly turned into a canine klutz.

Both owners are asking the wrong questions. Max isn't experiencing a belated doggy adolescence, and Molly hasn't decided to become a canine doofus. What the owners don't realize is that Max has lost much of his hearing, and Molly is dealing with the loss of her eyesight.

But do such losses mean that Max and Molly must now lead diminished lives? Not at all! Even the totally blind or deaf dog can continue to live a high-quality life — if the owner recognizes what's happened and does what's needed to help her dog adjust to such a loss. This chapter describes how age affects the canine eye and ear, lists symptoms of canine visual and audio problems, and recommends ways to help your dog survive and thrive despite such impairments, whether partial or total.

How's That? What's That? The Aging Eye and Ear

Any dog who's lived beyond a certain age is bound to suffer some loss of eyesight or hearing. Just like your grandfather who needed a hearing aid when he hit seniorhood, your dog is likely to experience at least some hearing loss when he reaches the canine equivalent of AARP age. And just like your mother (or yourself, as I know all too well), who needed bifocals when she left her youth behind, so, too, will your aging dog probably experience some loss of vision. Both such developments are normal and result from age-related changes to the eyes and ears.

As the eye ages, the elasticity of the lens diminishes. This loss of elasticity makes it tougher for dogs to focus on nearby objects (but no, bifocals aren't an option for dogs). The lens may also become cloudy, although such cloudiness doesn't necessarily result in a loss of vision. In addition, the pupil of the eye doesn't expand and contract as much as it does in a younger dog, which can cause your senior to have trouble seeing well in very bright light. Some dogs also have trouble seeing in darkness, but others maintain their night vision, at least temporarily.

Aging ears also change. Calcium deposits may form on the small bones inside the ear, or those bones may fuse. Either way, the eardrum responds more slowly to vibrations than it did in the past. This slower response is called *conduction deafness,* and it's quite common among aging dogs.

 Although some loss of eyesight and hearing is common in senior dogs, don't write off such losses as normal in your aging friend until you get an expert's opinion. If you discover that your aging canine's eyesight or hearing is partially or totally lost, take your dog to the vet for an evaluation.

Recognizing Signs of Trouble

Although some vision or hearing loss is common in older dogs, such changes also may indicate that abnormalities are afoot. Some of those abnormalities are confined to the eye or ear; others reflect problems that affect other parts of your dog's body. Keep reading for some common indicators that your senior pooch's eye or ear changes need veterinary attention — the sooner, the better.

Symptoms of ear problems

Ear troubles can beset dogs of any age (if my 1-year-old Golden Retriever, Allie, could talk, she'd tell you all about her ear infections) — but the senior dog with ear issues may be in worse shape than his younger counterpart. The reason: Ear troubles in seniors, especially if those problems haven't been treated effectively, have had much more time to cause permanent damage to the ear. Such damage may lead to partial or even total hearing loss. Some indicators of ear trouble include

- **Discharge from the ear:** Wax, goop, or a substance that resembles coffee grounds are all signs of trouble that require a veterinary examination.

- **Obvious odor:** A dog whose ears smell like baking bread or any other strong odor doesn't need deodorant, he needs a vet's attention.

- **Balance problems:** A dog who's having trouble walking straight or staying on his feet isn't suffering from too much partying. Instead, he may be having trouble with his inner ear — and needs to see his vet.

- **Snapping when touched unexpectedly:** A deaf or hearing-impaired dog is surprised more easily because he can't hear someone coming. If the approaching individual is behind him, he can't see who's coming, either. The resulting surprise may provoke a fearful snap or even a bite from the dog.

- **Sleeping changes:** A dog who's sleeping longer and/or is more difficult to awaken may be deaf. The reason: He can no longer hear the noises that used to arouse him from his slumber.

- **Consistent lack of response:** The senior dog who repeatedly fails to respond appropriately to noise needs to see his vet as soon as possible. Examples of inappropriate responses include continuing to sleep when you call his name or not coming into the kitchen when he hears someone opening the refrigerator door. (The latter, of course, applies only to dogs who've been food-oriented all their lives.) Dogs with *selective deafness* — in other words, those pooches who run in the opposite direction when you call their names but who materialize like magic when you open a can of dog food — don't fit into this category!

Frequently, a dog's ear problems result from an infection that's caused by either bacteria or yeast. For many dogs, such infections clear up with topical medications such as antibiotics and ear flushes that a vet prescribes.

For other dogs, though, ear infections are a chronic problem. That's because the canine ear canal drops vertically before taking a 90-degree turn to the eardrum. This twist-and-turn structure makes cleaning a challenge and traps moisture, resulting in an environment that's a yeast's, mite's, or bacteria's idea of heaven. A dog with drop ears, such as a Basset Hound or a Dachshund, is even more likely to develop chronic infections because their long, hanging ear flaps help to further seal in dirt and moisture.

Many experts believe that repeated ear infections are an allergic reaction. Food often is the culprit, particularly commonly ingested proteins such as beef and chicken, or commonly eaten carbohydrates such as wheat and corn. Determining the gastronomic culprit involves changing your dog's diet to one with a novel protein, such as venison, rabbit, or ostrich, and, perhaps, a novel carbohydrate such as sweet potato or barley. Vets can prescribe commercial diets, such as those from Innovative Veterinary Diets, made from these novel proteins.

If your dog's ears improve after three or four months on such a diet, you can add the potentially offending ingredients one at a time until the allergic reaction is triggered once more. After you determine which element(s) triggers the reaction, you remove it from your dog's diet. You may also choose to keep your dog on the novel diet indefinitely, rather than risk triggering another round of stinky ears or other allergic reaction.

Other pet-food companies, such as Nestle Purina and Hills Pet Foods, make dog foods that contain *hydrolyzed proteins*. The protein molecules in such diets are smaller than those proteins that cause an allergic reaction.

Holistic vets believe that a blood test provides valuable clues on what's causing a chronic ear infection, assuming the infection is an allergic reaction. However, many conventional vets are more likely to suggest a traditional allergy test, in which very small quantities of known allergens are injected under the skin in order to determine what the offenders are.

Many experts believe that a diet that consists of bones and raw food but is free of any grain or carbohydrates, helps eliminate the allergic response. Other experts, however, are less convinced that raw food diets benefit dogs; rather, they say that such food regimens can result in food poisoning or other adverse reactions. Check out the detailed discussion of raw food diets in Chapter 2.

Either way, treatment of ear infections is a crucial component of any program to maintain a senior dog's hearing. Sometimes, though, if the infections fail to respond to treatment, your dog needs surgery. The veterinary surgeon removes the vertical portion of the ear canal so that the horizontal portion opens directly to the outside of the ear. This alteration eases drainage and facilitates cleaning, making infections less likely.

If all else fails, a surgeon can remove the entire ear canal. Such surgery allows the ear to drain but also makes the dog almost totally deaf if performed on both ears. However, dogs whose ears require such treatment often have lost their hearing already.

Avoiding deafness isn't always possible, but regular ear exams and prompt treatment of infections can keep your dog's hearing sharper longer.

Symptoms of eye problems

Eye problems present many more symptoms than ear troubles do, perhaps because the eyes are vulnerable to a much wider range of diseases. Complicating this fact is that many symptoms of eye trouble indicate the presence of several possible diseases. Here are some danger signals that should send you and your dog straight to your vet:

- ✔ **Discharge from the eye:** Goopy, colored discharge signals a variety of eye conditions or irritations such as *keratoconjunctivitis sicca* (also known as dry eye), *corneal ulcer* (an injury to the cornea), and *conjunctivitis* (commonly known as pink eye).

- ✔ **Redness of the eye:** An eye that's red and inflamed may reflect one of several serious conditions, such as *glaucoma* (an increase of pressure inside the eye), keratoconjunctivitis sicca, and corneal ulcer.

- ✔ **Cloudiness of the eyes:** This cloudiness may be a sign of *cataracts* (sight-impairing cloudiness of the eye lens), which can hamper vision, or may simply herald the onset of a benign condition called *nuclear sclerosis* (normal cloudiness on the lens), which doesn't impair vision at all but may indicate the start of cataracts. Your vet can tell the difference.

- ✔ **Sudden loss of vision:** If your dog appears to have lost his eyesight very suddenly, an immediate trip to the vet is imperative. Such a loss may signal the presence of cataracts, glaucoma, or another serious condition. To save your dog's eyesight, you must seek treatment promptly.

- ✔ **Sensitivity to light:** A dog who squints at or avoids light may have conjunctivitis, keratoconjunctivitis sicca, structural problems involving the lashes and lids, a corneal ulcer, or glaucoma.

✔ **Frequent pawing of the eye area:** This clear sign of eye irritation may signal the onset of many conditions, including glaucoma and conjunctivitis.

✔ **Lack of change in pupil size:** Pupils that remain small may indicate the onset of *anterior uveitis* (a decrease of pressure inside the eye); consistently dilated pupils may signal the presence of glaucoma.

✔ **Small red ball in the eye corner:** A dog who sports a small red ball in the inner corner of the eye isn't feeling very sporting. He probably has *cherry eye,* which results when the tissue that holds the dog's tear-producing gland weakens, causing the gland to pop out of place and become visible.

You can find detailed descriptions of eye conditions that are more prevalent among seniors, such as glaucoma and cataracts, in Chapter 10.

In addition to symptoms that come directly from the eye, changes in your dog's behavior may reflect at least a partial loss of vision. Those changes include

✔ Reluctance to go up or down stairs

✔ Fearfulness in unfamiliar places

✔ Bumping into furniture

✔ Becoming a Velcro dog (in other words, the dog sticks very closely to you)

✔ Unwillingness to go outdoors at night

✔ Snapping if touched unexpectedly

✔ Sudden caution or hesitation in movement

These symptoms all signal that your dog may have a serious vision problem. Prompt veterinary attention is essential to save your dog's vision, or to help him cope with vision loss as painlessly as possible.

Helping Fido Cope

Although human beings are often devastated at the loss of sight or hearing, dogs don't appear to be as traumatized when such losses happen to them. A canine is remarkably adept at using his remaining senses to compensate for the one he's lost. For example, a blind dog often develops sharper hearing and a keen sense of smell to offset his loss of sight. A deaf dog quickly learns to respond to sightly or smelly cues to compensate for the loss of his hearing.

Still, your senior's adaptability doesn't preclude getting some help from you. Here are some ways that you can help your aging pooch companion not only survive but also thrive despite his loss of sight or hearing.

Minimize surprises

The dog whose sight or hearing is totally lost or even diminished often startles much more easily. That's because he's relying on one sense to do the work of two. Although canines' abilities to adapt are almost legendary, dogs can't totally offset the loss of the sense in question. The blind dog can't always hear the approach of a person he might've been able to see in his youth. The deaf dog who's asleep in a doorway isn't likely to wake up until an unsuspecting human steps over him. Either way, if the impaired pooch is surprised, he can become frightened — and in his fright, may snap at or even bite the person who has caught him unaware.

Forestalling such reactions is simple: Avoid surprising your dog. Make sure that your blind dog hears you coming — perhaps by clapping your hands or calling his name, so that he can orient himself to you through sound and smell. When he knows that you're close by, he won't be surprised and is less likely to react defensively.

A deaf dog needs a similar warning. Surprisingly, you may still be able to make certain sounds that will orient him to you. That's because despite being deaf, an individual can feel the vibrations that result from certain sounds. Clapping your hands and stomping your foot on the ground are two ways to let your deaf dog know that you're nearby.

Adapt your home

A dog who can't see relies on her hearing, sense of smell, and good memory to compensate for her loss of eyesight. Scents, sounds, and knowledge that she acquired before she lost her vision enable her to navigate familiar surroundings with little or no problem. Consequently, you may not realize that your senior pooch is blind until you change your home's décor, such as rearranging some furniture. That's when your dog will exhibit a telltale sign of blindness — bumping into things — because the rearranged room no longer has the cues and clues that previously enabled her to walk through the room with ease.

Now's not the time to explore the principles of Feng Shui in your home or make any other changes if they're not necessary. Out of consideration for your aging friend, leave your room the way it is if you possibly can.

But suppose you can't? What if, for example, you get a new wide-screen television for the family room and realize that it needs to go where the sleeper sofa is right now? How can you keep your blind dog from trying to hop up onto the TV?

The answer is to plan beforehand to capitalize on your dog's remaining senses — in this case, her sense of smell. Spray the sofa with a little bit of cologne for a few days before you get the wide-screen TV. The scent of the cologne will tell your dog where the sofa is. Then, before the TV arrives at your house, move the sofa to its new location and spray it again. Your dog will smell the cologne and realize the sofa is someplace else.

For the cologne-spritzing technique to work, don't use that particular scent for anything else, including your own toilette — unless you want your dog to wonder whether you've turned into the sofa.

Make your dog feel safe

A dog who can no longer hear or see becomes disoriented much more easily than a pooch who's retained all his senses. You may find that to prevent such disorientation and otherwise stay out of harm's way, your four-legged senior sticks much more closely to you than he did before. He knows what he's doing: He wants to stay safe, and you represent safety to him. Therefore, he glues himself to you.

Take your cues from your canine companion: Keep him close to you when you venture out in public. Even if he was reliable off leash in his youth, leash him up now whenever the two of you venture into the great wide world. You're not restricting him; you're giving him the gift of security by tethering him to you.

If he's used to going out into the yard by himself to do his business, you should start going with him, even if your yard is fenced. That way, if he becomes disoriented, you're right there to help him.

If your yard isn't fenced, it's better not to let your blind or deaf dog use the yard at all. Make sure you're there with him *and* you use a leash. By keeping him close to you, you prevent a tragedy that could result if his disorientation results in him wandering away from home and into the path of an oncoming vehicle, or even just getting lost.

Can dogs wear hearing aids?

Theoretically, yes — and enterprising individuals have attempted to design such devices for dogs. However, the high costs of such devices and the inability of many dogs to tolerate having the aids inserted into their ears make transforming this theoretical concept into everyday practice tough. If your dog is deaf, a classic song by The Beatles may be a good mantra for you: A dog without hearing can certainly "get by with a little help from [his] friends" — the friends, of course, being you and your family.

Exercise caution when bringing your blind or deaf dog into contact with other people and pooches. When taking a walk with your four-legged friend, don't let other people touch him without him being able to check them out first (a good rule to follow for any dog). If the people you see are unknown to you or are unpredictable, such as small children, it's probably better to cross the street and avoid them entirely. The same is true for unknown dogs.

Caution is also the buzzword when you have visitors. If your blind or deaf senior dog is skittish when visitors come to the house, give him a break: Confine him to a room with your scent (for example, your bedroom) or put him in his crate.

Communicate differently

Even though your dog can't hear you call or see you come, you can communicate with her. You simply need to take advantage of her remaining senses to compensate for the one she's lost:

- ✔ **Use a signal your dog can recognize.** Ideally, you taught your dog to respond to both voice and hand signals when you first trained her. If so, your ability to communicate with your dog won't change, even if she can no longer hear or see you. A deaf dog can respond to hand signals; a blind dog can respond to your voice.

- ✔ **Know that the nose knows.** If your dog doesn't know how to respond to both voice and hand signals, she can still learn. Get some treats that your pooch adores and set them aside for 10 or 15 minutes. Then, begin teaching a new command and use the treat's scent to guide her in the direction you want her to go.

  For example, to teach your dog to sit, hold the treat between your thumb and index finger, and make sure your dog is aware that you have the treat. (She lets you know by sniffing avidly at your hand. Let her sniff, but don't give her the treat — yet.) When you have your four-legged friend's attention, move the treat-laden hand up slowly until it's over her head. If your dog is blind, also say, "Sit"; if your dog is deaf, say nothing. Either way, your dog will follow the scent, and in doing so, will plant her butt on the ground (see Figure 7-1). When that happens, give her the treat. Keep repeating this process until she responds consistently to either the hand signal or voice command.

✔ **Flash her.** If your deaf dog can't hear you call, and she's in a dark area, you can still summon her. Just flash a porch light or a flashlight in her direction. The light orients her to you, at which point she's more than likely come to your side (especially if she can smell some treats!).

✔ **Don't coddle.** It's crucial to treat your blind or deaf dog not as an invalid, but simply as a dog who's different. Compensate for her loss by capitalizing on her other senses. By doing so, you help your four-legged friend maintain her confidence despite the fact that she no longer has five reliable senses.

Figure 7-1: If your dog shows signs of hearing loss, start teaching her to respond to hand signals.

Senior Super Dogs: Kimi winks

Nine-year-old Kimi, a Cocker Spaniel who lives with Lynn Whittaker of Alexandria, Virginia, always seems to be winking. Although the dog's clearly a happy camper and an energetic senior, the reason she's winking comes from a hazardous saga.

In November 2000, Whittaker noticed that her dog's left eye was starting to look red and — like any conscientious dog mom — took her four-legged friend to her regular vet. The vet examined both eyes, said the left eye was infected, and prescribed an antibiotic ointment. All went well for a few days until one Saturday night when Kimi's condition took an unexpected turn.

"When I got home [that night], I noticed that Kimi's right eye was extremely red," Whittaker recalls. "I knew it must have come on suddenly because when I put the ointment in her left eye — which was looking much better — earlier on Saturday, I had not noticed anything unusual. I thought perhaps the eye infection had spread to her right eye, so I wasn't terribly worried and didn't consider it an emergency."

Whittaker called her vet the following Monday and made an appointment for Kimi the next day. At her vet's office, Whittaker soon realized that what she'd thought was a minor setback for Kimi was actually a much more serious problem.

Kimi's concerned vet told Whittaker to take her dog to an ophthalmologist as soon as possible. The ophthalmologist, Eric Smith, VMD, DACVO, immediately pinpointed the cause of Kimi's eye problem: A detached retina and a hemorrhage that resulted in the loss of sight in that eye.

Although the cause of the retinal detachment and hemorrhage remained a mystery, Dr. Smith began treating the eye with anti-inflammatory agents. But several weeks later, Kimi faced a new challenge: Tests showed that she'd developed glaucoma. Initially, Dr. Smith prescribed four different medications to be dispensed three times a day to reduce the inflammation and likelihood of infection that glaucoma causes.

Soon, however, both dog and owner found that regimen to be tiring.

To eliminate the need for such a rigorous routine — and also to alleviate any pain and infection from the eye — Dr. Smith recommended the removal of inner eye contents, replacing them with a prosthetic. The surgery went well, but several months later, Kimi developed a tumor on

Courtesy of Lynn Whittaker

(continued)

(continued)

that eye. This development forced Dr. Smith to remove the entire eye, prosthetic, and tumor.

Today, Kimi looks as though she's perpetually winking and has recovered fully from the loss of her eye. For her part, Whittaker is happy just to have Kimi with her. "She's doing fine now," Whittaker says. "Her stitched-up eye area has healed nicely, and she seems to have recovered fully."

Chapter 8

Losing Mobility

Many aging dogs have more trouble getting around than they used to. They take longer to lie down and even longer to get up. Staircases your dog once scampered up become challenging or impossible to negotiate. Hopping up on a sofa or a bed for a nap is now beyond your dog's capacity, and a daily jog with a beloved human companion may become nothing more than a distant memory.

However, your creaky-jointed canine or even totally crippled dog can still have a full, happy life. In this chapter, I explain how even an aging pooch can rediscover the joys of "goin' mobile," as the legendary rock group The Who would say. I also describe why aging dogs have trouble getting around, offer ideas for preventing mobility challenges — or at least ways that you can hold them off for awhile — and suggest ways that you can make your senior dog more comfortable.

Why Aging Dogs Lose Mobility

Every morning I take a calcium supplement in an effort to forestall the effects of age on my bones, and almost every day I try to work in a brisk half-hour walk to keep my muscles and bones in decent working order. My young Golden Retriever, Allie, gives me plenty of incentive to get moving. Her bones and muscles give her the grace and stamina of youth. Someday, though, I know she'll face the same sort of granny gimpiness that I'm trying to avert in myself.

These old bones

In both humans and dogs, bone quality deteriorates during senior-hood. Bones become thinner and break more easily. For many women and some men, this bony change results in dowager's hump, also known as osteoporosis. Senior canines aren't likely to hunch over the way some senior humans do, but if a senior dog breaks a bone, his fracture will probably take longer to heal than it would have when he was younger.

As a dog's bones become thinner, his body's mechanisms that facil-itate the movement of bones deteriorate, too. *Cartilage,* the fibrous material that covers the joints, becomes worn and brittle. Because the cartilage deteriorates, the *joints* (the places where two bones intersect) no longer glide smoothly past each other. These devel-opments result in *arthritis,* a common senior canine malady (for more information on the causes and treatment of arthritis, flip to Chapter 10).

Muscle deterioration

Dogs' muscles are affected by age, too. Like nerve cells, muscle cells can't reproduce themselves. Consequently, when muscle cells die (like all cells are supposed to), no new cells are available to replace them. The not-so-surprising result is a loss of muscle mass, which can make recovery from injury or illness more difficult than before. Additionally, the muscle cells that do remain don't use energy as efficiently as before, and thus can't work as well.

Diseases that may impair your dog's mobility

In many cases, disease can cause your dog to lose mobility — for reasons as varied as the diseases themselves. The following dis-eases can impair your dog's ability to move:

- *Hip dysplasia:* This disease is a hereditary condition in which the leg bone doesn't fit properly into the hip joint. This disease can cripple the dog severely by the time he reaches seniorhood.

- *Degenerative myopathy (DM):* This condition is a progres-sive disease that some scientists believe results from the spinal cord being attacked by the dog's autoimmune system (see Chapter 10 for more information).

Although there's no such thing as a fountain of youth for either dogs or people, you can do a lot to slow the effects of aging on your canine's mobility. And for those dogs who've already slowed down, as an owner, you can take plenty of steps to help your pooch be more comfortable.

Staying on the Move

If you're trying to keep your senior pooch reasonably limber, the most important thing you can do is keep her moving.

Experts urge women to exercise in order to forestall osteoporosis, and both genders are advised to keep moving to combat arthritis pain. This use-it-or-lose-it principle applies to dogs, too. The typical senior canine tends to spend most of her day on the couch, which can accelerate her physical decline, particularly with respect to her mobility. That's because diminished exercise actually accelerates bone and muscle aging. Staying sedentary can speed up the loss of both muscle mass and bone density, which, of course, makes the affected dog even more inactive. A vicious cycle is born.

Although exercise is great for dogs of any age, certain activities are no-nos for the senior dog. For example, sitting up to beg and jumping off the couch should be consigned to your dog's history. Both activities can injure your dog's back, particularly if she's a long-bodied, short-legged breed such as a Dachshund or Basset Hound. Overdoing any physical activity is never a good idea for any dog. If your senior pants hard, slows up significantly, or just plain stops, take the hint and grab a break.

Staying on the move doesn't necessarily mean doing a doggy triathlon (is there even such a thing?), setting endurance records on a treadmill, or even engaging in a multi-mile hike. Every dog, senior or otherwise, is unique, and that uniqueness extends to her ability to engage in physical activity. I offer lots of ideas for exercises that are especially good for senior dogs and suggestions for helping dogs with mobility issues make the most of what they have in Chapter 3.

Making Changes to Your Dog's Lifestyle

Dogs are incredibly stoic and adaptable individuals, so a senior pooch with mobility issues will most likely do whatever he can to keep himself moving when necessary. But you can help him deal with his loss of locomotion by adjusting his environment, medications, and overall care to meet his current needs. In the following sections, I tell you how to accomplish all those tasks.

One of the toughest aspects of caring for a dog who's losing mobility is the feeling that you're alone in the task. Able Dogs, an electronic mailing list, can put you in touch with other owners of mobility-challenged dogs. You can find details at www.abledogs.net.

Adapting the environment

Getting around your home and into your car may be easy for you, but for a dog who has locomotion limitations, home turf and car entry may seem like obstacle courses. Slippery floors, steep stairs, high-car entrances, and chilly indoor temperatures can make your creaky-jointed pooch uncomfortable. You can make minor alterations that ease your pooch's pain and lessen the challenge of negotiating her home turf. Some alterations you may want to make include

- ✔ **Ramping up.** If your senior companion can't hop up into your car the way she used to, make it possible for her to forego hopping altogether. You can get a slanted ramp that lets her walk up into your car rather than jump into it — which gives her sore muscles and joints some much-needed relief and spares you from lifting her into the car (see Figure 8-1). One manufacturer, PetStep, offers its product in two different sizes. You can order a ramp directly from the manufacturer at www.petstep.com or call 877-738-7837 to find a retailer that sells them.

  When you're not using your doggy ramp, tuck it behind the driver's seat. Such placement prevents the ramp from becoming an airborne missile if you must stop suddenly.

- ✔ **Stepping up.** Senior dogs who can't get themselves up on a couch or human bed will probably welcome some carpeted steps to preclude the need for jumping. A company called Dog Bed Works sells such products in two-step, three-step, and four-step sizes. They're available at www.dogbedworks.com.

- ✔ **Bedding down.** Sure, your dog didn't mind sleeping on the cold, hard floor when she was younger — but now that she's older, she may enjoy having some heat and some cushioning. Soft, cushy beds can cradle your four-legged friend in soft-as-a-cloud comfort (see Figure 8-2). *Orthopedic beds* —also known as egg-crate beds, because the mattress looks like the inside of an empty egg carton — have special foam linings that can add to your dog's luxury. Some orthopedic beds even have heating elements to increase that sense of ease. You can find good dog beds, orthopedic and otherwise, at any pet superstore such as Petco or PETsMART, or from retailers such as Drs. Foster and Smith (www.doctorsfostersmith.com).

Figure 8-1: A ramp eliminates a senior dog's need to jump in and out of a vehicle.

©Karen Taylor

Figure 8-2: Let your senior rest on a soft, comfy bed.

To keep your senior comfy no matter where she is, try placing beds not only where she usually sleeps at night, but also at other favorite places in your home. There's no law against a dog having more than one bed!

✔ **Giving her some stockings.** Many older dogs have calluses on their elbows from years of lying on hard floors and other surfaces. The constant rubbing of the dogs' elbows on the floor causes the hair to wear away and the exposed skin to thicken. A callus can actually protect the elbows, but if it gets painful, a product called DogLeggs can help. The product looks like a stocking that's open at both ends, and it's lined with fleece. Simply pull the stocking over your dog's paw, onto her leg, and over her elbow. You can order one or more pairs of DogLeggs, which are custom-fit to your dog's measurements, by logging on to the company Web site at www.dogleggs.com or calling 800-313-1218.

✔ **De-flooring it.** Bare floors can be tough on your older pooch because they don't offer any traction. You could install wall-to-wall carpeting in your home, but a cheaper option is to add some rugs in strategic places. Make sure, though, that the rugs adhere to the floor either with their own backings or with backings that you buy. If you feed your senior in the kitchen, which probably has a bare floor, putting a rug in the feeding area can help her stay on all fours while she eats

✔ **Warming up.** Most elderly people are more sensitive to cold temperatures than younger folks are, and most elderly dogs are the same way. Your mobility-challenged senior will probably feel much more comfortable if you turn up your thermostat a couple of degrees in the winter and use a little less air conditioning in the summer.

✔ **Giving her a raise.** Or, more accurately, giving her dishes a raise. A dog whose back hurts or has trouble bending down will be grateful to eat from dishes that are lifted up from the floor. Many pet-supply companies sell platforms that you can set food bowls on; you can also rig up your own doggy place setting simply by placing the food bowls atop a low bench.

Do *not* raise your dog's dishes from the floor if she's at risk for *bloat,* a potentially deadly condition in which gas fills the stomach and compresses the surrounding organs. Dogs who are at risk include large dogs with narrow chests, dogs who've already had bloat, or dogs with one or more relatives who've had it. A dog's risk increases with age, and the condition can be fatal if left untreated. Check out Chapters 9 and 10 to find out more about bloat's symptoms. What you find out may save your senior's life.

Taking meds

You can get some medications at your local pharmacy to ease your pooch's pain and help him get moving — and your vet has plenty more. Here are some of the most commonly prescribed remedies for mobility-impaired dogs:

- ✔ **Non-steroidal anti-inflammatory drugs (NSAIDs):** *NSAIDs* are often the first choice of veterinarians for alleviating the pain that results from arthritis and other types of mobility impairment. Some NSAIDs, such as aspirin, are available over the counter. Others, such as Rimadyl and Deramaxx, are available only by prescription.

  Don't give your dog any NSAID until you consult your vet about dosage. Note, too, that NSAIDs can have side effects that range from a simple tummy upset to much more serious problems (see Chapter 10 for the most common side effects). And never, ever give your senior ibuprofen (in Advil and Motrin) or acetaminophen (in Tylenol); both compounds are toxic to dogs.

- ✔ **Nutraceuticals:** A *nutraceutical* is a food supplement that also serves as medicine. Glucosamine and chrondotin sulfate, both of which you can get from your vet, are two nutraceuticals that help relieve arthritis and other musculoskeletal pain.

You can find detailed descriptions of many of these meds, particularly the drugs for arthritis, in Chapter 10.

Getting adjusted

Chiropractic is a treatment system that adjusts the spinal column to promote healing and relieve pain. Practitioners, known as *chiropractors,* believe that many conditions, such as arthritis and incontinence, result from a lack of normal nerve function. A chiropractor's objective is to restore normal nerve function by manipulating and adjusting the spine's position. Such changes aren't just a matter of popping a vertebra back into place, though: Chiropractors have specific techniques and equipment designed to achieve the results they and their clients are looking for. After a series of treatments, patients find that they move with greater ease and less pain. Often, such results are obvious after a single treatment.

People aren't the only individuals who can benefit from chiropractic therapy; pooches do, too. As an example, my brother regularly brings his 13-year-old arthritic Dachshund to a veterinary chiropractor for a periodic adjustment. My brother says that his dog enters the chiropractor's office looking somewhat hunched over and walking with clear discomfort. After the chiropractor has manipulated the dog's spine, the Doxie leaves the office with a straight back and, if not a spring in his step, at least much more comfort for the next several weeks. Other animals have different results, depending on their ailments; in some instances, the results of one chiropractic session can last for months or even years.

Veterinary chiropractors are either doctors who've chosen to focus on animals or vets who've received post-graduate training in chiropractic. Either way, a certified veterinary chiropractor has received post-graduate training from one of three facilities in the United States and has passed an exam given by the American Veterinary Chiropractic Association. If you're interested in finding out more about veterinary chiropractics, or if you want to find a veterinary chiropractor for your senior dog, check out the association's Web site at www.animalchiropractic.org.

Other therapies that can help dogs with mobility impairment, particularly from arthritis, are massage and acupuncture. You can find out more about both these treatments by heading over to Chapter 4.

Trying physical therapy

Many people who have injuries that keep them from getting around comfortably opt for physical therapy (also known as rehabilitation) to help them recover. Such therapy is a must for athletes who want to return to the field after an injury, not to mention weekend warriors like my husband, who ruptured his Achilles tendon during his only attempt to play adult soccer. Physical therapy may involve working on a treadmill, exercising underwater, or having a trained therapist work your injured limb for you. Other forms of physical therapy include heat therapy, which helps relax the muscles and loosen the joints, and cold-pack therapy, which decreases swelling in an injured area (the reason for putting ice on a sprained ankle).

Not surprisingly, physical therapy has become a treatment option for our mobility-impaired canine companions, too. Vets, vet technicians, physical therapists, and physical therapist assistants can even enroll in a certificate program in canine rehabilitation at the University of Tennessee.

The course of professional physical therapy is as individual as the patient is. The length, frequency, and cost of treatment depend greatly on why the dog needs therapy in the first place.

For a list of facilities throughout the country that offer animal physical therapy and rehabilitation, or to find a physical therapist for your dog, go to `www.utc.edu/Faculty/David-Levine/#Clinics`. Dr. David Levine, a member of the faculty at the University of Tennessee program, compiled the information on this Web site. Handicapped Pets.com also offers a similar listing; go to `www.handicappedpets.com/AnimalRehab.htm`.

You can give your dog one of the most common and least expensive forms of physical therapy at home: A massage. For more info on how to massage your four-legged senior, head to Chapter 3.

Getting some wheels

Don't misinterpret my heading. I'm not suggesting that you get your limited-locomotion senior her own muscle car or any other equally flashy four-wheeled vehicle. However, two-wheeled vehicles such as dog wheelchairs (also known as dog carts) can do a lot to restore a mobility-challenged dog's ability to get where she wants to go, not to mention her zest for life.

A dog wheelchair has a harness that fits over your dog's chest and front legs, and two wheels in the back (see Figure 8-3). Your dog uses her front legs to pull the wheelchair along, while her hind legs drag in the back (booties can help protect her feet from the ravages of being dragged along).

Wheelchairs aren't just for dogs who've lost total use of their hind legs. They can also help senior pooches whose hind legs don't work as well as they used to. You can even get wheelchairs for quadriplegic dogs; these wheelchairs have four wheels, not two. Either way, your dog can frolic, and you can even bathe her while she's in her wheelchair.

Wheelchairs can be pricey: A chair for a small dog costs about $200. They're costly, in part, because each chair is custom-made. However, many companies also sell used wheelchairs for a considerably lower cost. Leasing a wheelchair is another option.

You can order a wheelchair for your dog from the following Web sites. Each site explains how to measure your dog before you place your order:

- **Doggon' Wheels:** `www.doggon.com`.

- **Eddie's Wheels:** `www.eddieswheels.com`. This site also has information on refurbished wheelchairs.

- **K9 Cart Company:** `www.k9carts.com`. This site also has information on nursing care for the mobility-impaired dog and questions to help you determine whether your senior is suited for a wheelchair.

✔ **Dewey's Wheelchairs for Dogs:**
  www.wheelchairsfordogs.com.

✔ **Pet Mobile:** www.pnx.com/petmobile.

Courtesy of Edie Galpin, GRREAT

Figure 8-3: This elderly Golden Retriever scoots around like a puppy with the doggy wheelchair.

When you acquire your dog's new wheelchair, you may need to assemble it. Your dog may need some time to become accustomed to the chair, too — although some dogs peel out as soon as they're strapped into the wheelchair harnesses, burning tire marks and leaving their owners behind in a cloud of dust.

Considering other ways to help

Some changes you can make on behalf of your senior dog can't be classified. Even though you can't easily categorize these changes doesn't make them any less useful for you and your senior pooch. Here are just a few more ways you can help your mobility-challenged buddy get more out of life:

✔ **Be patient.** Your dog's limited ability to get around means that she may not be able to respond to your commands as quickly as she used to. Sitting, lying down, and coming when called take at least a little longer for her to execute. Be patient with your pooch if she's slow and know that she's doing the best she can. And give her lots of love: She needs to know that you adore her, no matter what.

✔ **Give her a pedicure.** Any woman who's ever tried squeezing her tootsies into a pair of pointy-toed, stiletto-heeled designer shoes knows that they make her feet look good but feel awful after a couple of hours. For senior pooches, long toenails cause the same pain as those designer shoes do — but dogs don't have the pleasure of looking fashionable to compensate for such discomfort. Nails that are too long force your dog to walk on the front parts of her feet, as if she were wearing a pair of stilettos. Trimming her nails helps your dog keep her balance and reduces her walking difficulties (in Chapter 5, I offer a step-by-step primer on how to give your pooch a pedicure).

✔ **Neaten her feet.** Your long-haired pooch's pedicure will be for naught if you don't also trim the long hair that grows between the pads. Keeping this hair short boosts your dog's traction and reduces the likelihood of her slipping and sliding on floors or otherwise losing her balance.

✔ **Give her the no-slip.** If your senior has trouble keeping her balance on smooth floors, try a product that dog-show exhibitors use to help their dogs compete indoors: Show Foot Anti-Slip Spray. You can find this product on Web sites that cater to show dogs and performance dogs; you can also purchase the spray at Doggon' Wheels, a retailer that sells doggy wheelchairs and other mobility aids (go to www.doggon.com).

✔ **Give her a butt lift.** No, I'm not advocating an extreme makeover for your aging pooch; for canines, a butt lift involves no plastic surgery at all. If your dog's back legs tend to give out after walking awhile, changing your leash may help her retrieve her zest for strolling. A rear-end harness lifts up your pooch's tush, relieving some of the weight on her hind legs. That weight transfers to you when you hold the leash. The device is appropriately named Bottom's Up. To get more information, visit the company's Web site at www.bottoms upleash.com.

If you want to make your own doggy butt-lifter, you can create a sling for your dog. The sling can be a simple towel under your dog's abdomen or a firewood carrier. Unlike the Bottom's Up harness, though, slings are practical only when walking a short distance with your dog. If you're like me and are hopelessly klutzy when crafting makeshift slings or anything else, go to a Web site, such as Doggon' Wheels (www.doggon.com), where you can purchase a variety of slings.

✔ **Keep her sleek.** Excess weight adds to the stress on an aging dog's bones and joints. To ease your dog's discomfort and help her move more easily, find out what she actually weighs and then find out from your vet what her ideal weight is. If the former is significantly higher than the latter, you need to chat with your vet about your pooch's physique. Together, you can evaluate what's causing your pooch to pork out and, if appropriate, create a diet and exercise program that will help her regain her youthful figure. (In Chapter 2, I suggest ways you can help your dog cut her food intake, and in Chapter 3, I offer ideas for giving your senior more exercise, no matter how much or how little mobility she has.)

Canine obesity may have an underlying cause, such as hypothyroidism (where the body produces too little thyroid hormone) or Cushing's Disease (where the body produces too much adrenal hormone). Before you put your dog on any kind of reduced diet, have your vet run the appropriate tests to rule out such factors.

Senior Super Dogs: Zack leaves a legacy

When Edie Galpin of Belcamp, Maryland first heard about the 14-year-old Golden Retriever Zack who needed lots of help getting around, she didn't think she could provide the right kind of foster home for him. Although Galpin participates in Golden Retriever Rescue Education and Training, Inc. (GRREAT), and is a passionate believer in rescue, she held back when the call came to find a foster home for Zack — for what she thought was a very good reason.

"I live in a colonial house, with all the bedrooms upstairs, three steps by the front door [and] two out to the backyard," Galpin explains. "That was sooo not the kind of foster home they [GRREAT] were looking for for Zack. But, when absolutely no one stepped forward, I couldn't turn my back on him."

Thus, in June 2003, Zack came to stay with Galpin. When he arrived, though, the new foster mom was surprised and concerned by what she saw: Zack compensated for the progressive loss of control in his rear legs by hurling them forward, creating momentum to help him move. But there was just one problem: All too often his rear legs landed on the ground in a way that caused him to lose his balance and fall over. Sometimes he could pull himself up with his front legs, but other times he couldn't and would fall again.

Zack's locomotion problems, coupled with his inability to remain stable — which caused him to collapse in his output — may have made some pooches and people throw in the towel. But Galpin saw that Zack was by no means ready to go. He maintained a consuming passion, literally: He'd risk injuring himself just to score a stray morsel that fell on Galpin's kitchen floor.

And Zack still loved walking, with Galpin's help. She recalls, "I hopped behind and beside him like a three-legged locust, hanging on to him via a towel sling while he was on hard surfaces (sidewalks, crossing the road) and much of the time while he was on grass to prevent him from falling and possibly injuring himself." When he collapsed completely, Galpin picked him up and carried him home.

The Me-Tarzan-You-Zack routine soon put a strain on Galpin's shoulder, forcing her to cut back Zack's beloved ambles. As an alternative, she introduced Zack to the joys of swimming in the backyard pool. Despite his pool parties, though, Zack seemed to miss walking. In her desire to help her foster child, Galpin had an idea: getting a wheelchair for Zack.

At first, Galpin searched for a wheelchair that she could borrow and return when it was no longer needed. But her search proved fruitless, which left just one option: Buying a wheelchair. Like most rescue groups, GRREAT's funding is perpetually stretched — and a wheelchair for a 90-plus pound dog doesn't come cheap.

Still, GRREAT took up the challenge. Some volunteers searched for a wheelchair while others solicited money that they put in a special account called "Zack's Fund." By the time the group found a wheelchair, Zack's Fund had enough money to pay for it in full.

For all their fundraising efforts, seeing Zack's reaction to being in the wheelchair was their reward. He was sheerly delighted that the wheelchair enabled him to regain his mobility. Galpin felt humbled by his joy of motion. Zack had "the grace to accept help [that's needed] when the body fails, but the spirit is willing and loving."

Five weeks after Zack arrived at Galpin's home, he had a massive stroke that left his head spinning and his front legs as useless as his rear limbs. Both GRREAT and Galpin decided that the time had come to euthanize him. Gaplin recalls, "I held his head in my arms, crying into his neck, giving him kisses while he left."

Although Zack is gone, he left a legacy. His wheelchair now helps other mobility-impaired Golden Retrievers who enter GRREAT's foster-care program, and Zack's Fund continues to provide additional wheelchairs and aids for dogs who need them. For Galpin, Zack's all-too-brief time in her life provided lessons in humility, forgiveness, courage, and love — and it also gave her a sense of mission.

"Without him here, it truly wouldn't have entered my mind to research and hunt for assistance aids for mobility challenges, [or to know] how to deal with such issues, what does or doesn't work," Galpin says. What began as a simple search for a loaner wheelchair continues to help other GRREAT Golden Retrievers who need some wheels or other help to get where they want to go.

Courtesy of Edie Galpin, GRREAT Foster Home

Part III
Dealing with Diseases

"Don't be embarrassed, Mr. Gundle. Your dog isn't the first one to get a duck call lodged in his throat."

In this part . . .

*N*o matter how diligent you are, your senior dog will get sick at least occasionally. However, senior canines are typically beset by maladies that can be cured or, at least managed, if they're diagnosed early. In Part III, I describe common signs of illness or other trouble; outline symptoms, treatments, and prognoses for a host of illnesses that are more prevalent among seniors than their younger counterparts; and offer tips for keeping your aging canine's care from destroying your budget.

Chapter 9

Knowing When Your Dog's in Trouble

. . . .

In This Chapter

▶ Recognizing emergencies

▶ Understanding doggy symptoms

▶ Knowing when not to worry

. . . .

No matter how diligent you are, your senior dog will get sick at least once in awhile. Heredity, the ravages of old age, and the law of averages make the occasional illness hard to avoid, even for an older dog with a robust constitution.

However, not all senior-specific illnesses are serious, and even those that are often respond to treatment if you detect them early. But for the owner who's had many years to develop an attachment to her canine companion — or for the adopter who's just welcomed a needy senior into her home — it's difficult not to panic if her dog starts walking into walls, develops a lump in her leg, or suddenly sports a bright red eye.

A loving owner can find each of those symptoms frightening, but not all of them constitute a true emergency. This chapter describes a wide variety of symptoms that befall senior dogs — including the three mentioned in the previous paragraph — and help you decide when to take your dog to a vet or emergency clinic immediately, when to place a phone call to your vet, and when to just wait and see.

Get Thee to a Vet . . . Now!

The following section lists conditions and symptoms that should prompt an immediate trip to a vet or emergency clinic. All these symptoms and circumstances signal extremely serious and perhaps even life-threatening conditions. If your senior dog exhibits any of the signs described here, don't wait. Have someone else call ahead while you and your dog get into a car and high-tail it to a vet.

Blowing up like a balloon: Sudden bloating

Maybe those antacid commercials in which people's stomachs expand like balloons make you giggle, but if your senior dog's stomach exhibits similar behavior, it's no laughing matter. It's a matter of life or death — literally. If your dog's belly expands so much over a one-day period that it looks like someone pumped it full of air, you need to get him immediate attention. If he has this symptom, your dog often also becomes so restless that he can't get comfortable lying down. He may try to vomit.

The most likely cause of these symptoms — particularly if your dog is a large, deep-chested animal, like a Rottweiler or Great Dane — is *gastric dilation,* more commonly known as bloat. Other possible causes of expanding stomachs include rupture of an internal abscess and leakage of blood or lymph fluid into the abdominal cavity.

In any case, though, you need to get prompt veterinary attention to save your dog's life. Don't stop to call the vet to tell him that you're on your way — just get there. If the problem occurs after normal business hours, high-tail it to your closest emergency veterinary clinic.

Expansion of the abdomen is life-threatening if you don't deal with it immediately. Prompt veterinary attention is crucial.

Tossing her cookies: Persistent vomiting

All dogs upchuck at least occasionally. A tummy bug or other minor malady makes most pooches toss their cookies. And sometimes just plain hunger prompts a dog to regurgitate a little bit of yellow bile. These upchuck sessions are no big deal: A 12- to 24-hour fast followed by a bland diet of rice and boiled hamburger (or white-meat chicken) helps deal with stomach bugs, and prompt feeding prevents a hunger-induced hurl.

However, a dog who vomits frequently over several hours — particularly if the vomit contains blood or foreign material — may be dealing with a major malady, not a minor one. All kinds of things can cause such vomiting, including eating a foreign object, poisoning, pancreatitis, kidney disease, cancer, or inflammatory bowel syndrome. Some of these causes, such as poisoning, may place the dog's life in immediate danger. Others, such as inflammatory bowel disease, are often serious but rarely life-threatening over the short term. Unfortunately, though, only a vet can tell you what's causing your dog's vomiting — and to do that, she needs to see the dog.

Prompt veterinary intervention can make the difference between life and death for the affected dog with persistent vomiting. The cause may turn out not to be life-threatening, but it's not worth betting your dog's life on it. Get to a vet ASAP.

Retching — when your dog tries to vomit but can't — also gives you a sign that something is seriously amiss. A dog retches when he suffers from bloat or has a foreign body near where his esophagus opens into the stomach. A retching dog needs a vet's attention, *stat.*

 If you have reason to believe that your dog's been poisoned (for example, you see evidence that he ate something toxic, like a poinsettia plant), get to your vet quickly, but also have someone contact the ASPCA Animal Poison Control Center in Urbana, Illinois (phone 888-426-4435). The center is staffed with veterinary toxicologists who can determine exactly what antidote your pooch needs. Have your credit card ready when you call; the consultation costs $45. For more information about the center, log on to www.apcc. aspca.org.

It's a gusher! Significant bleeding

No matter how careful an owner you are, I can practically guarantee that you'll nick the quick of your dog's nail at least once. If (or more like when) this happens, you end up with a few minutes of bleeding that takes some time to stop but is nothing serious.

 A *styptic pen* or *styptic powder* — which men use to staunch bleeding from shaving nicks — can halt any bleeding from an overly clipped nail. If you don't have either on hand, though, try dipping your dog's paw into a small bowl of flour.

However, if your dog's bleeding from anywhere else, and the bleeding doesn't stop even after you've applied a pressure bandage for 10 or 20 minutes, you need to take him to a veterinary clinic. If bleeding for any length of time spurts or pulses outward, your dog needs immediate veterinary attention. Such bleeding often results from an injury to an *artery* (the type of blood vessel that leads away from the heart). And even if the bleeding stops after your senior cuts himself, consult a vet — your senior may need stitches.

All the gum colors of the rainbow

A dog's gums are normally pink, and any significant deviation from this color can signify a health issue that requires a vet's attention right away. Here's a list of some unusual gum colors and what they can mean:

- ✔ **White or pale gums:** May indicate anemia or shock

- ✔ **Blue gums:** Result from respiratory problems

- ✔ **Yellow gums:** May signal red blood cell destruction, liver disease, or gall bladder disease

- ✔ **Red gums:** May mean septic shock, severe infection, or hyperthermia

When your dog's a hottie: Hyperthermia

Too much heat is toxic to living beings, including dogs. A dog who overheats and develops *hyperthermia* may exhibit extreme panting with a dark red tongue and gums, profound depression, shallow or rapid breathing, confusion, and bloody vomiting. He also may have a rapid heartbeat, may quiver, and, subsequently, may collapse.

Such a dog needs immediate attention in order to save his life. While someone else calls your vet, find some way to cool down your dog quickly. Cool-down options include immersing your dog's body (but not the head) in a tub of cool water, spraying him with water from a garden hose, and applying cold water compresses to his face, neck, footpads, and armpits. At the same time, use a fan to keep air moving over your dog's body surface.

 Don't use ice water to cool down a hyperthermic dog. Ice can trigger *hypothermia* (flip to the next section) and a whole new set of problems.

As soon as your way-too-hot friend stabilizes, take him to a vet, even if he appears to be fine. A vet can treat your dog for shock, respiratory distress, or other problems that the excess heat may have caused.

The best way to deal with hyperthermia is to prevent the condition from occurring in the first place. Never leave your senior (or any other dog) in a parked car— not even in the shade with some windows rolled part way down. Avoid exercising your aging friend during the hottest part of the day. Finally, make sure that your senior has access to cool, fresh water at all times — especially during warm weather.

Avoiding a dog-sicle: Hypothermia

Too much cold, or *hypothermia,* can be just as disastrous to a dog as too much heat. Signs of hypothermia include cold limbs, deep shivering, rigid muscles, and lethargy. Traumatized, very thin, and metabolically ill dogs are especially prone to this condition.

In addition, senior dogs can be especially vulnerable to hypothermia because — like elderly humans — they have more trouble staying warm. If your senior exhibits the symptoms outlined in the previous paragraph, wrap her up in blankets, put her in your car, and get her to a vet pronto.

As with hyperthermia, the best way to deal with hypothermia is to prevent its occurrence. Don't take very long walks with your senior during the coldest days of winter, and if she must be out for more than a few minutes, put a doggy coat or sweater on her first. Don't make her stay outside for long during cold snaps, either.

In and out: Breathing problems

If your dog's breathing is labored in any way — for example, he pants heavily while at rest or struggles to get his breath at all — take him to your vet immediately. Your dog may be suffering from a respiratory disease or injury, such as heart or lung problems, a tumor in the lungs, pneumonia, or bruising of the lungs. Other possible culprits are heartworm, anemia (perhaps caused by an undetected internal injury), and obstructions in the respiratory tract. Even excess weight can force your four-legged friend to literally gasp for breath.

If your senior has a short nose, such as a Boxer, Boston Terrier, or Pug, monitoring him for any breathing problems is especially important. The short snouts on these breeds often have narrow nasal passages that can make breathing difficult, particularly during periods of stress, including heat.

A dog who's having trouble breathing may benefit from lying on his side. Helping such a dog stay calm can ease his breathing problem, too. But you absolutely have to do one thing: Get him to the vet.

And, incidentally, breathing problems don't involve just the internal respiratory system. Sometimes the nose knows that something's amiss and manifests that knowledge with a cloudy or bloody nasal discharge. If your dog's runny nose fits either description, especially if the runniness comes only from one nostril, you need to get yourself and your friend to the vet right away.

Obvious trauma

Years ago, when I knew much less about *canis familaris* than I do now, I took my very spry senior dog, Molly, and my preschool daughter to a nearby playground. My intrepid daughter, Julie, proceeded to scramble to the top of a way-too-high-for-her slide. For some reason that I'll never know, Molly raced up the slide behind her — and proceeded to perform a swan dive from the top of the slide back down to the ground. Once she hit the turf, she trotted over to my daughter, who'd landed safely at the bottom of the slide the conventional way. Because Molly appeared to be unhurt, even after I examined her, I didn't take her to my vet — but I should have.

If your senior dog experiences any clearly traumatic event, such as falling or getting hit by a car, take her to your vet immediately, even if she appears unhurt. Dogs can be incredibly stoic. Your senior pooch's show of apparent well-being may mask an internal injury that requires treatment. Play it safe and get her to a vet, no matter how fine she appears to be.

As for Molly, she and I were both very lucky. Her apparent lack of ill effect was for real, and she went on to live for another couple of years. But I would never take such a chance with a dog again, and neither should you.

Dealing with seizures

One dog may be just going about his business when he suddenly stops, becomes rigid, puts his head down and his tail between his legs, and begins to scream and whimper. His owners, believing he's in pain, try to comfort him — but the dog doesn't even seem to realize that his people are there.

Another dog suddenly slumps to the floor, writhing and foaming at the mouth, his legs moving all the while. His eyes become large, almost to the point of bulging, and his saliva is tainted with blood from having a bitten tongue.

Both dogs have undergone seizures, even though their actual behaviors were quite different from each other. The causes may be as different as their behavior.

Many conditions and illnesses can trigger seizures. A senior's seizure is more likely to result from another condition, such as kidney disease or a brain tumor. No matter what, he needs to see a vet as soon as possible after the seizure ends.

For more information about kidney disease, check out Chapter 10. And for info about canine cancer, flip to Chapter 11.

Falling down on the job: Sudden collapse

If your dog's legs suddenly give out from underneath her, you need to get her to the vet or animal clinic immediately — whether your four-legged friend loses consciousness or not. The many causes of collapse include seizures, heart problems, and the progression of a serious chronic or acute illness.

Sudden eye changes

Any sudden change in the appearance of your senior's eye, in addition to or rather than eyesight loss, is a good reason to bring your dog to a vet immediately. The big concern here is that the change — which may be redness of the white of the eye, a change in the color of the iris, or a change in the size of the pupil — may well reflect the presence of a serious eye disease that can lead to blindness. In fact, the dog may be blind already.

Sudden redness in your dog's eye can signal the presence of *glaucoma*, which inevitably leads to blindness if not treated promptly. Other signs of glaucoma include dilated pupils, sensitivity to light, and eyelid spasms. A red eye, small pupils, and a change in iris color may herald the onset of another serious eye condition, *anterior uveitis*.

You can read more about the diagnosis and treatment of glaucoma and other canine eye diseases in Chapters 7 and 10.

Walking drunk

If your dog starts to walk as though he's spent too much time at the local watering hole, his problem may be a lot more serious than a few too many beers. Possible causes include anti-freeze poisoning — which can be fatal — or a metabolic problem. Play it safe and get your dog to a vet right away.

Don't Give Aspirin, but Do Call in the Morning

The conditions listed in the following section may signal problems that may be serious but aren't life-threatening. Your best response to these problems is to call your vet as soon as possible and ask whether you need to bring your dog in for a look. If you first notice any of these symptoms after hours, you can wait until morning to call your vet.

Appetite changes

Every dog skips a meal occasionally: She may not be hungry, have an upset stomach, or may have just decided to be a picky pooch that day. Such fasts don't usually last more than one meal.

However, if your senior bypasses her breakfast (or dinner) more than once or twice, she may be more than just a little sick. Appetite loss often signals the presence of a serious medical problem. A call to your vet is in order.

A dog who suddenly becomes ravenous may have a problem, too. Increased food intake is a common symptom of diabetes and Cushing's Disease, two conditions that befall senior dogs more often than younger pooches (see Chapter 10). Both conditions require a vet's expertise for diagnosis and treatment.

Feed your senior two or three separate meals per day instead of leaving a full food dish on the floor at all times. Scheduled feedings enable you to detect a change in appetite more quickly than if you free-feed your four-legged friend. For more about how to feed your dog, flip to Chapter 2.

Unexplained weight gain or loss

If your dog's too thin, you want him to put on some pounds; if he's too thick, you want him to take pounds off. Either way, if you read Chapters 2 and 4, you have some good ideas on how to achieve either objective — and, in all probability, your dog's physique is responding accordingly. Such weight changes are good and you obviously shouldn't worry about them.

On the other hand, if your dog packs on poundage or wastes away to nothing for no apparent reason, you have cause for concern. Such changes — particularly when accompanied by other symptoms, such as appetite changes, lethargy, diarrhea, constipation, and changed water intake — can mean that your dog suffers from a serious problem. If you notice a change in your dog's physique, either on the plus side or the minus side, but can't figure out why, put in a call to your vet.

Drinking more or less

Water is crucial to sustaining all plant and animal life — but excessive water intake can be too much of a good thing. Increased thirst and drinking can occur if your dog has one of several conditions, including kidney disease, Cushing's Disease, and diabetes (discussed in Chapter 10). Your vet is the only person who can tell you what's going on, so pick up the phone and call.

If your senior drinks a lot less water than she used to, that can be a problem, too. Because older dogs have more trouble getting around than younger animals do, they may not drink as much water as before, which can lead to dehydration. Try putting several water dishes in different rooms of your home — particularly on different floors if you have a multi-story home. Make sure, too, that she knows about the additional watering stations; take the time to show her the extra bowls. If she still drinks much less water, put in a call to your vet.

 You can tell whether your dog is dehydrated by picking up the skin behind her neck. If the skin doesn't spring back into place within a few seconds of letting it go, her body needs fluids — and you need to take her to a vet immediately.

All stopped up: Constipation

If you've ever had the dubious pleasure of cleaning up the output of a dog with diarrhea, you may think that having a constipated canine would be just wonderful. However, the canine wouldn't agree with you — and after awhile, you wouldn't agree with you, either.

Sometimes, a dog's failure to poop results from a simple dietary imbalance, such as inadequate water intake or insufficient fiber; in such cases, correcting the imbalance corrects the constipation. Too little exercise and too much poundage — common problems among senior dogs — also can slow down a pooch's stool production. Getting your senior off the couch and out for a walk often can help get things moving.

Feeding a dog more often can help relieve simple constipation. When food enters the dog's stomach, his *gastro-colic reflex* (in other words, the poop ejector) kicks into action. Thus, more frequent meals mean more stimulation to the reflex — and, often, more frequent pooping.

But if your dog hasn't moved his bowels for more than a couple of days — even after you've made some adjustments — or if he tries but fails to get rid of his poop, you need to contact his vet. An intestinal blockage caused by a foreign object or a tumor may be the culprit.

The dreaded runs

I defy anyone reading this book to find a dog who has not had diarrhea at one time or another. Any canine I've ever known — senior or otherwise — has had at least one attack of the runs, and generally more. Often, those attacks occur because the dog eats something that she shouldn't or has a little bug of some sort. Those instances aren't necessarily a big deal. A 12-hour fast, followed by a bland diet, generally gives the gastrointestinal tract the time it needs to recover.

But when your dog's bowels work overtime for more than a day or so, call your vet. Call sooner if your dog exhibits any of the other symptoms listed in this chapter. Persistent diarrhea signals the possible presence of many conditions, some of which can be quite serious. It's important to enlist the help of your vet to find out which of those conditions your senior has.

A dog with diarrhea is a dog who's in danger of becoming dehydrated because she loses so much water every time she poops. Make an extra effort to give your senior a lot of water if she has the runs. If you grasp the skin on the back of her neck and it doesn't spring back into place a few seconds after you let go, she's already dehydrated — and needs a vet's attention immediately.

Lumps and bumps

You're petting your beloved senior pooch when suddenly you feel a lump under your hand. Your hand freezes in place, and a chill grips your body as you think, "Omigod — Bowser's got cancer." I know exactly how you feel because it's happened to me and more than one dog who I've loved.

I'm here to tell you that you may very well be wrong. However, you can't know for sure whether your lumpy friend has a benign tumor or a malignant growth until a vet tests the lump. The same goes for determining the seriousness of a malignant growth. Only a vet's expertise can tell you for sure what you're dealing with.

The bottom line here: If you find a new lump under your senior's skin or anywhere else on his body, call your vet as soon as possible during normal business hours and make an appointment for him to see your four-legged friend. But, in the meantime, don't panic. Your senior's lump is probably nothing to worry about.

Chapter 10 describes *lipomas*, which are generally harmless fatty tumors that are very common among senior dogs. I devote Chapter 11 entirely to canine cancer: how it's detected, how it's treated, and what the prognoses may be.

Bald is not beautiful on dogs

It's perfectly normal for many older human males to go bald, but that's not the case for older male dogs — or for female dogs, either. Seniors do experience a little thinning of their coats as they age. But if your senior's coat thins so much that she has bald spots, you need to take her to a vet.

Canine baldness can result from one of many conditions, depending on where the baldness occurs. For example, dogs with *hypothyroidism* (a condition in which the dog's level of thyroid hormone is too low) often lose fur in symmetrical patches on both sides of the body. Other symptoms of hypothyroidism include weight gain and lethargy.

Another condition that often causes symmetrical hair loss is *Cushing's Disease,* which results if the dog's adrenal gland secretes too much cortisol, a hormone. Other symptoms of Cushing's include weakening of the legs, lethargy, increased appetite and thirst, and the development of a potbelly. More about Cushing's symptoms, treatment, and prospects for recovery appear in Chapter 10.

Hair loss also may occur if a senior's food doesn't fulfill her nutritional requirements, particularly for fatty acids. If your senior's hair is thin and falling out and you feed her the El Cheapo generic brand of dog food from your local supermarket, switch her to a higher-quality product that comes from a pet superstore, specialty outlet, or your vet; you can also consider starting her on a raw food diet (see Chapter 2 for more info).

If itching accompanies the hair loss, your senior may be playing host to some unwanted parasites, such as fleas. Another malady that causes both itching and hair loss is *seborrhea,* which also may make the dog's skin become very flaky, greasy, and foul-smelling. Seborrhea is not a life-threatening condition, but it does require veterinary evaluation and treatment.

The bottom line here is that senior doggy baldness isn't normal — and needs the expertise of a veterinarian to determine its cause. Call your vet as soon as you notice bare patches on your older pooch's skin.

Bad doggy breath

Living with a dog stricken with halitosis is no fun. All too often, when a senior dog yawns, his people wish that they could give him a breath mint. But despite the well-known term (and occasional insult) "dog breath," you can help a foul-mouthed mutt or purebred with stinky breath. His people need not suffer in silence, and the dog need not suffer, either.

And, chances are, your dog is suffering. If, along with your senior's bad breath, he also has red gums and yellow teeth, he probably has periodontal disease. This all-too-common canine condition results when bacteria (also known as *plaque*) deposits build up on the teeth within hours after eating. In just a few days, the plaque hardens. If ignored, the gum begins to separate from the teeth and may lead to tooth loss. Meanwhile, your dog's teeth and gums may hurt so much that it's hard for him to eat.

But tooth loss isn't the only result of canine periodontal disease. Make no mistake — this disease is an infection, and this infection can spread to other parts of the body, including the dog's vital organs, such as the heart and lungs. Infections in any of these organs are extremely serious and can prove fatal.

You can find more information about how to deal with canine periodontal disease and how to prevent its occurrence in Chapter 5.

However, other conditions can cause your poochie to have hoochy breath. They include eating stinky food or stool, diseases such as diabetes or kidney disease, sinus problems, and autoimmune diseases. Most of these problems require a vet's attention; on the other hand, if your dog has eaten something stinky, such as poop, you probably already know it.

If your dog's breath has a urine or ammonia-like smell to it, he may have a serious kidney problem. Get him to your vet as soon as you can.

Stinky ears

Dogs with all-too-fragrant ears probably are pretty uncomfortable. They most likely have an ear infection, and such infections can be quite painful. If left untreated, the infection can cause your dog to lose her hearing.

The most common type of ear odor smells like baking bread. This odor results from a yeast infection. Other symptoms include frequent head shaking and a brown, goopy discharge that comes from the ears. To find out how to treat your dog's yeast infection, turn to Chapter 7. Bacteria also can cause ear infections.

Often, an ear infection is a sign of an underlying problem, such as allergies, hypothyroidism, disorders of the immune system, or tumors. You need to get a veterinary exam to figure out the root cause of the problem as well as the organism that's causing the infection. Then you have a reasonable chance of eliminating the infection with treatment.

A canine case of B.O.

If your dog's offensive aroma doesn't come from the mouth or ears, he may still have a problem. Canine body odor isn't necessarily normal, despite the existence of the term "doggy odor." If you know that your senior pooch hasn't rolled in something disgusting, his embarrassing (to you, not to him) aroma may reflect one of several conditions.

A common cause of canine stinkiness is *seborrhea,* a condition that also can cause hair loss, flaking, and greasy skin. Certain metabolic diseases may also cause your four-legged friend to smell foul. If the odor comes from a wound, suspect infection. Body odor is also symptomatic of cancer.

In any case, a Fido with B.O. needs to be evaluated by a vet — not only for his sake, but also for the sake of his people.

Dog-tired for no good reason

It's true that senior dogs often don't have as much energy as more youthful pooches do. An older dog probably tires more quickly than a younger one does. And no matter what your dog's age, a sustained period of exercise will wear her out. When my young-adult Golden Retriever comes back from a session at the local dog park, she heads to the couch or her crate to snooze.

However, a long-term drop in energy — particularly when accompanied by other symptoms — can mean that your dog suffers from one of a variety of problems. Your pooch may have anemia, kidney disease, liver disease, hypothyroidism, obesity, arthritis, or cancer. If your dog seems to suddenly lose energy and fails to regain it, you should make a call to your vet.

If you call or visit your vet for his advice about your senior's fatigue, try to describe other symptoms that your dog may be showing. Doing so can give your vet important clues as to the cause of your dog's lethargy and save valuable diagnostic time.

Acting out of character

Although we humans have had a regrettable tendency to separate our physical selves from our mental selves, dogs know better. Their behavior generally reflects how they feel. Often, a change in your senior dog's behavior indicates that all is not well.

A senior who seems forgetful, confused, or otherwise disoriented may suffer from canine *cognitive dysfunction syndrome* (CDS), which some people call "doggy Alzheimer's Disease" or "doggy senility." Typically, dogs with this condition don't seem to recognize their people, appear to have totally forgotten their bathroom manners, and drastically change their sleeping habits — they pace all night and sleep all day.

Other behavioral changes result from physical causes. For example, a dog who's in pain may suddenly avoid the petting sessions that he used to enjoy. The newly blind or deaf dog may suddenly become canine Velcro, sticking closely to you in order to feel more secure in his now sightless or silent world. Conversely, the blind or deaf dog may seem obstinate, suddenly refusing to come when you call him. A dog who sleeps significantly longer and more deeply than before may be deaf (noise no longer awakens him from his slumbers).

Lethargy and depression are signs of a host of dangerous conditions, ranging from severe bladder stones to hyperthermia.

If your dog's personality changes significantly, start looking for physical signs of trouble and put in a call to your vet. When you talk with your vet, describe not only your senior's behavioral changes, but also any physical changes that you've discovered.

Lameness (and I don't mean being uncool)

A dog who persistently favors one leg clearly has a problem and needs to visit her vet as soon as possible. But you don't need to make the visit immediately unless the lameness results from an obvious trauma, such as jumping from a high place or being hit by a car. Non-traumatic causes can range from arthritis to bone cancer; the prognosis, obviously, depends on the diagnosis.

Occasionally, a dog favors one leg and then the other; she's a kind of switch-limper. If your dog limps on both sides of her body (at different times, of course), she's not faking you out or trying to score some extra attention. Instead, she may have arthritis or a heart valve infection. Lyme Disease is another possibility, also prompting the need to see her vet.

Going bump in the night (and day)

A dog who bumps into furniture and clearly can't see where he's going obviously needs to see his vet. Only a vet can determine how much of his eyesight your dog has lost and whether treatment can restore his vision.

Sometimes, though, an elderly dog may walk smack into a wall even though he clearly can see. If he also vomits, the likely cause is *geriatric vestibular syndrome,* a condition that affects a senior dog's balance. This condition looks frightening — when I saw this happen to my elderly dog, I thought she was having a stroke — but you shouldn't worry. A vet can insert fluid under your dog's skin to keep him hydrated, and you should keep the dog as calm and quiet as possible. The condition usually resolves itself within a few days.

Sores that don't heal

A cut or sore that doesn't heal may signal a serious condition such as cancer, or a less serious (but frustrating) condition called *lick granuloma,* otherwise known as a hot spot. The latter occurs when a dog licks an area so often that the skin breaks; subsequently, the licking prevents the area from healing. Either way, the dog needs to see her vet, who can run the proper tests and determine the cause of the problem.

Changed bark

If your dog's bark sounds different than before, he may have a condition called *laryngeal paralysis.* This condition, which is particularly prevalent in older dogs and retrievers, also can cause a dog to have trouble breathing in hot weather. A changed bark may also indicate deafness — particularly if your dog doesn't come when you call him or is easily startled and reacts defensively. Have your vet check him out.

Head games

Dogs who do unusual things with their heads may have some serious problems — not emergencies, but certainly maladies that require a vet's assessment.

If your senior canine companion frequently presses her head against the wall and stays there, the reason is simple: Her head hurts. However, several things could be causing that headache, including a brain tumor, a stroke, Cushing's Disease, canine dementia, or liver disease.

The senior who bites at the air as though she's trying to catch an invisible insect may actually be having a seizure. Such a seizure could signal the presence of a brain tumor, infectious or inflammatory brain disease, or epilepsy.

A dog who looks as though she's perpetually cocking her head isn't necessarily trying to understand what you're saying or just trying to look cute. Instead, her persistent head tilt may signal the presence of a brain tumor or *vestibular disease* (a condition that affects the dog's balance).

Weird-looking poop

Poop that changes color or otherwise looks odd may signal a variety of problems, depending on the color and consistency:

✔ **Black or dark brown poop:** If your dog's doo is this color, it indicates bleeding — either the dog has swallowed his own blood, or the bleeding comes from the intestinal tract. Either way, such bleeding may result from a tumor, an ulcer, kidney or liver problems, or inflammatory bowel disease. Other possibilities include parasites, a bleeding tooth, bleeding in the mouth, dental disease, or even swallowing the blood that results from an overlicked paw.

✔ **Grayish, greasy looking poop:** This shade of poop may point to a problem in your pooch's pancreas, such as *exocrine pancreatic insufficiency,* or EPI. This condition occurs when the dog's pancreas doesn't produce enough enzymes to process the fats in his food. Special meds with digestive enzymes and a low-fat diet can correct this problem. Other possible causes of gray poop include a tumor or *pancreatitis* (inflammation of the pancreas).

Not Necessarily a Big Deal

Some conditions may or may not require veterinary attention, but either way, you shouldn't panic. Here are some conditions that fit this category:

✔ **Noisy inhalation:** Sometimes a dog starts to inhale loudly through his nose in a kind of spasm that resembles a human asthma attack. Vets call such breathing *reverse sneezing,* and you generally don't need to worry about it. In fact, you don't even need to call your vet; the condition usually abates within a few minutes.

✔ **Cloudy discharge from the penis:** Sometimes a male dog discharges a little bit of an opaque-looking substance from his penis. If your senior doggy guy is one such animal, experts suggest that you watch to see if he has any problems peeing. If not, the discharge probably is normal; if he does have difficulty peeing, you should call your vet.

✔ **Butt-dragging:** If your aging canine companion drags his bottom across the ground, you can be confident that nothing's seriously wrong. The most likely culprit is an infected or impacted anal gland. You can express your dog's anal glands yourself; just get a vet to show you how. But if you turn squeamish at messy jobs or are easily grossed out (I plead guilty here), let a vet or groomer do the expressing for you.

✔ **Bloody stool:** A small amount of fresh blood in a dog's stool is cause for concern, but it isn't an emergency. Generally, an inflamed large intestine causes the bleeding. A timely (but not immediate) visit to the vet lets you know what causes the inflammation and how you can treat it.

✔ **Bloody urine:** Dogs with excessively dark or blood-tinged urine — especially when accompanied by frequent peeing of small amounts of urine — often suffer from a urinary tract infection. This condition is uncomfortable for the dog and requires a vet's attention, but it's not an emergency, and you can usually treat it easily with antibiotics.

If your dog tries to pee but nothing comes out, get him to a vet as soon as possible; he may have stones in his urinary tract.

When to Ignore This Advice

Although the symptoms detailed in this chapter should help you distinguish among the urgent, serious, and not-so-serious medical problems your senior may face, sometimes you may have to ignore such advice if your instincts tell you otherwise. If your dog appears to be in trouble, and you sense that something's very wrong — even if you can't put your finger on what that something is — go with your gut and either contact or go to your vet. No responsible vet will give you a hard time for erring on the side of caution. In fact, most vets appreciate such diligence because they know that you know your dog better than they do.

As your dog ages, he benefits from your efforts to educate yourself about canine health, and your pocketbook may benefit, too. But in those instances where instinct conflicts with knowledge, let the former overrule the latter. The life you save could be your dog's.

Chapter 10

Understanding Common Senior-Dog Ailments

In This Chapter
▶ Knowing the symptoms of typical older-dog illnesses
▶ Preventing senior-dog ailments
▶ Treating aging dogs' woes

As your dog progresses through seniorhood, chances are that she — and you — will have to deal with one or more ailments that older pooches get more often than younger ones do. Such occurrences are invariably stressful not only to the pooches, but also to their people.

Any illness or medical problem reminds a caring owner that his canine companion is mortal, and that she's lived out most of her life span. Such awareness heightens the fear that this time, this illness may take your beloved four-legged friend away from you.

This chapter is designed to allay those fears by giving you some facts about 20-plus ailments that befall a higher proportion of the senior canine population than that of other doggy demographic groups. Such knowledge is power: the power to stop worrying and start really helping your dog when she needs you the most.

Where possible, I describe the most common symptoms, explain how a vet reaches a diagnosis, describe conventional and, where appropriate, holistic treatments, and outline the likely outcomes. I also include, where possible, some tips for preventing the onset of each ailment — or, at least, holding it off.

Going Mobile . . . Not!

A dog's ability to get around is likely to diminish when he becomes a senior, as I explain in Chapter 8. However, some diseases can cause a dog's locomotion to deteriorate further. Here are the most common conditions that affect a senior's mobility.

Arthritis

Arthritis is one of the most common illnesses that older dogs face, although dogs of any age can acquire the condition. The disease involves the *joints,* which are where the ends of bones come together; *cartilage,* which covers the bones that form the joints; and fluid, which lubricates the cartilage.

When the cartilage becomes worn and deteriorates, the bones that form the joint no longer glide smoothly past each other. Instead, the bones rub up against each other, with less fluid to lubricate them, and the joint becomes inflamed. The result: painful arthritis.

Years of wear and tear can lead to arthritis. In addition, excess weight, joint abnormalities such as hip dysplasia, previous injuries, and infections such as Lyme Disease can make a dog more susceptible to the condition. Genetics play a role, too: Labrador Retrievers, Golden Retrievers, and other large breeds are more likely to get arthritis than the general canine population.

Symptoms

The arthritic pooch generally has more trouble moving around than his more limber counterpart. He's likely to have trouble getting up from a nap or lying down to start one. He may be less than eager to go for walks, run, climb the stairs, or hop onto the couch. He may be especially stiff in the morning but may become more mobile later in the day. If just one joint is affected, he probably avoids putting weight on the affected limb.

Diagnosis

Because the symptoms of arthritis are similar to those of other diseases, and because arthritis can result from other conditions, a veterinary examination is necessary to confirm a diagnosis. The vet examines the entire body, including the affected limb(s), and may take X-rays of the joints that seem to be affected. The vet may also test the dog for Lyme Disease.

Treatment

A wide variety of treatments is available to relieve the pain of the canine arthritis patient:

✔ **Non-steroidal anti-inflammatory drugs (NSAIDs):** From common aspirin to state-of-the-art meds such as Rimadyl and Deramaxx, NSAIDs are usually very effective in combating arthritis pain and inflammation. However, they also can have side effects that range from unpleasant to dangerous. Your vet is likely to prescribe the lowest possible dosage that will relieve pain for your senior. The vet will also warn you to watch for side effects such as diarrhea, vomiting, increased urination, decreased appetite, and depression.

Don't give your arthritic dog either ibuprofen (the active ingredient in Advil or Motrin) or acetaminophen (the active ingredient in Tylenol). Even though both drugs help relieve pain in people with little or no difficulty, both can have toxic side effects on dogs.

✔ **Nutraceuticals:** Nutritional supplements that help relieve disease symptoms such as pain and stiffness are called *nutraceuticals.* Medical experts have found two nutraceuticals, *glucosamine* and *chrondotin sulfate,* to be especially effective against arthritis. They come in several forms: injection, liquid, and tablet. Among the better known meds manufactured with these nutraceuticals are Glycoflex, Adequan, and Cosequin.

✔ **Acupuncture:** This traditional Chinese healing method is gaining increasing acceptance in the modern-day veterinary community as a way to relieve arthritis pain. I discuss the principles behind acupuncture in Chapter 3, along with another hands-on healing method: massage.

To find a vet who's trained in acupuncture, log on to the International Veterinary Acupuncture Society (IVAS) Web site at www.ivas.org or the American Academy of Veterinary Acupuncture Web site at www.aava.org. Both sites contain searchable directories of veterinary acupuncturists; the vets in the IVAS directory are certified in veterinary acupuncture.

✔ **Dietary adjustments:** Many arthritic dogs are overweight, and such excess poundage puts additional strain on their already stressed joints. For that reason, a vet almost certainly will recommend that the portly arthritic pooch start a reducing diet. The vet can help you develop such a diet or select a weight-reducing commercial food. Find more help for the portly pet in Chapter 2.

✔ **Exercise:** An arthritic dog benefits from staying on the move — in moderation. A daily walk or two, regular swim sessions, or other gentle exercise can help strengthen the muscles and ligaments of the canine arthritis patient and keep him a little more limber. Your vet can help you develop an exercise program that's right for your senior canine companion.

✔ **Creature comforts:** Your achy pooch undoubtedly appreciates a little bit of help in navigating some of the challenges that confront an arthritic canine. Soft beds, ramps, and slip-free flooring all help cushion sore joints and prevent additional injury. I cover more on making adjustments to accommodate the not-so-mobile dog in Chapter 7.

Raising the food bowl may make eating more comfortable for the arthritic pooch, but if your dog is susceptible to bloat, leave the food on the floor. A raised food bowl can increase a dog's chances of acquiring this deadly condition.

✔ **Surgery:** In certain instances, surgical procedures such as hip replacement and *femoral head ostectomy* (where a surgeon removes the ball-and-socket joint and closes up the resulting gap) can give a new lease on life to a dog with severe arthritis. These and similar procedures can cost several thousands of dollars, though, so they make the most sense for dogs who aren't getting relief through non-surgical treatment. Your vet can help you decide whether surgery is right for your arthritic dog.

Prognosis

Depending on the treatment method and the severity of the condition, many dogs gain significant relief from their arthritis aches and pains and maintain a high quality of life.

Prevention

Keeping your dog fit and trim is probably the best thing you can do to forestall, if not prevent, age-induced arthritis. In addition, your vet can prescribe either a glucosamine or glucosamine-and-chrondotin nutraceutical for your senior, both of which may help to prevent the onset of this disease.

To prevent the arthritis that results from tick-borne illnesses such as Lyme Disease, get your vet's advice about selecting an appropriate tick-control product and check your four-legged friend for ticks any time he's been cavorting in high grass or other gathering places for such insects.

Degenerative myelopathy

Degenerative myelopathy (DM) is a progressive disease that eventually results in paralysis. Although it's long been thought to be a problem mainly for older German Shepherds, cases also have been reported in Boxers, Old English Sheepdogs, Kerry Blue Terriers, Cardigan Welsh Corgis, Chesapeake Bay Retrievers, Huskies, Irish Setters, Belgian Shepherds, Rhodesian Ridgebacks, Weimaraners, and Collies.

Although the cause of DM isn't clear, some researchers believe that it's an autoimmune disease in which the dog's immune system attacks the spinal cord. The disease generally strikes dogs over 5 years of age.

Symptoms

Symptoms of DM include loss of coordination in the hind legs, bowel and bladder incontinence, foot dragging, and wobbling. As the disease progresses, the dog loses the use of his rear legs, and then his front legs. Eventually, the respiratory system fails.

Diagnosis

The only way to come up with a definitive diagnosis of DM is through an autopsy. However, a veterinarian can deduce the presence of DM by performing tests that rule out other conditions that cause similar symptoms, such as disk disease or cancer. Such tests include a neurological exam, X-rays, and *myelography* (injection of a dye around the spinal cord to make the cord easier to see in X-rays).

Treatment

Most vets say that DM can't be treated, only managed. Moderate exercise, particularly swimming, may slow down the progression of the disease.

Dr. Roger Clemmons, a veterinarian at the University of Florida, developed a diet that he says halts the symptoms of 80 percent of dogs whose DM is identified early. The diet consists of a mixture of cooked pork chop, tofu, cooked brown rice, olive oil, molasses, cooked carrots, spinach, green bell peppers, and broccoli. Ground ginger, raw garlic, dry mustard, and bone meal are added to the mixture before serving.

Prognosis

Unfortunately, DM usually results in the dog's death — either naturally or via euthanasia — within 18 months of diagnosis.

Prevention

Dr. Clemmons believes that the diet he's developed may prevent the development of DM in healthy dogs. However, no proven prevention method currently exists.

Vestibular syndrome

Vestibular syndrome (also known as *geriatric vestibular syndrome* or *peripheral vestibular syndrome*) is fairly common among middle-aged and older dogs, and can occur with any breed (or mixture). The condition affects the dog's balance, and may make it tough for him to get around. Although it's frightening to watch, vestibular syndrome is usually much less serious than it looks — and it generally doesn't last long. The cause is unknown.

Symptoms

The dog may lose his balance, lean to one side, and tilt his head. He may try to walk straight ahead but end up walking diagonally. He also may vomit and probably will refuse to eat or drink.

Diagnosis

A physical exam can confirm a diagnosis of vestibular syndrome.

Treatment

Vets usually just try to make a canine vestibular patient comfortable. Treatment focuses mainly on keeping the dog hydrated, even though he probably won't drink any water. Vets can get around that problem, though: They simply insert fluids through a tube into an area that's under the skin but on top of any muscles. The body slowly absorbs the fluids, similar to the way a timed-release human medication works. This method is called *subcutaneous administration*.

The condition may appear to be a stroke. Dogs do get strokes, but far less often than people do. Canine strokes also may be more difficult to detect than human strokes, although an MRI can help. Treatment often consists simply of letting the dog rest.

If you're looking for veterinary MRI services in your area, the Iams Company may be planning to open advanced imaging facilities near you; call 866-473-8674 to find out. In addition, some veterinary schools may have access to imaging technology.

Prognosis

Vestibular syndrome often strikes quickly; your dog may seem fine one minute but start walking like a drunken sailor the next. However, the condition usually doesn't last long — typically no more than a few days. If recovery doesn't become evident within a couple of days after the symptoms appear, have your vet re-examine your dog to see whether another problem is causing the symptoms.

Prevention

No known method for preventing vestibular syndrome exists, but you may want to keep the Jack Daniels out of your dog's reach so that you don't mistake vestibular syndrome for just plain overindulgence.

From the Inside Out

Often, a senior dog's medical malady originates from inside his body, beyond the reach of human vision. Eventually, though, these inside jobs exhibit external symptoms.

Bloat

For human beings, feeling bloated usually is no big deal. Their tummies expand when they've eaten a way-too-spicy chili dog, when they're feeling a tad irregular, or (for the relatively young women) they start retaining water at a certain time of month. Sure, such feelings are uncomfortable, but they're nothing to get into a swivet about.

For dogs, though, being bloated is a situation for their people to be alarmed over; it's a serious, deadly condition. A dog with bloat experiences great discomfort when gas fills her stomach and begins to compress the surrounding organs; experts call this *gastric dilation*. In some cases, the gas causes the stomach to rotate partially or fully on its axis, closing off both ends. Partial rotation is known as *gastric torsion;* rotation of 180 degrees or more is known as *gastric dilation volvulus (GDV)*.

Certain dogs are more vulnerable to bloat than others. Large, deep-chested breeds such as Rottweilers, Great Danes, and Doberman Pinschers have an especially high risk, as do overweight dogs, fast-eating dogs, and dogs whose diets consist mainly of kibble (dry food). A dog who drinks lots of water or exercises vigorously after a meal also is a candidate for bloat. Other possible risk factors are being male and having a fearful temperament.

Many researchers believe that dogs who are already at risk for bloat become even more vulnerable to it as they age. And as if that weren't enough, they still face another age-related risk factor: the all-too-common practice of raising the food dish off the floor in order to make eating more comfortable for the arthritic dog.

Symptoms

The dog who's developing bloat is likely to become extremely restless and to whine over a period of several hours to one day. At the same time, his abdomen will begin to swell and will feel tight to the touch, and he'll show clear signs of discomfort. He also may salivate and drool excessively, stretch and look at his abdomen, and appear anxious. He may try but fail to vomit and/or poop. He also may go into shock; if so, he may collapse, have pale gums, and have a rapid but weak pulse. Failure to treat these symptoms can lead to the dog's death.

If your dog develops any of these symptoms, immediately bring him to a vet. Don't even stop to phone and say you're on your way; have someone else make that call. Your dog's life depends on obtaining expert care as quickly as possible.

Diagnosis

A vet giving your dog a physical exam may be all that's necessary to confirm a case of gastric dilation. X-rays can determine whether the stomach has rotated and, if so, how much.

Treatment

If the dog is in shock, a vet administers intravenous fluids and medications designed to stabilize the animal. To decompress the abdomen, the vet may pass a tube into the stomach. The vet may also perform surgery (called *gastropexy*) to return the stomach to its normal position and to permanently anchor it to the body wall.

Prognosis

Research shows that more than 1 in 4 dogs with GDV (where the stomach rotated 180 degrees or more) die from the condition. The outlook is more hopeful if treatment begins before an affected dog goes into shock.

Prevention

Some vets believe that for high-risk dogs, a preventive gastropexy is a good idea — and, in any case, gastropexy is needed to prevent a recurrence. Other suggested preventive measures include

- Keeping your dog's food bowl on the floor
- Feeding your dog at least two small meals per day rather than one large meal
- Limiting exercise for two or three hours after a meal

  ✔ Limiting water intake for 30 minutes after eating

  ✔ Moistening dry kibble with water (if your dog is on an all-kibble diet)

  ✔ Limiting stress, particularly at meal times (see Chapter 2 for ideas)

Cushing's Disease

Cushing's Disease, also known as *hyperadrenocorticism,* results when a dog's adrenal glands produce too much cortisol. The condition is quite common among older dogs and occurs in one of three ways.

Occasionally, a dog develops a medically induced form of Cushing's when she's been given steroids over a long period of time to treat another health condition. The Cushing's symptoms generally disappear if the steroids are discontinued.

Most dogs get Cushing's Disease because of a small tumor that develops on the pituitary gland, which regulates bodily growth and other functions. The tumor — which usually isn't cancerous — prompts the adrenal glands, which regulate a variety of bodily functions, to grow larger and to produce too much cortisol (which affects metabolism and immunity). In some cases, however, the disease originates from a tumor on the adrenal glands themselves.

Certain breeds are more vulnerable to Cushing's Disease than others; among them are Dachshunds, Labrador Retrievers, Golden Retrievers, Beagles, Poodles, Boxers, German Shepherds, and most terriers, including Boston and Yorkshire Terriers. However, dogs of any breed can get the disease.

Symptoms

The most common symptoms of Cushing's Disease include

  ✔ Darkening and thinning of the skin

  ✔ Drinking more water than normal

  ✔ Gaining weight

  ✔ Growing a potbelly

  ✔ Increasing appetite

  ✔ Losing hair on both sides of the body

  ✔ Urinating more often than normal

  ✔ Weakening of the legs

Although the following symptoms aren't as common, be aware that your dog's behavior also may change. He may become lethargic, pant excessively, be restless during the night, seek out cool surfaces to lie down on, and experience seizures.

Diagnosis

Because the symptoms of Cushing's are similar to those that signal the onset of other diseases, such as kidney failure and diabetes, a vet needs to conduct a number of diagnostic tests to determine what's causing the dog's problems. A vet may perform a complete blood count (CBC) and a blood chemistry profile. If those tests show higher-than-normal levels of white blood cells, liver enzymes, and cholesterol, the vet probably will do additional testing that's designed to confirm a Cushing's diagnosis.

Treatment

The treatment of Cushing's Disease depends on which type of the disease the dog has. For one type, known by the big dogs in medicine as *pituitary-dependent hyperadrenocorticism,* prescription medication reduces the cortisol levels in the blood just fine and doesn't require tumor removal. But for the other type, known as *adrenal-dependent hyperadrenocorticism,* the vet will likely opt for surgically removing the tumor, because this type of tumor is more likely to be cancerous.

Removing the tumor requires removing the affected gland. However, this surgery can be quite complicated. A decision on whether to proceed with surgery should depend on the dog's age, presence of other conditions besides Cushing's Disease, the type of tumor on the adrenal gland (benign or malignant) and, if malignant, whether the cancer has begun to spread elsewhere in the dog's body.

Prognosis

The outlook for the canine Cushing's Disease patient depends, at least in part, on which variety the dog has.

A dog whose Cushing's Disease originates in the adrenal gland is cured of the disease if the tumor and one gland are removed. The same is true if both adrenal glands are removed, but such dogs need lifelong medication to replace the hormones that the adrenal glands produced.

For dogs whose Cushing's originates from the pituitary gland, the prognosis is somewhat murkier. Treatment can relieve the symptoms, improve the dog's quality of life, and perhaps lengthen life by several years. The long-term outlook depends on what other health issues the dog has.

Prevention

Cushing's Disease that originates in either the adrenal or pituitary gland can't be prevented. To prevent medically induced Cushing's Disease, dosages of steroids (to treat other conditions) should be kept as low as possible.

Diabetes

Diabetes — or, more exactly, *diabetes mellitus* — is the disease that results when a dog's pancreas doesn't produce enough *insulin,* a hormone that helps the body process sugar in the blood. Occasionally, the disease occurs because the pancreas does produce insulin, but for some reason the body can't use it.

Older dogs — particularly if they're overweight — are at greater risk for diabetes than their younger and/or skinnier counterparts. Any breed can get it, although Miniature Schnauzers, Miniature Poodles, Samoyeds, and Pugs may be predisposed to the disease. Overall, females are twice as likely to get the disease as males.

Symptoms

The primary symptoms of diabetes include increased thirst and urination, weight loss despite an increased appetite, and cloudiness of the eye.

Diagnosis

The symptoms of diabetes are similar to those of other conditions, such as Cushing's Disease and kidney problems, so diagnostic tests are necessary. Many of the tests are designed to measure the level of sugar (glucose) in the blood and urine. The tests include a complete blood count (CBC) and urinalysis.

If one or both eyes are cloudy or the dog suddenly loses his sight, he may also have cataracts, which often are caused by diabetes. Examination by a veterinary ophthalmologist can confirm a cataracts diagnosis.

Treatment

As is the case for human diabetic patients, injections of insulin are the primary treatment for diabetes in dogs. The injections supply the insulin that the body can't produce or process by itself. You can find out how to inject the insulin into your dog yourself; your vet can show you how. Injections usually occur twice a day.

Blood tests can help the vet determine how much glucose is in the blood and help him make any necessary adjustments. Your vet probably will need to adjust the amount of insulin injected periodically for the rest of the dog's life.

It's crucial to give your dog the right amount of insulin every time you inject. An insulin overdose can cause a dog to act weak, to become disoriented, and to drool and tremble. If your dog's conscious, offer food immediately and get him to his vet as soon as possible. If your dog's unconscious, apply some Karo syrup or honey to the gums — and, again, take him to a vet as soon as possible. Make sure that any food you offer contains sugar; diet syrups and foods don't contain enough sugar to revive a dog in a diabetic coma.

The overweight canine diabetic will be placed on a reducing diet, and all diabetic doggies benefit from regular meals and consistent exercise every day.

Prognosis

Diabetes has no cure — but the owner who commits to a lifelong program of medication, nutritional management, and regular exercise for the senior can enable the animal to live a long and healthy life.

Prevention

Keeping your senior from porking out or packing on too many pounds may help prevent diabetes in a few instances.

Heart disease

Canine heart disease comes in many forms. Some forms are genetic in origin, but others tend to strike in early to middle age. However, one heart condition that strikes older dogs far more often than younger pooches is *chronic valvular heart disease (CVD)*.

As the name implies, CVD is a progressive condition that affects the valves of the heart. The valves degenerate and thicken, which interferes with the heart's ability to pump blood efficiently. If left untreated, the disease can cause the heart to enlarge and lead to the accumulation of fluid in the lungs, both of which are classic signs of congestive heart failure.

CVD is quite common among older dogs. Smaller dogs, whether purebred or mixed, tend to acquire this condition more often than larger ones. Especially vulnerable breeds include Cavalier King Charles Spaniels, Poodles, Yorkshire Terriers, and Dachshunds.

Symptoms

A dog who tires easily, coughs often, has difficulty breathing, and has a swollen abdomen and/or faints may have CVD or heart failure. Such a dog also may lose her appetite.

Diagnosis

To exclude other diseases that have symptoms similar to CVD, such as a birth defect of the heart, heart muscle disease, pneumonia, lung cancer, or bronchitis, a vet runs several diagnostic tests in addition to conducting a physical exam. Such tests often include an *electrocardiogram* (a recording of the heart's electrical activity) to detect abnormalities in the heart rhythm; a chest X-ray to examine the size of the heart and to check for fluid in the lungs; and blood tests to rule out heartworm. An *echocardiogram* (an ultrasound examination of the heart) can confirm the diagnosis.

Treatment

If your dog's CVD is mild, your vet may choose not to treat the disease at all, but instead to simply monitor your senior's condition. If your dog's CVD is severe or has progressed to heart failure, your vet is likely to prescribe the following drugs:

- ✔ A diuretic such as Lasix to remove the fluid that's accumulated around the heart or abdomen
- ✔ A strengthener for the heart, such as Lanoxin
- ✔ A vasodilator, such as Enacard, to help the heart pump blood more easily

The vet may also suggest that you feed your senior a low-salt diet and no longer include table scraps on her menu.

Prognosis

Generally, CVD isn't curable; it can only be managed. However, treatment can improve your senior's quality of life and prolong it for several years.

Prevention

Unfortunately, CVD isn't preventable.

Kidney failure

Chronic kidney failure, also known as chronic renal failure, is another problem that's more prevalent in older dogs than younger pooches, although dogs of any age can fall prey to this condition. Any breed can experience chronic kidney failure, too, although Cocker Spaniels, Lhasa Apsos, Shih Tzu, Norwegian Elkhounds, Doberman Pinschers, Soft-Coated Wheaten Terriers, Golden Retrievers, Bull Terriers, Cairn Terriers, German Shepherds, and Samoyeds are especially vulnerable to the disease. Other risk factors include urinary tract infections, high blood pressure, and diabetes.

Sometimes, the kidneys suddenly fail due to trauma or exposure to poison; when this happens, the dog is said to have *acute kidney failure. Chronic kidney failure* can result if an episode of acute kidney failure causes permanent damage to those organs.

Healthy kidneys filter toxins and waste products from the blood and discharge what's left to the bladder. The bladder then releases this material, which is — you guessed it — urine. As a dog ages, his kidneys lose some efficiency, but a dog with kidney failure has little or no kidney function. Consequently, the toxins that should've discharged from the body build up in the blood instead. At that point, the dog shows clear signs of illness, even though the disease probably has been progressing for some time.

Symptoms

A dog with chronic kidney failure is thirstier than normal, needs to pee much more often, and may have bathroom accidents. He may be lethargic and lose his appetite. In addition, his breath may smell like ammonia.

Diagnosis

Because many symptoms of kidney failure are similar to those of other health problems, such as urinary tract infections, Cushing's Disease, diabetes, and liver disease, a vet will conduct a number of tests to arrive at a conclusive diagnosis. In addition to a physical exam, the vet will analyze your dog's urine and run blood tests. Other possible tests include X-rays or ultrasounds of the kidneys.

Treatment

A special diet with low concentrations of phosphorus and protein or one that contains easily digested proteins called *hydrolyzed proteins* is the most common course of action to treat canine kidney failure patients. Such diets are formulated to reduce the impaired kidneys' workload. Several major pet-food companies manufacture such diets, all of which require a vet's prescription. Another option is to make the food yourself, under your vet's supervision; however, doing so is very time-consuming. Check out Chapter 2 for information on homemade dog food.

Your dog's vet may also prescribe vitamin and fatty acid supplements or blood pressure medication. And because many dogs with kidney failure are in desperate need of fluids, your vet may have you perform fluid therapy on your dog — this therapy involves inserting a mixture of fluids under his skin to keep him hydrated. The vet shows you how to do this, so don't worry.

The owner of a dog with chronic kidney failure should plan on bringing his pooch to the vet for evaluation at least every couple of months.

Prognosis

Chronic kidney disease can't be cured, but its progression can be slowed when it's caught early enough. The condition is very serious, though, and over the long term, the dog's prognosis is guarded, at best.

Prevention

In some cases, chronic kidney disease is hereditary; for that reason, you shouldn't breed an affected dog. Early detection can extend both the quality and length of an affected dog's life.

Reproductive infections

By the time a dog crosses the bridge between middle age and seniorhood, his people probably aren't thinking of breeding him — even if, in his earlier life, he was a canine studmuffin (or she was a canine hottie). But even when a dog's humans decide that his sex life should be part of the past, the reproductive system may make its presence known, usually in the form of one or more health problems.

For female dogs, the main problem is *pyometra,* an infection of the uterus that can be fatal if left untreated. Male dogs may experience *prostatitis,* an infection of the prostate gland.

Symptoms

A dog with pyometra is likely to develop the condition within eight weeks of her previous heat cycle. Symptoms include a foul-smelling, green-brown discharge from her vagina, increased thirst and urination, vomiting, appetite loss, and fever.

The dog with prostate problems loses his appetite, moves stiffly and is hunched up, and feels pain when you touch his abdomen. He may be constipated, be in pain when he urinates, and his urine may be cloudy or bloody-looking. If the dog mates (and, given his discomfort, that prospect is problematic) with a female dog, puppies may not result, causing his owner to wonder why he apparently is infertile.

Diagnosis

If the vet suspects a dog has pyometra, he'll perform a physical exam, order blood tests and a urinalysis and, perhaps, X-ray the reproductive area. The vet will also probably want to know when the dog's most recent heat occurred, because the condition generally occurs soon afterward

To diagnose prostatitis, the vet will perform similar procedures.

Treatment

For both males and females, surgical removal of the reproductive organs is essential. The vet is also likely to prescribe antibiotics to knock out the infection that prompted the need for the spaying or neutering in the first place.

Prognosis

If the condition is diagnosed and treated in time, the dog can make a full recovery — and won't miss having a sex life, either.

Prevention

Spaying completely eliminates a female dog's chances of developing pyometra because she has no uterus for the infection to develop in. Neutering a male puppy no later than 6 months of age can reduce his likelihood of developing prostatitis. Research has shown that intact male dogs are much more vulnerable to prostatitis than neutered males are.

The Eyes Have It

Although most senior dogs don't see as well as they did when they were younger, some pooches' windows to the world get clouded by disease as well as normal aging. Here are some conditions that get in the way of a senior's ability to see.

Cataracts

Cataracts are, quite simply, a clouding of the eye lens. Cataracts occur when the normal mechanics of the lens changes, and the normal balance of water and protein in the eye alter, allowing excess water to enter the lens.

Symptoms

A dog with cataracts has a whitish cloudiness in one or both eyes. If the cataracts have progressed sufficiently, she may show signs of vision loss.

Almost all senior dogs eventually develop a blue-gray color rather than a white color on their eyes. Although many people mistake this development for cataracts, it's far more likely that such dogs have *nuclear stenosis,* which has little effect on the dog's ability to see.

Diagnosis

An eye examination by a veterinary ophthalmologist can confirm the presence of cataracts. The dog also may undergo a blood test to determine whether he's dealing with underlying causes of the cataracts, such as diabetes.

Treatment

The only cure for cataracts is having surgery to remove the affected lens. However, not all dogs with cataracts are good candidates for such surgery. A dog with diabetes or an elderly dog in failing health is probably better off simply getting treatment for any inflammation that the cataracts have caused — and of course, taking steps wherever possible to restore the animal's overall health.

However, a healthy older dog can do fine with surgery, but the owner must be willing to spend at least $2,000 for such surgery and another $1,000 or so for artificially implanted lenses. You also need to consider whether you're willing to commit yourself to weeks of post-operative care for your canine patient. In addition to giving her eye drops to control any post-surgical inflammation, you also have to restrict your dog's activities for several weeks after the surgery.

Many experts suggest leaving cataracts alone if they're small and aren't really interfering with your dog's vision. A dog with a cataract in only one eye also may be better off without undergoing surgery, which carries some risks even for healthy older dogs.

Prognosis

If a senior is a good candidate for cataract surgery and still maintains some sight in the affected eye, prospects are excellent for a successful procedure and improved eyesight.

Prevention

Unfortunately, no proven methods currently prevent cataracts in dogs whose conditions aren't caused by another disease, such as diabetes. However, research on human patients suggests that regular Vitamin E supplements may help thwart cataract development in people. Don't start giving your dog Vitamin E supplements on your own, though; consult your vet first.

Conjunctivitis

Also known as "pink eye," *conjunctivitis* is an inflammation of the *conjunctiva* — the tissue that surrounds the eyeball and eyelids. This common canine eye ailment has many causes, including bacterial or viral infections, foreign bodies in the eye, irritation from shampoos and dips, allergies, and a wide range of underlying eye diseases.

Older dogs are especially vulnerable to conjunctivitis because their eyes lose the ability to tear as they age. This lack of tearing may result in the development of dry eye (see the section, "Dry eye," in this chapter). That condition can, in turn, lead to conjunctivitis.

Symptoms

A dog with conjunctivitis shows clear signs of discomfort in the eye area. In addition to redness in the white parts of the eye and/or the eyelids, the animal may squint or even paw at the affected eye. The eye probably will emit a discharge, although the nature of the discharge often depends on the underlying cause of the conjunctivitis.

Diagnosis

When a vet suspects that a patient has pink eye, he'll probably administer a Schirmer Tear Test, which gauges the amount of tears the dog can produce in one minute. The vet will also carefully examine the affected eye and will be especially alert to the presence of abrasions or other injuries to the eye.

Treatment

To treat a pink-eyed pooch, the vet tries to determine what caused the condition in the first place. If the vet finds the cause, treatment focuses on eliminating the underlying problem as well as alleviating the discomfort from the conjunctivitis itself. If the vet doesn't uncover a specific cause, he generally prescribes a topical antibiotic and/or corticosteroid to reduce irritation and eliminate infection.

Prognosis

Conjunctivitis clears up relatively quickly if the underlying cause is discovered and eliminated. If the cause is unknown, treatment of the symptoms is nevertheless helpful in most instances.

Prevention

Most of the time, you can't prevent conjunctivitis, although you can limit the severity of the condition by taking your dog to the vet as soon as you suspect any trouble. However, taking care to prevent foreign objects from entering your dog's eye — for example, stop letting your dog stick his head out the car window as you motor down the highway — can limit the possibilities of getting conjunctivitis for that reason.

Dry eye

Dry eye, formally known as *keratoconjunctivitis sicca,* or *KCS,* results when a dog's eye doesn't produce enough tears. Causes of dry eye include skin allergies, side effects of certain drugs, and, of course, age. Among some breeds, such as Cocker Spaniels, Bulldogs, and West Highland Terriers, the condition is relatively common. Without treatment, the surface of the cornea can become damaged, which can greatly increase the discomfort she already feels and lead to blindness.

Symptoms

A dog with dry eye develops a red eye that discharges thick mucus. She may also squint to relieve her discomfort or paw at her eyes. Those eyes may look as though they've gotten too many visits from Mr. Sandman: Crusty material appears at the corners.

Diagnosis

To diagnose dry eye, a vet gives the dog a Schirmer Tear Test, which measures the amount of tears the dog produces in one minute. If the amount is lower than normal, a dry eye diagnosis is likely.

Treatment

Twice-daily administration of cyclosporine cream or liquid can increase the dog's own tear production. Artificial tears and antibiotic eye meds also can help. Wiping away the eye cruddies at the corners is also a good idea; just soak a cotton ball with warm water and wipe gently. The water will soften the crusts. In most cases, treatment continues for the rest of the dog's life.

Prognosis

Dry eye responds very well to appropriate treatment.

Prevention

You can reduce the chances of long-haired dogs (such as Bearded Collies and Old English Sheepdogs) developing KCS by making sure that their bangs are kept clean and are either trimmed or tied away from their faces.

Glaucoma

Glaucoma results when the fluid within the eye, which normally drains into the circulatory system, is blocked from making such an exit. Consequently, the fluid accumulates and takes up space in the eye, causing fluid pressure within the eye to increase. As the pressure increases, the optic nerve becomes irreversibly damaged. Without treatment, the dog loses sight in the eye.

Some breeds are particularly susceptible to glaucoma. They include the Beagle, Cocker Spaniel, Jack Russell Terrier, Siberian Husky, Alaskan Malamute, Bassett Hound, Chow Chow, Akita, Sharpei, Poodle, Maltese, Welsh Terrier, and Shih Tzu. Older dogs manifest the disease far more often than younger pooches do.

Veterinarians and scientists divide glaucoma into two classes: primary and secondary. *Primary glaucoma* occurs in dogs who are born with malformations in the eye that block the outflow of liquid from the eye and cause pressure to build up within; often, this affects both eyes. *Secondary glaucoma* means that the disease was caused by another condition, such as swelling of the lens or tumors in the eye.

Symptoms

A sudden bright redness in the eye is a common symptom of glaucoma. Other signs include light sensitivity, dilated pupils, loss of vision, eyelid spasms, eye enlargement, discoloration or cloudiness of the cornea, and rubbing or pawing of the eye area. The dog also may tilt his head on the same side as the affected eye in order to relieve the pressure.

If your dog develops any symptoms that suggest glaucoma, don't delay: Get him to a vet immediately. Unlike human glaucoma, the canine version of this disease can be extremely aggressive — so fast-moving that the dog can lose his sight in the affected eye within just a few days unless he's treated right away.

Diagnosis

To diagnose glaucoma, the vet or veterinary ophthalmologist measures the amount of pressure within the eye. If secondary glaucoma is suspected, the vet may perform blood and urine tests to determine the underlying cause and may use X-rays or an ultrasound to locate a possible tumor.

Treatment

Treatment depends on whether any sight remains in the affected eye. If the eye retains some sight, surgery to either diminish the production of fluid or to bypass the blockage can help. To reduce pressure within the eye, prescribed medications can help.

When the pupil no longer responds to light, your dog loses his vision in the affected eye. At that point, the best course of action is often to remove the eye in order to eliminate any infection or pain that results from the disease. For cosmetic purposes, you can get your dog a prosthetic eye to replace the eye that's been removed.

Prognosis

A dog with glaucoma eventually loses sight in the affected eye — and often, the other eye is affected later. However, prompt treatment can put off the inevitable, often for quite a while.

Prevention

Some veterinary ophthalmologists believe breeds that are at relatively high risk for glaucoma should be screened twice a year for the disease, particularly if one or both of the dog's parents already have the condition. Such screenings don't prevent glaucoma, but they do increase the odds of catching the disease early on.

For a dog who already has primary glaucoma in one eye, treating the other eye can delay the onset of the disease there.

The Not-So-Best of the Rest

Some senior-specific maladies don't lend themselves so easily to classification. Here I list three of those conditions.

Cognitive dysfunction syndrome

Just as human brains age, so do the brains of dogs. Almost every dog experiences some deterioration of mental function as she journeys through seniorhood — but for some dogs, the decline is dramatic. These dogs may be experiencing *canine cognitive dysfunction syndrome (CDS),* which also is known as "doggy Alzheimer's Disease" or "doggy dementia."

CDS is believed to occur when proteins form deposits of plaque on the brain. The process is similar but not identical to what happens to the brains of human Alzheimer's patients.

Symptoms

A dog with CDS may exhibit a wide range of behavioral changes, including

- Anxiety
- Barking or whining for no apparent reason
- Changed sleep cycle: sleeping most of the day, being awake at night
- Confusion
- Difficulty navigating stairs and other obstacles
- Disorientation
- Failure to obey familiar commands or directions
- Failure to recognize familiar people
- Housetraining lapses
- Less interest in people
- New fears or phobias
- Uncharacteristic aggressiveness

Diagnosis

Because some symptoms of CDS also may indicate the presence of other diseases, a vet needs to perform several diagnostic tests. These tests help eliminate other possible causes of a dog's symptoms and can help confirm a CDS diagnosis.

The tests may include a neurological exam, a complete blood chemistry, a urinalysis, thyroid and adrenocortical hormone level tests, and computed tomography (CT) scans or magnetic resonance imaging (MRI) scans.

Treatment

Until the late 1990s, no effective treatment for CDS existed. However, that unhappy state of affairs changed with the debut of Anipryl, a drug the U.S. Food and Drug Administration (FDA) approved specifically to help reduce the symptoms of CDS. Anipryl is available by prescription from your vet.

Another CDS treatment comes from Hills Pet Foods: Prescription Diet Canine b/d. The company says that this food is specifically designed to combat the effects of aging on the canine brain, even when your dog is showing the most extreme CDS symptoms. This product also is available only from your vet.

Prognosis

Unfortunately, just as researchers haven't found a cure for human Alzheimer's Disease, they haven't found a cure for CDS, either. However, treatment can extend the length of time that your senior's mental functions stay at a reasonably high level. Eventually, though, CDS symptoms return and incapacitate the dog completely.

Prevention

Ultimately, CDS isn't preventable. However, you can forestall the effects of this condition and even normal canine mental aging if you keep your dog both mentally and physically stimulated. As noted in Chapter 4, it's not only possible, but also advisable to teach an old dog new tricks. Age-appropriate exercise helps your dog stay healthier physically and boosts his mental capabilities.

Lipoma

Just about every senior dog develops at least one soft lump under her skin, and your senior's not likely to be an exception. In all likelihood, you'll find such a lump when you groom, massage, or just pet your pooch. You can't know for sure what the lump is until it's tested. Chances are, though, that the lump is just a benign tumor called a *lipoma* — or, to keep it nice and simple, a fatty tumor.

Symptoms

A lipoma can be located anywhere on the body, but common locations are underneath the front leg where the limb joins the body, on the chest, and on the groin. The lump usually feels soft and spongy. When you pick up the surrounding skin, the lump is usually within the skin rather than underneath it, and you can move it around easily.

Generally, a dog with a lipoma has no other symptoms, unless the tumor is located in an area that's irritated by motion or is so large that it interferes with the dog's ability to move.

Diagnosis

A vet can determine what type of lump your dog has by inserting a needle directly into the lump and extracting fluid. This procedure is called *aspiration*. Microscopic examination of the fluid results in a diagnosis of lipoma if cancer cells aren't present — or, in rare cases, it's diagnosed as cancer if such cells are found in the fluid. However, needle aspirates aren't completely foolproof; sometimes an aspirate will extract only normal cells and leave stray cancer cells behind. For that reason, your vet may follow a needle aspirate with a biopsy of tissue, just to be on the safe side.

Treatment

Unless the lipoma grows, causes your dog discomfort, or interferes with her mobility, leaving it alone is your best course of action — or, rather, non-action. If the tumor is causing a problem, you can have it removed surgically.

Prognosis

Lipomas are usually harmless. In rare instances, they may become cancerous or grow to a size that impedes your dog's ability to move normally. As with any condition your dog has, monitoring the lump is a good idea. If the lump grows or shows other changes, take your dog back to the vet for a re-exam.

Prevention

Lipomas seem to be an inevitable manifestation of canine aging. You can't prevent them — but generally, you don't need to.

Tooth and gum disease

Rare is the senior dog who doesn't have some dental issues. A senior's had a lifetime to accumulate gunk on her teeth and gums, especially if her owners haven't taken the time to brush her teeth on a regular basis. If the dog is small and has overcrowded or mis-aligned teeth, dental problems are even more likely to occur.

The accumulated gunk starts as *plaque,* which is a colorless but bacteria-laden film that adheres to the teeth. If the plaque isn't removed — either by the dog's own chewing or by the owner brushing her teeth — it hardens into brown or yellow tartar that adheres to the gum line. The gums redden and become tender and inflamed. Eventually, the gums begin to pull away from the teeth, allowing more bacteria to accumulate in the resulting gaps. The same bacteria can enter the bloodstream, travel to vital organs, and cause life-threatening infections in those places.

Symptoms

Bad breath, yellowish or brownish teeth, bleeding gums, pain while eating or chewing, and tooth loss are the most common signs of canine tooth and gum disease. The affected senior also may be somewhat subdued in her behavior.

Diagnosis

Your vet can give your senior a visual examination of the teeth to confirm a diagnosis of canine dental disease.

Treatment

Treatment of gum and tooth disease starts with a full cleaning, which is performed under anesthesia. Before the procedure, however, the vet will perform a complete blood chemistry (CBC) and other tests to determine whether the dog can tolerate the anesthetic. If anesthesia isn't advisable, your vet may scale the tartar off by hand — provided that the dog is extremely cooperative.

The dental cleaning includes removing tartar from the teeth and pulling any loose teeth. The vet may prescribe antibiotics afterward to fight off any infections that have contributed to the dog's dental disease.

Prognosis

A thorough cleaning can halt tooth and gum disease dead in its tracks. Keeping the disease at bay requires the owner's commitment to starting and maintaining a good oral health program that includes brushing the teeth, providing appropriate chew toys, and having the dog's teeth professionally cleaned once a year, or as often as your vet feels such cleanings are necessary.

Prevention

You can keep tooth and gum disease in check by taking an active role in maintaining your senior's oral health. Here's how:

- **Brush the teeth.** A daily brushing removes the particles that form disease-causing plaque. For directions on how to brush your canine's canines (not to mention all the other teeth), check out Chapter 5.

- **Feed for health.** Several pet-food companies, including Hills and Iams, either manufacture special diets to promote dental health or add ingredients to their foods that help keep dogs' mouths healthy.

- **Let her chew.** Help your senior pooch keep her teeth clean by providing proper chew toys. Rawhide chews are a good choice, as long as you don't let your dog have too many (overdoing the rawhide can upset a dog's stomach).

- **Lay off the hard stuff.** Avoid offering your dog very hard chew toys or even everyday stuff like ice cubes. They can break the teeth, particularly if the teeth are already weakened.

- **Bone up.** Holistic veterinarians highly recommend feeding a raw, meaty bone to a dog at least once a week — both to clean the teeth and to provide some doggy-style entertainment.

Senior Super Dogs: P-Dog takes his lump

Although he's approaching his ninth birthday, P-Dog hasn't slowed down. The Beagle-Shepherd mix still enjoys taking long hikes with his people, chasing after those crazy squirrels in his yard, and scaling whatever log piles and hillsides come his way. But physical prowess isn't this senior dog's only accomplishment, says his owner, Alissa Schwipps of Danville, Indiana (an editor on this book).

Courtesy of Greg and Alissa Schwipps

"From day one of our friendship, P-Dog has been a source of love and support I can rely on," says Schwipps, who adopted the dog when he was a puppy. "Keeping me grounded has been his special accomplishment."

The idea of losing that source of love and companionship prematurely is horrifying to anyone — which is why Schwipps says her stomach did a nervous two-step when she found a walnut-sized lump on P-Dog's left hind leg. The lump was soft and spongy, but Schwipps could touch and manipulate the lump without causing any apparent discomfort to her canine companion.

Still, says Schwipps, "I worried, 'How long has this lump been here? I'm such a terrible [dog] parent; how could I have not noticed it? Could the lump be cancerous?' " The latter thought was especially terrifying to Schwipps, because her parents were forced to euthanize a beloved Golden Retriever when a lump on that dog's leg grew to the size of a softball.

Those worries prompted Schwipps to take P-Dog to her vet the very next day. "I wanted to get P-Dog help as soon as possible, if he needed it," says Schwipps. "More than anything, I wanted to hear the vet say that the lump wasn't cancerous."

The vet, Dr. Jim Chastain of Animal Hospital of Avon, examined the lump and removed some liquid. When he examined the liquid under the microscope, he found only non-cancerous cells, much to Schwipps's relief.

"Dr. Chastain explained that dogs sometimes get fatty deposits in their old age," Schwipps explains. "The lumps are nothing to worry about unless they grow larger and distract the dog. Thankfully, P-Dog's lump hasn't grown, and it hasn't slowed him down a bit!"

With that happy result, Schwipps and her husband have faith that P-Dog will remain their energetic best friend for years to come.

Chapter 11

Coping with Canine Cancer

. . . .

In This Chapter

▶ Recognizing signs of cancer

▶ Knowing the different types of cancer

▶ Treating your dog's cancer

▶ Finding a cancer specialist

▶ Balancing treatment pluses and minuses

▶ Preventing cancer

. . . .

*O*ne of the most frightening experiences a senior dog owner can have is hearing the vet say, "It's cancer."

So far, I've heard those words uttered twice by my vet. The first time, I wasn't surprised; I'd found a suspicious lump on 16-year-old Molly's groin and taken her to my vet for evaluation. But the second time I heard those words, I was flabbergasted; I never dreamed that 7-year-old Cory's digestive difficulties — previously diagnosed as a food allergy — would turn out to be a cancer of the digestive tract. Both times, though, I felt my stomach lurch and a chill run down my spine.

A cancer diagnosis can devastate anyone. If your senior dog receives that diagnosis, you'll be pretty upset but you'll be far from alone. According to a report from Hills Pet Food Company, at least 1 in 4 dogs will develop cancer during his lifetime.

Not so long ago, a cancer diagnosis amounted to an automatic death sentence for the unfortunate victim, human or canine. Today, though, the prognosis can be quite different. Although a cancer diagnosis for a senior dog is certainly serious, as an owner, you don't necessarily have to plan on euthanizing your pooch. Depending on your dog's situation, his prognosis may be a lot better than you think. In this chapter, I explain why cancer doesn't always kill, describe the most common canine cancers, and offer advice on how senior dogs and their people can cope with a cancer diagnosis and its aftermath.

Concerning Cancer

Cancer results when abnormal cells in the body grow uncontrollably and destroy normal tissue. Doctors and veterinarians may use the terms "cancer" and "malignancy" interchangeably.

One way to think of cancer is as an invasion. Specifically, damaged or altered cells overpower the normal ones. Normal cells are supposed to die when damaged, but cancer cells take on the trappings of immortality: They don't die. Without treatment, these immortal cells overwhelm their normal counterparts and disrupt the normal workings of the dog's body.

Which dogs are at risk?

Many factors can boost the odds that a dog will get cancer. Those factors include

- **Age:** According to the Animal Cancer Center at Colorado State University, 50 percent of dogs and cats develop cancer if they live 10 years or longer. In part, this huge percentage is a sign of success, at least from a veterinary perspective, because advances in veterinary medicine have enabled more dogs to reach seniorhood. And because more dogs are reaching seniorhood, the seniors are more likely to develop cancer than youthful pooches are. In addition, the wear and tear of accumulating years can make a senior dog more vulnerable to cancer than his youthful counterpart, who hasn't had as much time to strain his working parts.

- **Heredity:** Cancer often runs in families, so a dog with relatives who've had cancer is more likely to draw a cancer diagnosis than a dog whose forebearers have been cancer free.

- **Body type:** Scientists have found that physical characteristics may predispose a dog to developing a particular cancer. Large dogs, for example, may be more prone to developing bone cancer, or *osteosarcoma,* because their legs must tolerate the stress of the dogs' weight. Dark-skinned dogs seem more prone to developing *melanoma,* a skin tumor that can be cancerous for a canine.

- **Breed:** Although dogs of any breed — or mix — can develop cancer, certain breeds are more likely to develop different forms of cancer. For example, English Setters are among the breeds that appear predisposed to developing breast cancer, and Boxers are one of the breeds that have higher odds of developing mast cell cancer (a kind of skin cancer), compared to the overall canine population. Only a few types of dogs may be affected by some cancers; for example, almost all cases of *histocitosis of Bernese Mountain Dogs* occur in that breed.

✔ **Sun exposure:** A light-skinned, thin-haired pooch who likes to sunbathe may find himself with a case of skin cancer later in life. Just like with people, sun exposure can cause damage to skin cells that leads to cancer.

Not every tumor is cancerous

At the risk of repeating myself, let me state again: Not every canine lump or tumor heralds the onset of cancer. Plenty of abnormal swellings, lumps, or bumps are basically harmless, or at least, not very serious. If your senior dog's diagnosed with one of the tumors in the following list, you can rest easy.

✔ **Lipomas:** These soft, spongy lumps are nothing more than a harmless accumulation of fat cells and are often called "fatty tumors." Lipomas usually don't appear until a dog is middle-aged or older. You can find out more about lipomas in Chapter 10.

✔ **Warts:** If your four-legged friend develops one or more lumps that look like cauliflower, chances are he has plain old warts. They're not serious, but you can't do much about them, other than let nature take its course. Sometimes, however, a growth that looks like a wart can be a cancerous tumor, so have your vet look at any wart your pooch appears to be sporting.

✔ **Hematomas:** A blood-filled lump may appear on the ear of a dog who's been shaking her head a lot, and thus caused fragile blood vessels to break. This lump, or *hematoma,* needs a vet's attention, not only to drain the lump itself but also to deal with the ear infection or parasites that may have triggered the head-shaking in the first place.

✔ **Sebaceous cysts:** These red bumps may remind you of the zits you had when you were a teenager, but they're completely different. Sebaceous cysts aren't filled with pus; they're filled with *keratin* (a protein that looks a bit like cheese). They're not serious, but they can be uncomfortable, so have your vet either drain the cysts or remove them altogether.

Even if a lump appears to be harmless, you need a vet's evaluation to confirm your hunch. If your senior sports a lump you haven't seen before, call your vet.

Reading the Signs

Discovering the condition early is crucial to a successful outcome against cancer. Just like with people, early detection of a dog's malignant tumor often greatly increases the odds of vanquishing it. Because you're with your senior every day, you have the role of early detector. Here's what the American Veterinary Medical Association says you should look for:

- **Abnormal swellings that persist or continue to grow:** I'd go further and say that any lump that appears suddenly needs a vet's evaluation. Chances are, the lump is harmless (see the preceding "Not every tumor is cancerous" section on harmless lumps) — but you won't know until a pro looks at it. If an earlier lump was diagnosed as being harmless but later starts to grow, you need to have it re-tested.

- **Sores that don't heal:** A cut or sore that doesn't heal indicates that all's not well within your dog's body — and the reason could be the onset of cancer.

- **Weight loss that can't be explained:** If your dog pares off poundage through a supervised weight-loss diet, that's okay. But if your dog starts losing weight for no apparent reason, he needs to see his vet pronto.

- **Loss of appetite:** Compare your dog's current eating pattern with his usual dining habits. If his interest in eating declines further or if he refuses to eat a favorite food, take him to the vet.

- **Bleeding or discharge from any body opening:** Obviously, I'm not talking about a cut or a minor open wound that bleeds a little bit; that's normal. However, if your dog has blood or other discharge emerging from his nostrils, mouth, ears, anus, or urethra, this isn't normal, and a vet needs to evaluate him.

  If your dog has blood in his urine, it probably doesn't indicate the presence of cancer. A urinary tract infection, or UTI, is a more likely cause. A UTI isn't serious if caught early, and it responds well to treatment with antibiotics prescribed by your vet.

- **Offensive odor:** Your dog might stink for plenty of reasons, from rolling in a disgusting substance to eating his poop. Ear infections also can cause your dog to smell less than terrific, and dental disease inevitably leads to gross dog breath. An inexplicable offensive odor, though, can mean that something serious is amiss with your dog. Get him to a vet as soon as possible.

Smelly ears and bad breath also need a vet's attention, even though you probably already know the causes. Untreated ear infections can cause deafness; untreated dental disease can lead to an infection of your dog's vital organs that can be fatal.

✔ **Difficulty eating or swallowing:** Eating problems may result from painful teeth and gums, but they also can result from a tumor that's blocking the esophagus. If your senior's having trouble eating or swallowing, have your vet give him a look.

✔ **Hesitation to exercise or loss of stamina:** Don't automatically attribute your senior dog's loss of endurance to age. If your four-legged friend needs to stop and rest during a walk that he usually completes with ease, he needs to see the vet.

✔ **Persistent lameness or stiffness:** Although arthritis often causes old-dog mobility problems, you shouldn't assume your dog is gimpy because of arthritis. A vet can check to see whether a tumor is causing the problem.

✔ **Difficulty pooping, peeing, or breathing:** If your senior dog can't poop, he may simply be constipated. On the other hand, he may be suffering from a blockage that prevents pooping — and a tumor may cause that blockage. Peeing problems may result from a blockage caused by crystals in the urine or from a tumor. Breathing problems may indicate a heart ailment or a tumor. The bottom line: Get your dog checked out if any of these normal bodily functions suddenly become problematic.

Looking for the Cause

If you detect a possible problem, your vet can perform several tests to determine whether cancer is the cause. The tests she uses depend on where the problem is: whether it's on the surface (usually in the form of a lump) or is internal.

For example, if your senior's skin sports a suspicious lump, the vet is likely to *aspirate* it: insert a needle into the lump to withdraw some of the fluid within. She'll examine the fluid under a microscope or send it to an outside lab. If the sample shows abnormal cells, the next step she'll take is to surgically remove a piece of the tumor itself for microscopic examination, or a *biopsy*. With a large tumor, the vet may decide to perform a biopsy even if the aspirate shows only normal cells, because the aspiration may have missed cells that aren't normal.

By taking a biopsy, the vet can not only determine whether the tissue is a cancerous tumor, but she can also determine how serious the cancer is. If the tumor isn't cancerous, it's generally left alone unless it's bothering the dog.

If your dog's problem is internal, the vet's diagnostic techniques change because the tumor isn't visible. Vets use imaging tools such as X-rays and ultrasound to locate an internal tumor, and less frequently, magnetic resonance imaging (MRI). Sometimes, though, conventional imaging doesn't locate a suspected tumor; in such cases, the vet may suggest performing exploratory surgery. If such imaging does pinpoint a tumor's location, the vet probably will recommend surgery to remove the mass and perform a biopsy.

Developing a Battle Plan

Once your vet discovers a tumor and evaluates it or has an outside lab perform the evaluation, he'll work with you to develop a treatment plan for your senior. The treatment plan may involve not only your vet, but also specialists such as a *veterinary oncologist* — a vet who specializes in treating cancer (see the "Consulting a Specialist" section later in this chapter).

The techniques I discuss in the following sections are used to treat different types of cancer. Sometimes these techniques are used singly but, more often, they're used in combination. However they're used, they have a common objective: to remove the cancerous tumor and keep it from coming back. If that objective is unattainable, these same techniques can slow the cancer's growth and extend the dog's life.

Surgery

Unless your senior's cancer is very advanced or is a systemic variety like lymphoma, your vet or oncologist probably will recommend surgery as the first step in treating your dog. Surgery aims to remove your dog's tumor. Depending on where the tumor is located and what type of cancer your dog has, surgery can extend your dog's life by several months or more, or even result in a complete cure.

Even in cases where the entire tumor can't be removed, surgery may still be a good idea because it can reduce the size of the tumor — or, in vet-speak, "debulk" the tumor — so that chemotherapy and radiation can be more effective (see the sections "Chemotherapy" and "Radiation therapy" later in this chapter).

Research frontiers

Scientists are hard at work finding out how canine cancer starts and how to defeat it. Much of their research focuses on *gene therapy:* understanding the genetic mechanisms that change a normal cell into a cancerous cell, and developing new weapons to reverse those mechanisms. The results of this research can help not only dogs, but also people who develop cancer.

For example, researchers discovered that a certain type of gene that causes a cell to age and die isn't present in cancer cells. This discovery led researchers to develop a technique that replaces the missing gene, thus stimulating the dog's own ability to fight the tumor.

Other researchers focus on the opposite situation: a cell that has an unneeded copy of the gene that regulates cellular growth. Normal cells with just one of these genes grow normally, but the extra gene sets in motion the uncontrolled proliferation of cells that characterizes cancer. Consequently, these scientists are focusing on finding a way to disrupt the functioning of the duplicate gene and restore normal cell growth to the dog's body.

A number of organizations fund canine cancer studies, including the American Kennel Club Canine Health Foundation (www.akcchf.org) and the Morris Animal Foundation (www.morrisanimalfoundation.org). These and other groups provide funding for preliminary studies that, when successful, lead to clinical trials of the treatment that's been developed (I discuss clinical trials in more detail in the "All about clinical trials" sidebar in this chapter).

Your vet is likely to use the term *margins* when he discusses tumor removal surgery with you. If he does, he's saying that he not only wants to remove the tumor, but also the tissue that surrounds it. By removing the surrounding tissue, he's attempting to make sure that any cancerous cells that have begun to spread from the tumor are also removed. For example, if your dog has a mast cell tumor, the surgeon will aim to remove the tumor with *wide margins:* at least 3 centimeters of surrounding tissue. The more cancerous cells are removed, the better your senior's prognosis is.

Surgery always carries some risk, especially for a senior dog. So your vet or oncologist will order blood work on your dog before undertaking the surgery. The vet or oncologist tests your dog's blood sample for a variety of components to make sure that he can tolerate the anesthesia. He may also use X-rays, ultrasound, or even magnetic resonance imaging (MRI) to locate the tumor and determine whether it's spread.

Chemotherapy

Chemotherapy is when your vet or oncologist administers a series of powerful drugs that are designed to kill your dog's cancer, or at least slow its rate of growth. By prescribing drugs that are highly toxic to the tumor, vets are trying to poison the cancer.

I wouldn't be surprised if the prospect of chemotherapy scares some human cancer patients as much or even more than the actual cancer diagnosis does. Such fear is understandable: The human chemo patient often loses all her hair, suffers considerable nausea, and generally feels incredibly lousy.

However, dogs seem to tolerate chemotherapy much better than humans do. Two reasons account for this difference between canine and human chemo patients: Dogs receive lower doses of the drugs than people, and canine cancer therapy combines fewer drugs than human cancer therapy does. Consequently, a senior dog on chemo usually doesn't go bald and suffers little or no nausea.

Dogs who have cancer are prescribed many of the same drugs that are used for people who have cancer. In both instances, the drugs prescribed depend on what variety of cancer the patient has. Some drugs dogs are prescribed must be injected by a vet; others can be given by mouth at home. The duration of chemotherapy depends on the type and stage of cancer your dog has.

Most vets and oncologists agree that chemotherapy alone doesn't cure a dog's cancer. However, chemo can extend your dog's life and improve his quality of life by reducing the discomfort and pain the cancer may cause. When vets use chemotherapy in combination with other therapies, a cure is possible.

Radiation therapy

Radiation therapy aims extremely strong X-ray beams — many times stronger than what you're exposed to in a chest X-ray — at a targeted area in order to kill a cancer. Radiation therapy is designed to kill the tumor cells and spare the normal cells, although both cancerous tissue and normal tissue are affected.

Vets use radiation therapy when a dog has an inoperable or inaccessible tumor, and the results of the treatment are often effective in eliminating the cancer. In other cases, radiation can't kill a tumor completely, but it can slow the tumor's growth, which allows the patient to be more comfortable — often for a considerable length of time. In the future, the effectiveness of radiation therapy probably will increase as researchers find ways to target the radiation more precisely.

A dog usually requires several radiation treatments per week over the course of a few weeks. Dogs who are undergoing the treatment need to be anesthetized beforehand because the treatment requires the patient to lie still (usually impossible for most pooches!). Afterward, your dog may be a little unsteady from the procedure, as much from the anesthesia as from the radiation. In addition, she may lose her hair in the treated area, and the hair may be a different color when it grows back. Her skin color may change, too. Soreness in her mouth is another possible side effect.

Nutritional therapy

The right diet serves two purposes in treating a senior dog's cancer: It can help revive his flagging appetite, and it may actually help fight the cancer.

Dogs who have cancer often don't feel much like eating. For example, a dog who's receiving radiation therapy can have the uncomfortable side effect of a raw, sore mouth, which makes eating less than fun. This diminished interest in eating comes at exactly the wrong time, though, because a dog with cancer needs as much good nutrition as possible.

You can do a lot to stimulate your four-legged friend's interest in eating:

- ✔ Pour some water on her food to soften it, making it easier for her to chew.

- ✔ Heat her food — perhaps a minute or two in your microwave — to release the aroma that may tempt her appetite.

- ✔ Feed her by hand to start her eating on her own — it can be just the help that she needs.

Sometimes a dog does eat but loses weight nevertheless. This situation occurs because the tumor is stealing the nutrients that the rest of her body needs. In effect, the tumor is starving the dog. Anti-cancer foods aim to reverse that effect: to starve the tumor and feed the dog. Researchers discovered that a diet relatively high in proteins and fats but lower in carbohydrates can do just that. The Hills Pet Food Company developed a diet for the canine cancer patient called Canine n/d. The diet's available by prescription only. Your vet also may be able to help you develop a diet that you can cook yourself.

All about clinical trials

In *clinical trials,* scientists who've developed a *hypothesis* — in these cases, a possible treatment for cancer in dogs — need to test that hypothesis to see whether it's right. For scientists who study canine cancer, they must test their remedies on dogs who already have cancer.

If your dog's cancer has progressed to the point where no other remedies are available, enrolling him in a clinical trial might help prolong his life. Having your dog participate in a trial can also help other dogs who already have cancer or will acquire this condition in the future.

Before you decide to enroll your dog in a clinical trial, consider these factors:

✔ **You may have to make a significant time commitment.** Clinical trials are often conducted at vet schools and require the dog to be on the premises, so if you don't live near a vet school, you may need to drive some distance and leave him there in order to participate. To prevent such difficulties, many descriptions of clinical trials stipulate that participants must live within 100 miles of the facility where the trial is being conducted.

✔ **You may also have to pony up some money.** In many trials, the owner has to pay for diagnostic tests, which can run several hundred dollars. However, you'll usually get the actual treatments for free.

Your vet may know of a clinical trial that your dog might benefit from participating in. In addition, the Animal Cancer Institute maintains a listing of current trials. Visit its Web site at www.animalcancerinstitute.com.

Don't feed your canine cancer patient raw food if she's undergoing chemotherapy. Your dog's immune system isn't up to par, and raw food can make her feel a lot worse.

Your vet may also suggest supplementing your dog's food with antioxidants, such as Vitamins C and E, and fatty acids, such fish body oil. Both types of supplements may help slow the rate of tumor growth.

Hot and cold therapy

Two temperature-oriented tactics may enhance the primary strategy (surgery, radiation and/or chemotherapy) for conquering your senior's cancer. Both are administered by veterinarians.

One method involves putting heat on a tumor. This method, *hyperthermia,* employs heating devices to raise a tumor's temperature, which results in the deaths of the tumor cells. The treatment isn't widely available and is still being studied to determine its effectiveness. Preliminary findings indicate that hyperthermia can make radiation more effective in treating some cancers. However, the treatment may cause damage to normal cells as well as to cancerous cells.

The opposite treatment may help, if the dog's tumor is small. This treatment, called *cryosurgery,* uses liquid nitrogen to freeze and kill very small tumors on the eyelid, mouth, or face. Cryosurgery isn't used often, but, in some cases, it can be a viable option. The skin or hair may change color as a result of the procedure.

Not Just One Disease

Cancer isn't a single disease but a collection of more than 100 diseases that have one thing in common: uncontrolled cell growth. As the section "Looking for the Cause" earlier in this chapter explains, the method for diagnosing any of these diseases generally depends on whether the suspected cancer is outside the body, (such as on the skin), or inside the body (such as on an internal organ). Some types of cancer are more common than others. I describe the cancers that are most likely to strike senior dogs in the following sections, and I clue you in to the treatments your vet or oncologist may recommend for each type.

Mast cell tumors

Mast cell tumor, or *mastocytoma,* is a skin cancer that's quite common among older dogs. It occurs most often in Boxers, Pugs, and Rhodesian Ridgebacks, but any breed (or mix) can get it. A mast cell tumor often occurs on the trunk, abdomen, or upper portion of a limb, and may feel similar to a fatty tumor. Vets confirm the diagnosis with a needle aspiration (for more on aspiration, see the section "Looking for the Cause" in this chapter).

Treatment typically starts with a surgeon removing the tumor and at least 3 centimeters of surrounding tissue as well. The tumor is graded from 1 through 4. A Grade 1 tumor is a small growth that's very distinct from the surrounding tissue and generally doesn't need any treatment beyond surgery to remove it. A Grade 2 tumor isn't quite as distinct. It requires surgery, but a vet or oncologist probably also will recommend chemotherapy and/or radiation. A Grade 3 tumor isn't very distinct from the surrounding tissue. A Grade 3 tumor is considered the most aggressive tumor; the prospect for a cure is guarded, at best.

Melanoma

A melanoma is a type of skin tumor, but melanoma in dogs can differ from melanoma in people. Human melanomas generally are malignant, but canine melanomas may not be. Melanomas on a dog's skin are more likely to be benign, while those that appear on the mouth or toes stand a better chance of being cancerous.

A malignant melanoma that's relatively small has a better chance of being cured than a larger growth does. The standard treatment includes surgery to remove the tumor and surrounding tissue, and chemotherapy. More novel treatments such as *immunotherapy*, which stimulates the body's own defenses against cancer, and *gene therapy*, which involves inserting cancer-fighting genes into the animal's body, are on the horizon.

Lymphoma

Lymphoma, also known as *lymphosarcoma*, is a cancer of the *lymphatic system* (the system of vessels and clear liquid that bathes the body tissues) that primarily affects dogs who are middle-aged and older. Boxers, German Shepherds, Golden Retrievers, Scottish Terriers, West Highland White Terriers, and Pointers may be more susceptible than other breeds.

Lymphoma can take one of several forms:

- *Bone marrow,* which is called *leukemia* if the cancer is confined to this area
- *Cutaneous,* which involves the skin
- *External,* which involves the lymph nodes
- *Gastrointestinal,* which involves the digestive tract
- *Mediastinal,* which involves the chest

Chemotherapy, particularly with steroids, can be very effective in slowing down the progress of lymphoma and can give your canine patient several months or even an additional year of high-quality living. Unfortunately, lymphoma cannot be cured.

Hemangiosarcoma

Hemangiosarcoma is a highly aggressive cancer that starts in the cells that line the spleen or blood vessels. However, a tumor can form almost anywhere in the body because blood vessels are found everywhere.

German Shepherds, Golden Retrievers, Great Danes, Boxers, English Setters, and Pointers seem to acquire this condition more often than most breeds, but any dog can get it. The condition also tends to strike middle-aged dogs or seniors and is more common in males than females.

Treatment can include surgery to remove an affected organ, such as the spleen, and chemotherapy. However, these treatments prolong your dog's life, at best. Within a few months of diagnosis, your dog will usually die.

Brain tumor

If your older dog's behavior changes or she starts having seizures, she may be suffering from *meningioma,* a tumor that starts on the brain's outer covering. A veterinary neurologist can remove the tumor if your senior is healthy enough for surgery.

Unfortunately, meningioma tends to recur. Surgery extends the dog's life, as does chemotherapy, by about a year. If your dog's overall health is good, that extra year is likely to be quality time, as opposed to continued debilitation if the meningioma isn't treated.

Breast cancer

If your senior female dog hasn't been spayed, she's at high risk for developing breast cancer. Some breeds' females have far better than an even chance of developing this all-too-common form of canine cancer by the age of 10 if they haven't been spayed. By contrast, the spayed female of any breed (or mix) hardly ever falls prey to the condition.

Canine breast cancer can take one of several forms, such as a mast cell tumor, lymphoma, or glandular type of cancer that is located in the breast.

The best hope for curing your canine's breast cancer is to catch it early and agree to surgery that removes not only the affected breast but also the other nine on the dog's body, along with some lymph nodes. Spaying your dog is also a good idea because it can help prevent recurrence — and if the tumor does recur, it will be easier to detect. Radiation can help senior dogs with some inoperable cancers and prevent recurrence.

Your senior's prognosis depends on how advanced the disease is. Just as with human beings, early detection ups the odds of curing your canine's breast cancer.

Prostate cancer

Human guys who get prostate cancer may get a better break than canine guys do. That's because prostate cancer in dogs is usually more aggressive than its human counterpart. In addition, the canine prostate may not be where the cancer originated; for example, bladder cancer that's *metastasized* (or spread) may land in the prostate. But both human and canine victims of prostate cancer have one important trait in common: They're in the older contingents of their overall populations.

Chemotherapy is the treatment of choice, but dogs with prostate cancer rarely survive beyond a year after diagnosis.

Osteosarcoma

Osteosarcoma, or bone cancer, tends to strike larger, big-boned dogs such as Golden Retrievers (an example is the Golden who played the title role in the Disney movie *Air Bud*) and Great Danes. The tumor is usually found in one of the dog's legs. Treatment usually consists of amputating the limb, which can be followed by chemotherapy or radiation, all of which can give the dog a few extra months of quality time.

An exciting new treatment, however, is *bone replacement therapy,* which spares your dog's limb and can lengthen his survival time. The treatment consists of surgically removing the diseased part of the affected bone and replacing it with healthy bone from another part of the patient's body. Such surgery is usually just one component of the dog's treatment; chemotherapy and/or radiation usually is prescribed to limit the growth of tumor cells that have spread beyond the bone. Early use of bone replacement therapy has been promising, enabling a dog to survive a year or so longer than may otherwise have been the case. In at least one instance, a dog survived for several years after being diagnosed and receiving bone replacement therapy.

Consulting a Specialist

Clearly, there's good news on the canine-cancer front: Scientists are finding out a great deal about how different cancers develop and how they can be treated. The downside to such rapidly expanding knowledge is that your own vet may have trouble keeping up with the new technology and techniques. That's when a specialist in treating animal cancers — a *veterinary oncologist* — can help.

Finding help online

Dealing with your senior dog's cancer can be overwhelming. You need to put your hands on valid, timely information and also deal with any fear you feel about what lies ahead for you and your canine companion. Fortunately, the Internet offers plenty of information and support for owners who have a dog with cancer. Here are just a few helpful sites:

✔ **The Perseus Foundation (www.perseusfoundation.org):** An educational foundation that provides information about canine cancer and an online locator for a veterinary oncologist.

✔ **Oncolink (www.oncolink.com/types/section.cfm?c=22&s=69):** Compiled by the cancer-research arm of the University of Pennsylvania in Philadelphia, this Web site has an extensive animal cancer section that includes information on current research and clinical trials.

✔ **Veterinary Cancer Society (www.vetcancersociety.org):** This association of veterinary oncologists provides information about canine cancer and links to veterinary schools that are conducting clinical trials.

✔ **Canine Cancer Awareness (www.caninecancerawareness.org):** This nonprofit group provides information on its Web site about several common canine cancers, treatment options (including diet and holistic therapies), and links to support groups for owners of pets with cancer.

A vet doesn't become an oncologist overnight. She needs to complete a residency in animal cancer treatment at an appropriate facility and pass two tests that demonstrate her knowledge of oncology. If she succeeds, she earns a certification from the American College of Veterinary Internal Medicine (ACVIM) as a veterinary oncologist.

When your senior is diagnosed with cancer, your vet may choose to treat the dog herself. More likely, though, she'll refer you to a veterinary oncologist — and in any case, you can find one on your own to help with your dog's treatment. Here's how to find a veterinary oncologist who can assess your senior's condition, recommend options, and provide treatment that may not be available from your regular vet:

✔ **Look for referral centers.** If you live in a major metropolitan area, chances are that you have at least one large veterinary clinic nearby. Such clinics often include not only general practice vets but also veterinary specialists such as an oncologist. If you find such a clinic and want to visit the oncologist, ask your vet to give you a referral.

✔ **Check out vet schools.** Many large universities have schools of veterinary medicine, and those schools frequently include animal cancer research facilities. The veterinary oncologists who work in these facilities usually treat animal cancer patients, too. Again, ask your vet for a referral.

✔ **Search online.** At least two private groups — ACVIM and the Perseus Foundation — have searchable online databases that enable you to locate a veterinary oncologist near you. ACVIM's Web site is www.acvim.org, and the Perseus Foundation's site is www.perseusfoundation.org.

Striking a Balance

Although veterinary scientists have made some impressive gains in the fight against canine cancer, that fight is still very much a work in progress. In many cases, canine cancer can't be cured; instead, the latest medical strides prolong the dog's life. Sometimes, though, life-prolonging treatment doesn't mean that the extra time will be good for you or your dog.

For any canine cancer patient, the owner needs to balance quantity of time with the quality of time, the needs of the dog with the needs of the rest of the family, and short-term desires with long-term realities. Answering the following questions can help you figure out what's best for you, your senior, and your other loved ones.

✔ **How much time will treatment give my dog?** A treatment plan that gives your senior only a few months of additional time with you may not be justified, particularly if that treatment is likely to be debilitating. However, if treatment can prolong his life by more than six months, it's probably worth considering. Even a prognosis of less than six months can be a good option — if your dog can live a normal life during most of that time. Those extra months can give you the time you need to come to terms with your dog's condition and prepare to say goodbye.

✔ **How will the treatment affect my dog?** The quality of your dog's life during treatment should be a crucial factor in your decision-making. Many dogs sail through chemotherapy with few problems, unlike many humans. On the other hand, if your dog's cancer is very advanced or if he's already in poor condition from the cancer or another illness, prolonging his life with cancer treatment may not make much sense.

✔ **Can I afford it?** Cancer treatments can cost a lot of time as well as money. Special diets, chemotherapy, surgery, and radiation can put a significant dent in your wallet. And if your dog is being treated at a veterinary clinic that's far away from home, you'll need to spend some time getting him to and from that clinic and perhaps stay with him while he's there over several weeks. To find ways to hold down treatment costs, check out Chapter 12.

Don't assume that treating for cancer is an all-or-nothing proposition. You can decide not only whether to treat the cancer, but how much to treat it. Your vet, veterinary oncologist, and your family can help you figure out what's best for your senior — and for you.

Preventing Cancer

In a perfect world, no dog would ever get cancer — or at least every cancer would be cured. Alas, no such perfection exists. So although many canine cancers can be treated and, at times, cured, a senior's best defense against these diseases may be to not get any of them in the first place.

Unfortunately, the art of cancer prevention is still in its infancy. Scientists don't know how to avert most malignancies, and the prevention measures that are known don't carry any guarantees. However, the suggestions below can boost the odds against your dog getting cancer, sometimes significantly. They also help maintain your dog's overall health.

✔ **Spay or neuter.** The altered senior is much less likely to develop reproductive cancers than the intact pooch. A female spayed before her first or second heat cycle stands much less chance of developing breast cancer, which is quite common among unspayed female dogs. And of course, she can't develop uterine cancer at all. A neutered male dog can't develop cancer of the testicles, which is fairly common among intact males.

But if your senior hasn't been spayed or neutered, don't forego the procedure because you think it's too late to do any good. Even if your senior hasn't been altered yet, doing so now can still limit his or her risk of acquiring a reproductive cancer.

✔ **Stop smoking.** Yes, you (did you think I meant your dog?). Scientists believe that dogs who live with smokers may be more likely to get lung cancer and bladder cancer than those who live in smoke-free homes. Quitting smoking doesn't only prolong your life, it may prolong your dog's life, too. If you can't quit, at least take your cigarette break outside.

✔ **Give her the skinny.** Cancer is one of the many conditions that's more likely to befall fat pooches than dogs who are more svelte. More info on keeping your senior sleek is in Chapter 2.

- ✔ **Limit sun exposure.** Don't allow your senior to soak up rays, especially if her hair is white or her coat is thin. Dogs with these traits can up their odds of acquiring skin cancer if they indulge in sunbathing. Such indulgence, alas, can be lethal. Keep your dog out of the midday sun, and limit sun exposure at other times. Putting a T-shirt on exposed skin, such as on the tummy, also can help.

Senior Super Dogs: Taali's tale

Ten-year-old Taali knows what it means to win. The accomplished canine is both a United States and Canadian champion in her breed, Ibizan Hound — and "was number one in Canada," says her proud owner, Carol Dickerson Kauffman of Indiana, Pennsylvania. Outside the conformation ring, the dog has shown proficiency in hunting, obedience, lure coursing, and therapy work. But since January 2002, this multi-talented canine has been engaged in a contest in which winning is more important to her — and to Kauffman — than ever before.

January 2002 was when Kauffman found a lump on Taali's left hind leg. Doctors surgically removed the lump, performed a biopsy, and

Courtesy of Carol Dickerson Kauffman

found that it was a Grade 2 mast cell cancer. Kauffman had no question about how to treat Taali's cancer — she would pursue the best treatment available and make Taali the number-one priority in her life.

That commitment has cost Kauffman greatly in time, money, and gas. Taali's treatment consisted of 16 radiation treatments daily for nearly three weeks at the Veterinary Referral Clinic in Cleveland, Ohio — 170 miles from Kauffman's home. But knowing that the cure rate for such treatment was 85 percent balanced those costs for Kauffman.

Taali's treatment went well. "Each treatment took about a half hour," Kauffman recalls. "The radiation made Taali a bit unsteady for about a half hour after she was returned to me. Otherwise, she was her happy self — playing, sleeping, and eating normally."

When the treatment ended, Taali showed no signs of cancer for almost 18 months. But in August 2003, Kauffman found another lump — and once again, the diagnosis was a Grade 2 mast cell tumor. After Taali recovered from surgery to remove the tumor, Taali and Kauffman returned to the Cleveland clinic. This time, the prognosis was a little less optimistic. Still, hope remained — this time, in the form of chemotherapy.

"When Taali returned to the clinic in August 2003, she was given a prognosis of two to four months," Kauffman says. "But with chemotherapy, there was a 70 percent chance of a year ahead of her."

Kauffman opted for the chemotherapy, which began with weekly injections at the clinic and two oral medications every other day. Two months later, Taali's injections were cut back to every two weeks, and one of the oral meds was discontinued. By late January 2004, Taali was getting injections only once a month; the oral medication continued.

Despite the travel, mental strain, and financial outlay — well over $5,000 so far — Kauffman's glad she aggressively treated her dog's cancer. "I have no regrets," she says. "And the chemotherapy doesn't appear to have altered Taali's enjoyment and quality of life. We continue to hunt five days a week; she's holding her weight and is happy, loving, and enjoying daily life."

Chapter 12

Addressing the Bottom Line

Mandy, an 8-year-old Pointer, had an unfortunate encounter with a truck, and she clearly fared worse than the truck did. Her injuries included shock, a crushed pelvis, dislocated rear legs, and two dislocated vertebrae. Surgery and physical therapy could alleviate all of Mandy's problems, but the price would be hefty: about $8,000.

Laddie, a 7-year-old Sheltie, put himself on a total fast — and, in the process, put his owner into a panic. To find out what was coming between Laddie and his interest in eating, the vet needed to run extensive tests, accompanied by several days of hospitalization and continuous intravenous feeding. The tab: more than $3,000.

Dexter, a 12-year-old Lab mix, was limping painfully. His concerned owner brought him to his vet, who suspected arthritis and prescribed a glycosamine supplement. However, the supplement didn't help; Dexter continued to hobble around his home. At that point, the vet said that magnetic resonance imaging (MRI) could possibly pinpoint the cause of Dexter's gimpy gait — but the procedure would cost more than $1,200.

Such costs aren't chump change for Mandy, Laddie, and Dexter's owners — and those prices aren't unusual. Cutting-edge veterinary medical procedures, such as pacemakers, chemotherapy, MRIs, and hip replacements (to name a few), enable more dogs to live longer and better than ever before. However, such procedures may also wreak havoc on the budgets of such dogs' owners. But you can contain your senior canine's health-care costs. In this chapter, I give you ways to put a leash on your senior dog's veterinary expenses without compromising his (or your) quality of life.

Why the Sticker Shock?

No doubt about it, people are paying more money than ever before to provide veterinary care for their senior dogs and other animal companions. An article in *Consumer Reports* noted that in 2001, American dog and cat owners spent a whopping $18.2 billion on veterinary care, which was triple the amount they paid ten years earlier. It's a safe bet that the nation's senior dogs and cats, who comprise some 40 percent of America's canine and feline populations, account for a significant percentage of that spending. The same article also stated that over the same ten-year period, the cost of the average veterinary visit nearly doubled — to $99 for dogs. Personally, I'd be thrilled if I could reduce the vet bills that I pay to just $99 per visit — but I'm not willing to sacrifice the quality of my dog's veterinary care just to save a few bucks.

I'm not alone in my insistence that the four-legged members of my family have the best care that my husband's and my hard-earned money can buy. Plenty of pet owners share my feelings, and our unwillingness to give our critters nothing less than the best is probably the biggest factor behind the rise in veterinary costs. Today, most people consider their pooches to be full-fledged members of their families, and they're no more willing to stint on medical care for their dogs than they are for their children or for themselves.

Fortunately, the veterinary profession responded to this demand from pet owners by offering diagnostic and therapeutic options that were unheard of a generation ago. Just as Grandpa can receive a pacemaker to regulate his heartbeat, so can Grandpa's dog. Just as Grandma can take medicine to relieve her arthritis, Grandma's dog can take arthritis medicine to relieve her creaky joints. And just as chemotherapy and radiation have reduced the death rate for people with cancer, the same therapies have a similar effect on canines with cancer.

Of course, all this cutting-edge veterinary medicine doesn't come cheap. Sticker shock is one likely outcome of any visit to a vet to diagnose a dog's problem — and that shock isn't reserved for dogs over a certain age. Not so many years ago, my family and I paid more than $1,000 for surgery to remove a sock that our 3-year-old Shetland Sheepdog had inadvertently swallowed during a rousing session of Keep-Away. Did we think twice about forking over the money to pay for our dog's surgery? No way.

Senior dogs are more likely to need expensive surgery and other costly procedures than their younger counterparts, ingested socks notwithstanding. Certain conditions, such as heart disease, kidney disease, cancer, diabetes, glaucoma, cataracts, and arthritis, tend to strike the senior canine far more often than they do the more youthful pooch, and dealing with these conditions entails forking over more than a little money to pay for their treatment. And even if your senior isn't undergoing an expensive medical procedure, just gauging the state of her health costs quite a bit more than pocket change. A baseline screening of your aging dog's vital functions can cost several hundred dollars, and subsequent screenings also may run in the three-figure range.

Although taking care of a senior dog is likely to become at least a little pricey, the hits to your bottom line need not be unlimited. You can curtail at least some of the sticker shock that seems to have become a necessary evil of 21st-century veterinary care without diminishing the quality of that care. Several options are open to the caring but cost-conscious owner. Some save just a few bucks; others help you hold on to considerably more money.

Cutting Costs

Unfortunately for the cash-strapped dog owner, senior pooches and their people don't have the option of being eligible for a canine equivalent of Medicare, Medicaid, or other government programs designed to help the aging human pay his medical bills. When it comes to containing canine health-care costs, owners must depend on their own research, ingenuity, and ability to separate fact from fiction. That said, a little bit of all or even one of those qualities can help you give your aging canine companion the best of care without draining your savings account or damaging your credit rating. The following sections suggest some options to help you keep both your budget and your Bowser at least reasonably healthy.

Insuring your pooch

Although health insurance for pets has been around for about 40 years, the concept didn't really begin to catch on in the United States until the late 1990s. The largest U.S. pet insurer, Veterinary Pet Insurance (www.petinsurance.com), reports that between 2000 and 2003, the number of pets covered by its policies doubled.

To find a reputable pet health insurance company, ask your vet what insurance plans she accepts.

On paper, at least, the concept of pet health insurance looks like a no-brainer. Effective health insurance, whether for pets or for people, makes quality healthcare affordable. Paying a pre-set amount (the *premium*) throughout the year helps reduce the amount of money that the insured individual must pay for a costly medical procedure or drug. Instead of paying $65 for a dermatologist's appointment, you may pay only $10. Instead of paying $500 a month for a costly but effective acne treatment, you may pay about $25. Not a bad deal, any way you look at it.

For many people, purchasing health insurance for their canine companions doesn't seem to be a bad deal, either. These satisfied individuals report that their insurance plans have more than paid for themselves when they've been presented with a large or unexpected bill for their dog's care. However, other people have come to a different conclusion: They've found that paying for pet insurance actually ends up costing them more money than their dog's medical bills without insurance would have. Whether you and your dog fit into the *yay* or *nay* category depends on many factors:

- ✔ The plan you choose

- ✔ Your dog's age

- ✔ Any conditions or problems that your dog has before you choose insurance

- ✔ The conditions or problems that your dog encounters after you choose insurance

Your own health-care philosophy also factors into this equation. If you're committed to providing holistic care for your dog, you're likely to find that most pet health insurance policies don't cover such care. To determine whether buying health insurance for your senior dog is a good cost-saving strategy for you, take the following steps:

1. **Study the policies.**

   Pet health insurance plans aren't identical. Many are traditional fee-for-service plans that allow you to choose the vet or clinic you want but require you to submit a claim to the insurance company to be reimbursed for covered services. However, at this writing, at least one plan functioned more like a health maintenance organization (HMO), in which an owner gets more coverage for routine care but may choose among only those vets who subscribe to the plan.

2. **Study your dog.**

   Some dogs, especially seniors, don't qualify for some insurance coverage or even for any insurance at all. For example, one pet insurer doesn't cover dogs over 9 years of age; another doesn't approve a first-time policy to dogs over 10 unless you send additional medical records and lab reports along with the application.

Those insurers who do provide coverage for seniors often charge higher premiums than they do for younger dogs. In early 2004, one major pet insurer charged $239 annually to cover a 1-year-old Dachshund. The same insurer charged $583 per year to cover a 10-year-old wiener dog.

In addition, many plans don't cover pre-existing conditions — and seniors probably have more of those conditions than younger dogs do. For example, if the vet diagnosed your senior dog with kidney disease before you bought a pet health insurance policy, your new policy probably doesn't cover treatment for that disease.

3. Crunch some numbers.

Even if your senior dog qualifies for an insurance plan and has no pre-existing conditions, buying pet health insurance may not be worth the money. To determine whether insurance is cost-effective for you and your dog, find out what your vet charges for procedures such as blood work, teeth cleaning, and surgical anesthesia. Then, compare those charges with the insurance company's reimbursements for each. If you find a big gap between the two, you may want to think twice about spending money on a policy. You may draw the same conclusion if the policy you're considering requires you to pay a lot of money for procedures before any reimbursement kicks in (in insurance-speak, a high *deductible*) or if the policy imposes any limits on coverage.

Your numbers may crunch a lot differently if you're lucky enough to work for a company that offers pet health insurance as an employee benefit. Some reports indicate that, at the end of 2003, more than 700 companies offered such benefits to their animal-loving employees. If your company is one of those 700 (just ask your human resources department), take the time to find out more.

Is pet insurance out of the question for senior dogs? I can't give you a simple yes or no answer. It depends on you, your dog, the policy, and the numbers — and what happens when all those factors interact.

Visiting your local pharmacy

Sure, buying your senior dog's prescription drugs from your vet is convenient. However, convenience often comes with a price. Veterinarians and veterinary clinics often mark up the prices of drugs that you buy directly from them — sometimes a lot.

Several years ago, a veterinary ophthalmologist charged me $25 for a small bottle of eye drops for my dog, but I found out later that

I could have bought the same drops elsewhere for considerably less. *Elsewhere* was my neighborhood pharmacy, which sold the eye drops for about one third of the cost that the ophthalmologist charged me.

The eye drops aren't an isolated example. A dog with allergies can get relief from the itching with an antihistamine called Hydroxyzene that my local vet sells for $15.20 per bottle of 40 tablets. But two bottles of over-the-counter Benadryl, which you can find at just about any pharmacy, does the job equally well — at a price $4 less than the product offered at my vet's.

Of course, not every product prescribed for your pooch comes cheaper at the corner drug store or has a cheaper equivalent. But you may be able to save money on the product you need by putting up with a teeny bit of inconvenience (meaning the drive to the pharmacy rather than one-stop shopping at the vet's). If you opt to cut your senior dog's drug costs in this way, keep these points in mind:

- ✔ **Just ask.** When your vet prescribes a new medication for your aging canine companion, ask your vet if you can find the drug available at commercial pharmacies or if such pharmacies carry a drug that serves the same purpose as the drug that she prescribes.

- ✔ **Compare.** If you need to replenish your senior dog's current meds, don't automatically run to the vet's for a new supply. Instead, call a couple of local pharmacies to see whether they have that drug available, in what units they sell the drug, and at what price.

- ✔ **Tell your vet.** If you find that you can get the same drug cheaper from the pharmacy than from the vet, tell her. The vet can tailor the prescription dosage instructions to the amounts that you find commercially available. She may even offer to sell you the drug from the office's supply for the same price as the pharmacy.

Don't ever give your dog an over-the-counter product for people until you consult your vet. Your vet can tell you whether the product you're considering is okay for your dog. Some aren't: My local pharmacy's generic antihistamine contains acetaminophen (the active ingredient in Tylenol), which is toxic to dogs.

Compounding your savings

The cost-conscious senior dog owner can buy prescription medicine from a *compounding pharmacy.* These pharmacies prepare customized medications for their patients, human or canine.

Compounded meds often cost less than those dispensed by vets. For one thing, the compounder has access to more drugs than a vet does, which reduces the compounder's ordering costs. In addition, customizing a prescription to the specific needs of the dog gives the owner more meds for his money. An owner who gives his senior dog prescription meds designed for people may need to use that medicine in ways that the manufacturer didn't intend and thus waste some of the good stuff. You can get compounded drug dosages tailored to the dog's needs, eliminating the need for painstaking divisions and wasting any medicine.

If you choose to buy your senior dog's medications from a compounding pharmacy, make sure that you bring your veterinarian into the loop. Only by working with your vet can you be sure that the compounding pharmacist is formulating the right medication for your four-legged friend.

To find a compounding pharmacy in your area, consult the online referral service offered by the International Academy of Compounding Pharmacists (www.iacprx.org/referral_service/index.html).

Ordering your meds online

Online pharmacies — either conventional or compounding — offer another way to save money on prescription drugs for your aging pooch. Often, such pharmacies sell prescription meds at prices considerably lower than what a vet or even a local pharmacy may charge. The owner of a senior dog who needs a continuous supply of one or more prescription drugs to treat a chronic condition may find these savings especially welcome.

That said, you can run into considerable pitfalls when buying meds online, mainly because some not-so-legitimate enterprises are out there, along with the legitimate Web-based pharmacies. Not-so-legit outfits may offer to sell you the meds you need for your dog without a vet's prescription. As the U.S. Food and Drug Administration (FDA) explains, bypassing your vet (or your own doctor, if you buy online meds for yourself), means you run the risk of getting a contaminated product, a counterfeit product, the wrong product, an outdated product, the wrong dosage of a product — or no product at all.

Do such pitfalls mean that cost-conscious owners of senior dogs should forego online pharmacies? Not at all! Instead, owners just need to make sure that they're dealing with a legitimate Web-based company.

Here's what the FDA suggests would-be customers of online pharmacies should do:

- ✔ **Check out the pharmacy.** Log on to the searchable online database Web site of the National Association of Boards of Pharmacy (www.nabp.net/vipps/intro.asp) or call 847-698-6227 to determine whether an online pharmacy is licensed and in good standing.

- ✔ **Involve your vet.** Any legitimate online pharmacy requires your vet to e-mail or fax the prescription for the drug that you want to buy. If the pharmacy that you're considering promises to sell you the drug for the first time without having to go through your vet, look elsewhere.

- ✔ **Buy American.** At this writing, buying drugs from foreign Web sites or other overseas suppliers isn't a good idea. Importing foreign drugs into the United States is illegal — although that could change — and the U.S. government can't do much to help you if an online pharmacy rips you off. Make sure that any pharmacy you deal with provides a U.S. mailing address and telephone number to contact if you have a problem.

- ✔ **Look for real people.** The FDA recommends steering clear of any site that doesn't have access to a registered pharmacist who can answer customers' questions.

- ✔ **Safeguard your privacy.** Beware the pharmacy that doesn't display an easy-to-understand privacy and security policy. Steer clear, too, of any site that asks you to provide personal information, such as a credit card number or Social Security number, on an unsecured connection (your Web browser tells you whether the connection is secure or not).

Cashing in on promos

Sometimes your own veterinarian offers you some keys to the kingdom of financial comfort — or, at least, a way to hold on to a few more of your hard-earned greenbacks. That's because many clinics bundle a collection of services into one package and offer that package at a price well below what those services would cost if you bought them individually. Often, the vet's office ties such services to a particular theme.

For your senior, the most applicable promotion probably centers around a period that focuses on older pets. During this time, a vet or clinic may offer a package of services associated with a baseline health examination for the senior canine. Such services typically include measurements of vital signs; collecting and analyzing urine, stool, and blood samples; and checking the eyes, ears, teeth, skin, and body for signs of trouble. If priced individually, these services may cost several hundred dollars; a promo may shave 10 percent or more off those costs.

The U.S. doesn't have a nationwide, coordinated celebration of the older dog. Instead, clinics decide for themselves when to celebrate the senior pooch and offer discounts on services targeted to graying canines. Some clinics offer year-round discounts; others discount services for seniors one day per week, one week per month, or one month per year. You just need to ask your vet about her specific policies.

Veterinary and other services often have periods similar to senior pet promos that focus on Adopt-a-Senior Pet month, which the American Society for the Prevention of Cruelty to Animals and other humane organizations celebrate in November. If your newly adopted senior dog came from an animal shelter, your local vet may be willing to cut the prices of initial screening services. Again, you just have to ask.

Another common promotional period occurs during National Pet Dental Health Month in February. The American Veterinary Dental College, American Veterinary Medical Association, and other organizations use this time to step up their efforts to educate pet owners about the importance of good oral health for animal companions. Not coincidentally, veterinarians use this time to offer discounted dental services to their clients' pets. You can find out more about keeping senior dogs' teeth healthy in Chapter 5.

Little savings can mean a lot

Not every cost-control measure has to net *beaucoup* bucks. Even an effort that results in little more than pocket change can, when combined with other efforts, add up to significant savings, over time. Bringing in a stool sample yourself rather than having the vet obtain it may result in a savings of only a couple of dollars — but if you bring in three or four such samples per year, you can treat yourself to an extra visit to Starbucks.

You can also buy canned dog food in bulk — in other words, by the case rather than by the individual can — and save $5 per case of a certain high-quality premium dog food. If your dog consumes one case per month, you can save $60 per year. You can almost buy yourself a facial with that money or treat yourself and a friend to a gourmet meal at a fancy restaurant — or you can add that money to a special senior doggy savings account. No matter how you look at it, every little bit helps.

Senior dogs aren't the only individuals who can get price breaks for their care. If you're a senior human, you may qualify for a variety of discounted services for your dog, regardless of his age. You may be able to find such discounts not only from your vet, but also from other facilities that provide veterinary services, such as your local animal shelter.

Talking with your vet

Promos aren't the only way that your vet can help if you can't handle an unexpected medical expense for your senior. True, your vet probably doesn't run a credit bureau, and he certainly can't afford to give away a lot of services. After all, he's in the business not only because he loves dogs and cats and is committed to their care, but he's also looking to make a living. However, I've found that vets often are willing to help their clients find ways to deal with hefty expenses. Here are some examples:

- A woman whose Great Dane had Addison's Disease — a chronic condition that required several hundred dollars worth of medicine each month — persuaded her vet to sell her the meds without the customary mark-up. She saved a significant 40 percent.

- A family whose dog required several thousand dollars worth of diagnostic tests and surgery before the vet discovered an incurable cancer opted to euthanize the animal. The clinic didn't charge the family for the euthanasia or related services.

Any vet can tell you that although he can make a living caring for animals, he's not likely to get rich — and that he never expected to. In other words, most people become veterinarians mainly because of a compassion for animals, and that compassion usually extends to human clients, as well as to their canine companions.

So talk with your vet if money is a problem. At the very least, he's probably willing to work out a payment plan with you; at best, he may find a way to give you a break on the cost of some services. You have nothing to lose by asking, but you could well have some savings to gain.

Shopping around

Many humane organizations offer financial assistance to help low-income pet owners defray the expenses of caring for a senior dog. Such programs are based locally and require some diligent detective work to uncover; but if you find that you can't pay for your senior dog's health-care expenses, such a search may be worth your while. Your vet, local animal shelter, or local dog rescue group may also have information. An Internet search can also help: Log on to Google (`www.google.com`) and type "low income," "pet owners," and "discounts" into the search box.

Planning Ahead to Cut Costs

Your best bet for dealing with sky-high veterinary bills is to get ready for those bills before they occur. The following sections give you some plan-ahead options that can help you prepare to pay for your senior dog's veterinary care — and one option that can help minimize the payments you'll need to make.

Getting regular checkups

Want to really hold down your senior dog's vet bills? Then take her for regular checkups: twice a year, at minimum, and without fail. These exams don't necessarily include shots — and, in fact, most seniors' exams probably shouldn't, as I explain in Chapter 5.

That twice-yearly date with your vet uncovers potentially serious senior health problems early. Early detection of an illness or other problematic health condition not only can increase your senior's chances of full recovery, but also can boost the likelihood that you can help with simpler and less expensive treatment than would be the case if you had discovered the problem later.

And don't limit your checkups to those that the vet gives your senior. Do a weekly check yourself. When you brush or groom your four-legged friend, pay close attention to the condition of her skin, coat, and teeth. If you find any lumps, bumps, skin flakiness, or rashes, put in a call to your vet.

 Your sense of smell isn't nearly as sensitive as your dog's — but your nose still knows when your canine companion has a problem. You should sniff your senior dog's ears regularly and get close enough to her to catch a whiff of her breath. A yeasty or other foul odor coming from the ears signals a possible infection; hoochy breath may herald the onset of gum disease or kidney problems. I talk more about all these conditions in Chapter 10.

Giving yourself some credit

Sometimes, you just don't have the cash to cover a medical emergency (although, if you plan ahead, that shortfall is less likely), particularly if the cost of resolving that emergency approaches the four-figure level. I remember all too well the way I blanched when presented with the $1,000 estimate for removing the sock that had found its way to my Sheltie's tummy.

Fortunately, though, I had good credit. For the times when the cash isn't there, or when you're too bleary to deal with financial complexities (like the middle of the night, which is when I had to produce the $1,000 needed for that sock removal surgery), a credit card can save the day, not to mention the dog.

I'm not advocating paying any and all vet bills with plastic, and I'm not suggesting that running up a boatload of debt is okay. However, the intelligent use of credit — having a credit card on hand, paying as much of the bill as you can each month (ideally, the whole thing), and staying well below your credit limit — is a legitimate way to take care of your senior during those times when the last thing you can think about is money.

Paying your pooch

Financial planners and other experts who deplore Americans' low savings rates usually place one remedy at the top of their lists of savings-boosting recommendations: Pay yourself before you pay anyone else, bill collectors included. Of course, by paying yourself, these financial whizzes aren't suggesting that you write yourself a check and go out on yet another spending spree (that may be why Americans' savings rates are so low in the first place). Instead, the experts want you to write yourself a check and deposit it into a savings account or money market fund. Regular deposits into such a fund eventually grow those deposits into a comfortable nest egg that you can tap for emergencies.

The same principle holds true for your senior dog. Yes, you need to pay her. Fortunately for you, she's not likely to take that check and dash out to the nearest dog boutique to get that bejeweled collar she's been longing for. No, your payment to her should go straight into an account set aside to cover her future veterinary bills.

Regular deposits into your senior's medical account can accumulate quickly. Twenty dollars per week, for example, grows into more than $1,000 a year: more than enough to pay for a routine exam and many other moderately priced veterinary services. Plus, you get a little bit of interest or some dividend payments to add a little more to your stash. Add some of the savings that you net from following the other suggestions in this chapter, and you have a decent-sized fund that you can tap if you and your senior need it.

Part IV
Bidding a Fond Farewell

The 5th Wave   By Rich Tennant

PET CEMETERY

"Bob's had a hard time letting go."

In this part . . .

Although many dogs enjoy lengthy seniorhoods, no dog lives forever. As your senior ages, her mortality will become increasingly evident. As a caring owner, you need to prepare your dog, your family, and yourself for the time when she's no longer with you. In Part IV, I help you make the final season of your dog's life a time of celebration, help you decide when to say goodbye, and enable you to cope with the loss of your beloved four-legged friend.

Chapter 13

Preparing to Say Goodbye

In This Chapter

▶ Keeping your senior dog comfortable

▶ Deciding when to say goodbye to your dog

▶ Preparing children for your dog's passing

▶ Making arrangements before euthanizing

▶ Choosing your after-care option

••

*L*ike most people in the 21st century, I play multiple roles: wife, mother, daughter, sister, and writer, among others. I adore my husband and daughter, and I'm fortunate to have good relationships with my parents and brother. I'm equally fortunate because I can make a living doing what I love. All in all, I'm a very lucky woman, and I'm grateful for the blessings I've been given. But despite those blessings, I'd consider my life to be lacking unless I could also play the role of dog owner.

That's why, for more than 25 years, a dog's been part of my life. During that quarter century, I've lived with three dogs but never more than one at a time. Molly, my first dog, lived nearly 17 years. Cory, who came into my life after Molly died, lived only 7 years. Soon after, my family and I welcomed Allie, who's now 15 months old. We've experienced the joys of living with dogs, and we've experienced the sorrows, too.

If living with a dog is like a rose, then a dog's short life span is the thorn. The sweetness and joy that come from living with a dog are pierced by the pain that occurs when you lose that dog. The odds are overwhelming that such a loss will occur, because dogs don't live as long as people do. When you bring a dog into your life, you also bring the eventual pain you'll feel when that dog dies.

No matter how healthy your senior dog is now, the time you have with him is finite. His passing will come sooner rather than later, and when that passing does come, it will hurt. But you can temper that pain now by making this time a period of sweetness and celebration, and by planning ahead to make the end of that time as stress-free as possible. In this chapter, I help you do both.

Ensuring Continued Comfort for Your Senior Dog

To bring joy into this closing chapter of your dog's life, you may need to change the way you think about her care. Instead of trying just one more possible remedy for the serious illness she has, you may need to start thinking about simply keeping her comfortable and happy. However, making that transition is easier said than done. Most owners have a hard time deciding when to shift from cure to care and figuring out just how to implement that shift.

Deciding when to end treatment

Humans' understanding of canine health and how to treat doggy health problems has expanded exponentially in the last few decades. Not so long ago, many people would have euthanized a senior dog with cancer, a paralyzed senior, a senior who'd lost her eyesight or hearing, or even an incontinent senior. Today, though, most caring dog owners wouldn't automatically put any such dog to sleep.

Most of today's owners realize that many dogs who have these ailments can still lead high-quality lives. The owner of a dog with cancer can extend her dog's life not only with surgery, but also with chemotherapy and radiation (for more on these treatments, see Chapter 11). The owner of a partially paralyzed dog can purchase a doggy wheelchair and also provide his canine companion with physical therapy to help her regain some mobility (for more on doggy wheelchairs and physical therapy, see Chapter 8). The owner of a blind or deaf dog can make adjustments that enhance the animal's capacity to cope (for more info on the adjustments you can make, see Chapter 7). An owner who has an incontinent dog understands that his pet may have a curable illness and can work with his vet to determine what that illness is (for more on seniors' potty problems, check out Chapter 6).

However, the fact that such remedies are available doesn't mean they're always appropriate. Sometimes foregoing treatment and simply keeping your dog comfortable during the evening of her life is the best decision. Making that decision is especially appropriate when you know that your dog's condition is terminal. However, knowing when to say "when" can be extremely difficult for you, as your dog's companion.

Making the decision to end aggressive treatment is tough because the patient — your beloved senior dog — often can't tell you what she wants or even how she feels. And even if she could tell you, she may not want to. Research shows that dogs and cats instinctively try to hide their pain, perhaps because in the wild, an animal who exhibits pain often becomes another animal's prey. Such instinctive self-protectiveness means that you need to decode your dog's responses to treatment yourself. Your four-legged friend won't tell you that a treatment has stopped working or that it never worked in the first place; you have to observe that fact.

Another reason you may have trouble saying "enough" is because, by doing so, you're essentially giving up. You're acknowledging that nothing more can reasonably be done to help your senior dog, and that her life has entered its final act. You're closing the door on hope. When you close that door, you open another one: the door that gives you access to your own emotional pain and suffering.

Those difficulties and the very individual nature of each dog's condition make the decision to stop treatment highly personal. No one can make this decision for you — least of all me, a mere author. However, here are some pointers you can use to help you make the do-we-continue decision that's right for your beloved senior:

- ✔ **Really, really look at your dog.** Pay close attention to your senior and try to be objective about her condition. Is she noticeably better since she began treatment? Is she suffering any side effects that interfere with her quality of life? Does she still take pleasure in at least some of the activities that she's always enjoyed?

- ✔ **Have a heart-to-heart with your vet.** If you're starting to have doubts about continuing treatment for your senior, make an appointment to have a frank discussion with your vet about your dog's condition, treatment, and prognosis. Your vet won't tell you what to do, but if you listen carefully, you may get a sense as to what he really thinks is the proper course of action.

  A good way to find out what your vet is thinking is to ask him what he would do if his dog were in this situation.

- ✔ **Get a second opinion.** If your chat with your vet doesn't shed light on where he stands, ask for a referral to another vet. A truly professional vet will be happy to suggest a colleague with whom you can discuss your senior's future.

- ✔ **Do some research.** The discussions you have with any vet will be much more productive if you've taken the time to find out more about your senior's condition beforehand. Logging on to the Internet and visiting a few reputable veterinary Web sites can give you at least some of the facts you need. Good sites to visit include

- **Petplace:** petplace.com
- **VetInfo:** vetinfo.com
- **VetMedCenter:** vetmedcenter.com
- **VeterinaryPartner:** veterinarypartner.com

✔ **Evaluate your priorities.** Sometimes separating your own interests from those of your senior is hard, but when you're trying to decide whether to continue treatment, such separation is crucial. Keeping your dog with you as long as possible may be your natural objective because the thought of parting with her is unbearable. What may be unbearable for your senior, though, is continuing treatment if that treatment is interfering with her ability to enjoy life. When you're unsure about making any decision regarding your dog's welfare versus your own, asking "Is this good for my dog?" always helps. The answer to that question almost always pushes your decision-making in the right direction.

Creating a canine hospice

If you've decided that it's in your senior's best interest to stop aggressive treatment for a terminal condition such as cancer, kidney failure, Cushing's Disease, or dilated myopathy, you can still take steps to keep him happy, content, and comfortable. You can continue to give care, but your goal with such care changes.

Instead of trying to cure his condition or prolong his life, you now provide tender loving care to your four-legged friend and try to minimize any pain or distress that he feels. In essence, you provide *hospice* care to your senior. Hospice is a philosophy rather than a place, although many facilities offer hospice care to humans. The principles behind hospice care for a dog are the same as they are for a person: to provide the patient with a safe, comfortable, and caring end-of-life experience after efforts to cure a disease have been exhausted.

Depending on your senior's condition, providing hospice care may require extensive nursing such as giving injections, preparing special diets, providing fluids through an IV, or simply giving your dog a pill and plenty of stroking. However easy or difficult giving the medical care is, you make every effort to avoid transporting your dog to a vet or anywhere else; to the furthest extent possible, your dog receives his medical care at home. The end result of hospice care for a dog is (barring miracles) death from euthanasia or natural causes, but his death occurs in a way that minimizes his stress while giving his owner time to accept her dog's impending passing.

Experts suggest that owners who are considering hospice care for their senior take the following steps:

✔ **Get prepared.** Consider hospice care for your senior as soon as she's diagnosed with a terminal or progressive illness, not when she's clearly on her last legs. Even if your senior's currently on meds that extend her longevity, it's not too soon to prepare for end-of-life care.

✔ **Do some research.** You'll make better hospice-care decisions if you take the time to find out what hospice care entails. Check out these Web sites:

   • **American Animal Hospital Association:** www. healthypet.com/Library/animal_bond-17.html

   • **American Association of Human-Animal Bond Veterinarians:** aahabv.org/hospice.htm

   • **Nikki Hospice Foundation for Pets:** www.csum. edu/pethospice

✔ **Keep your vet in the loop.** Your vet can provide crucial support and information as you begin your senior's end-of-life care. Ask whether your vet is willing to make house calls; if not, request a referral to a vet who does and who can work as a partner with you and your regular vet.

If you need to find a vet who makes house calls on your own, log on to the American Association of Housecall Veterinarians Web site (www.athomevet.org). You can search a database of vets from all over the United States who treat patients in their homes.

Getting Ready for Your Senior Dog's Passing

I'm not going to tell you that euthanizing a dog isn't painful for the people who must make that decision, because such a statement would be untrue. But I can say — thanks to my own experiences, conversations with friends, and interviews with experts — that you can limit the stress of having to take your beloved friend's life, starting with what you do beforehand.

Preparing yourself

Death is a mystery, and that mystery is what frightens the living. Not knowing exactly what will happen during your senior's euthanasia procedure makes the decision to do so that much more difficult. To ease that difficulty, and to get ready for what's to come, try to do the following:

- **Know your options.** Releasing your canine companion from pain need not traumatize either of you. You have alternatives to bundling your freaked-out friend into a car, driving to the vet's, and handing her over for the procedure. In the "Making Arrangements for Euthanasia" section later in this chapter and in Chapter 14, you find out about more humane, less traumatic options for both you and your senior when the time comes to bid each other farewell.

- **Find out what will happen.** Finding out exactly what will occur when your senior is euthanized isn't morbid. Your vet can describe the process he uses (for more information on what typically happens when an animal is euthanized, go to Chapter 14). He also can help you decide whether you should stay for the procedure or not.

- **Talk to other people.** Your vet and other pet owners can provide sympathetic ears as you talk out your feelings. Consider calling a pet-loss hot line, too; they can help you deal with the grief you feel before a pet's death as well as after. In Chapter 15, I suggest how to find these hot lines and also suggest ways you can find a pet-loss support group or a one-on-one grief counselor.

Preparing others, including your children

Unless you and your senior dog are a pack of two, others in your household also are trying to deal with his impending death. If the other household members are adults like yourself, you can all prepare together: You can talk with each other, comfort each other, and come to an agreement regarding your canine companion's future.

When those family members are children, though, the adults' pain increases. Deciding to euthanize a senior dog is difficult enough, but having to tell a child what's going to happen makes the process even tougher. I had to tell my own daughter about a dog's imminent death on two occasions: when she was 5 years old and when she was 13. Both times were equally painful.

As a parent, your first instinct is to limit your child's pain as much as possible. However, experts explain that when the cause of your children's pain is a pet's demise, protectiveness isn't in a child's best interest. Your child will deal with your senior dog's impending death in a healthier manner and will heal more quickly if you're open and honest about what's going on.

Here are some pointers if you're a parent who has to tell her children about a pet's impending death:

- ✔ **Be direct.** When you tell your child about your senior dog's condition, tell it like it is: Your dog is dying or will die soon. Euphemisms such as "putting your dog to sleep" can backfire; after your dog dies, your child may be afraid to go to sleep.

- ✔ **Be honest.** You may be tempted to tell your child that your dog ran away or you gave him to someone else to take care of. Doing so may spare your child the pain of knowing the pet has died, but it can also cause another kind of pain: Your child may wonder why you gave his dog to someone else or why the dog ran away. The consequences are even worse if your child discovers the truth about his dog's fate from someone else. He'd realize that you lied to him and understandably would have a hard time trusting you again.

- ✔ **Show your own sadness.** Letting your children see your sadness can be a way of giving them permission to show their grief, and grieving together affirms that your senior has been a well-loved member of the family.

- ✔ **Consider your child's age.** Children deal with death in ways that may surprise or even shock their parents, but parents need to understand that grief takes many forms. For example, I was very upset when my then-5-year-old daughter announced three days after our dog died that she was "over it." Fortunately, some wise friends pointed out to me that by making such an announcement; my daughter was clearly showing that she wasn't "over it" at all.

- ✔ **Tell other caregivers.** If your child is in preschool or elementary school, tell her teacher what's going on. Her teacher can monitor your child's behavior, offer comfort, keep you informed about how your child's doing, and head off possible problems. For instance, I told my daughter's kindergarten teacher about our dog's impending death and sent a follow-up note to the school after the dog died. Because her teacher was aware of the situation, she intervened when a librarian decided to read the class a book about getting a dog for Christmas (our dog had died just after Thanksgiving).

> ✔ **Read together.** Several good books are available that can help your child (and yourself) come to terms with the impending loss of your senior, especially when you read them together. My personal favorite is *The Tenth Good Thing About Barney* by Judith Viorst (Aladdin Library). Other good books are *For Every Dog an Angel* by Christine Davis (Lighthearted Press); *I'll Always Love You* by Hans Wilhelm (Dragonfly); and *Dog Heaven* by Cynthia Rylant (Scholastic).

Making Arrangements for Euthanasia

Euthanizing a beloved senior dog is probably the most traumatic experience you'll face in your time with her. Because you loved your senior well, you can't avoid the pain that comes with such a loss. But the fact that such losses are painful doesn't mean you also must subject yourself or your dog to unnecessary indignities.

When you and your senior arrive at your vet's for the euthanasia appointment, you don't want to be sitting out in the waiting room with other owners around. You don't want your pet to freak out the way she usually does when she visits the vet. And you certainly don't want to have to figure out how to pay the bill afterward, when your shock and grief may feel overwhelming.

With a little advance planning, you can avoid much of the stress, if not the pain, of having to say goodbye to your senior. Here are some helpful ideas.

Finding the right place

Determine where the euthanasia will take place well before the procedure. Basically, you have two options: having your senior euthanized at home or having your senior euthanized at your vet's office.

Advantages and disadvantages of euthanizing at home

Many owners want their senior dogs to take their last breaths at home. These owners believe that an at-home euthanasia is less stressful for their seniors because they don't hear the sounds or smell the odors that they would encounter at an animal hospital.

Euthanizing your senior at home is a good option if your dog is too large or too ill for you to transport easily to a veterinary clinic. Ending your dog's life at home also allows you to control the environment in which your dog passes away: You can give your senior all the creature comforts you want. And if you euthanize your dog at home, you don't have to face strangers in a waiting room.

One final advantage of putting a senior dog to sleep at home is that the other pets in the family can see the dog's body, and thus come to terms with his death. Seeing the body gives your other pets the closure they need. Many experts contend that without having this opportunity, other pets in the family may search endlessly for the deceased dog and even suffer symptoms of depression, such as appetite loss and lethargy (for more on helping your pets deal with their grief, see Chapter 14).

However, at-home euthanasia also has some disadvantages. One disadvantage is that your regular vet may not make house calls. If euthanizing at home is important to you, you need to find a vet who can perform the procedure in your home, and that's a hassle you may not want to grapple with right now.

To find a vet who will euthanize your dog at your home, log on to the American Association of Housecall Veterinarians Web site (www.athomevet.org). There you'll find a searchable database that will help you locate a house-call vet in your area.

Another possible downside to euthanizing your senior at home is how you may feel afterward. In the days immediately following your dog's passing, you may have a hard time entering or even walking past the room where his death occurred.

Advantages and disadvantages of euthanizing at a veterinary clinic

Euthanizing your senior at your veterinary clinic offers two important advantages: It allows your home to remain a much-needed refuge for you and your family as you come to terms with your dog's death, and a vet you know and trust performs the procedure.

The disadvantages are clear: lack of privacy for you and your family in your time of grief, lack of creature comforts for your senior dog, and the inability to control the proceedings. However, you can overcome those challenges and other potential problems with just a little forethought. Here's how:

✔ **Bring your home to the vet.** Bring something from home to help your senior stay calm and feel comforted before and during the procedure. When I brought my senior, Molly, to the vet's for euthanization, I brought her bed with us so she would feel its familiar cushiness and smell the odors she knew as she passed away.

If your dog's bed is too big to bring to the vet's, consider bringing a favorite toy or an unlaundered T-shirt that you've worn. The familiar object and smell will comfort your dog — and you — during the procedure.

✔ **Pay beforehand.** Most clinics gladly accept your payment hours or even days before your dog is euthanized. Paying beforehand eliminates the stress that would result if you had to pay the bill immediately after the procedure or the pain caused by getting the bill in the mail after your dog's death.

✔ **Ease your senior's stress.** If your senior gets upset when she goes to the vet's office, find a way to make her journey less stressful. Your vet can prescribe a mild tranquilizer that you can give your dog an hour or two before the appointment. A tranquilizer will help your senior relax and travel with more ease than she normally does.

✔ **Book the last appointment of the day.** At day's end, your vet won't need to rush off to the next appointment, so he can spend time with you and your dog.

✔ **Ask for privacy.** When you make your appointment or stop by to pay the bill before the procedure, ask the receptionist whether you and your dog can use a separate entrance to the clinic. If there is a separate entrance, you and your senior won't have to walk through and wait in the public reception area amid a bunch of human and canine strangers.

Deciding whether to stay

Deciding whether you want to stay with your dog while he's being euthanized is highly personal. Many people, myself included, choose to stay with their senior dogs in order to comfort the animals and to provide themselves some closure. I'm glad I witnessed Molly's death and that my face was the last thing she saw.

However, witnessing the procedure may not be good for you if you're not prepared for what may happen during your senior's euthanasia. The tremors that may occur after death, the voiding of the bowels and bladder, and a dog's vocalization during the procedure can all unnerve an already traumatized owner.

Find out what you can about the process and try to be objective as you consider whether to stay or go. If you fear that you'll lose control, re-think sticking around. A sobbing, wailing owner will only frighten the dog and make the vet's job that much tougher. If you opt to leave, rest assured that your dog will pass away remembering your love and feeling the gentle touch of your vet's hand.

The question of whether children should witness a dog's euthanasia is problematic. Many vets advise against allowing a child under the age of 10 to see the dog die; vets contend that seeing a beloved dog's death may traumatize a young child. On the other hand, an older child or teenager may want to be with the dog when she's euthanized. As long as your vet is okay with the child's presence, let your child decide; don't try to force him to choose either way.

Don't assume that euthanizing your dog at the clinic means that your other pets can't be there. Ask your vet whether the other canine pack members can be there. Your vet may consent, especially if you bring the dogs in to see your senior's body after the procedure rather than while the euthanasia takes place.

Deciding about After-Care

As with bill paying, deciding what you want done with your senior's body is an issue you usually can deal with before, the death of your dog.

Group cremation

If cost is a concern, the least expensive way to dispose of your dog's remains is to have them cremated along with those of other animals. This option is called *group cremation*. Your vet can take care of this option; you simply leave your dog's body at the clinic after he's been euthanized. You can also take your dog's body to your local animal shelter for group cremation.

In addition to saving money, a group cremation is the best choice if you feel squeamish about handling your dog's remains or cremains. Those people who believe that money is better spent helping living dogs than memorializing dead ones may find that group cremation is the way to go.

Obviously, group cremation isn't a good choice if you want to keep your senior's cremains, bury the dog yourself, or have him buried in a private pet cemetery.

Individual cremation

Choose *individual cremation* if you want your senior's cremains returned to you. After your dog is cremated, the veterinary clinic or a pet crematorium returns the cremains to you in a box.

You can keep the ashes in a decorative urn in your home or scatter them somewhere outdoors. Some owners scatter the ashes in an open area as a way of signifying their senior's liberation from illness and pain. Others bury the ashes in an outdoor area, such as under a tree the dog loved or a place where the dog liked to play.

Many pet cemeteries cremate dogs' remains. To find one, start with Moira Allen's Pet Loss Support site at www.pet-loss.net, which includes a comprehensive list of pet cemeteries, sorted by state. Another resource is the International Association of Pet Cemeteries' members' list at www.iaopc.com/memberlist.htm.

Burial

Burying your senior's remains at home can make you feel that your beloved dog is with you in death as well as in life. As desirable as that option may seem, exercising that option can be complicated. If you live in a townhouse or apartment, of course, home burial is out of the question because there's no place to bury your dog. But even if you live in a suburban, single-family house, home burial may be out of the question if your county or town prohibits it. And even if home burial is permitted in your municipality, it may not be such a good idea. If you move out of your house, you may not feel very good about leaving your dog's remains behind. In addition, a grave needs to be dug quite deeply to prevent the remains from becoming a health hazard or being disturbed by wild animals.

 Your vet can tell you whether home burial is okay where you live. If, however, you're determined to bury your pet at home, you'll find a wide variety of dignified, attractive markers, statues, and headstones you can use to mark the burial site. Pet cemeteries and other pet-oriented businesses sell such items; check the classified ads in any newspaper pet section or in a pet magazine. A tree or bush is another way you can mark your senior's grave.

Or you can inter your senior at a pet cemetery. Almost every state in the United States has at least one pet cemetery. Burying your senior at a pet cemetery carries almost all the advantages and none of the disadvantages of home burial: Your senior's remains will be properly cared for, won't be disturbed, and won't run afoul of local ordinances. You'll also have a place to visit your senior for as long as you need to, which may help you deal more effectively with your dog's death. Still, home burial has two advantages over burial in a cemetery: You can visit your pet's grave easily — and, obviously, home burial costs less than a burial at a pet cemetery.

In Chapter 15, I discuss ways you can pay tribute to a deceased senior dog, no matter what your after-care decision is.

Chapter 14

Knowing When It's Time

. . . .

In This Chapter

▶ Making the decision to euthanize your senior dog

▶ Knowing what to expect during euthanasia

▶ Coping when your dog dies at home

▶ Managing insensitive people

▶ Dealing with your dog's unexpected death

. . . .

*A*ny dog lover will tell you that few events in life are more traumatic than having to euthanize a beloved canine companion. Whether you and your pooch are a pack of two or part of a pack of twenty-two doesn't matter. Exercising the power of life or death over your four-legged friend is almost overwhelming, even though letting go can be a great gift to give your dog if and when the time comes.

But how do you know when that time occurs? How can you really know when the time has come to let your dog go? How should you determine whether the two of you have reached the end of your road together?

Dealing with those questions is one reason why the whole idea of euthanizing a dog is so difficult. Another reason is that you may not know what happens during the actual euthanasia process. You may wonder whether the procedure is painful for your senior, whether he understands what's going on, or whether he'll just go to sleep.

This chapter helps you deal with all those questions — either by providing direct answers or, where appropriate, helping you find the answers that are right for you and your beloved senior.

Making the Decision

You may already realize that your senior's days are numbered, and you may already have decided to stop aggressive treatment for her condition. However, her continued presence may belie your anticipation of what's to come and may even tempt you to postpone the inevitable.

Such temptation is totally understandable. Your senior dog may have been part of your life for so long that she almost feels like part of you. Or maybe you adopted her fairly recently from a rescue group and bonded with her almost overnight. No matter how long she's been with you, though, the idea of your senior being gone may be impossible to contemplate. Your heart may feel as though it's shredding into small pieces at the thought of her death, or it may feel like a heavy weight in your chest.

Either way, you hurt — badly. And that feeling is appropriate: You're trying to face the loss of a beloved being in your life. But figuring out when that loss should occur may be a little easier if you can answer the following questions:

- ✔ **How's my dog doing?** Is your senior still active or at least engaged in the world around her? Is she still eating? Is she in pain that can't be relieved? Does she still interact with you, or is she so miserable that she barely recognizes you or anyone else in the family? A dog who's clearly enjoying life may be able to stick around a little longer. An obviously miserable dog may well be ready to say goodbye.

- ✔ **What's my dog telling me?** Often, a senior dog who wants to stick around will convey that message in a way her human can't possibly misinterpret. My 16-year-old mixed poodle, Molly, became quite affectionate and active — in fact, almost jaunty — while I was trying to decide whether she should have surgery to remove her cancerous tumor. I listened to her, and chose to go ahead with the surgery, which gave her several more months of a high-quality life and me time to come to terms with her mortality.

  Conversely, when the tumor returned several months later and my vet told me that the cancer had spread, Molly was spending most of her time sleeping. One notable exception to her nearly constant slumbering occurred, though: the evening that she looked up, placed her head on my chest, and stared directly at me. I knew immediately what she was trying to tell me, and I had her euthanized the next day.

- ✔ **How do I feel?** Although the decision whether or not to euthanize your senior should focus mostly on your dog's condition, assessing your own state of mind is okay, too. If your dog has a terminal illness but still seems healthy, you may feel it's too soon to have her euthanized. On the other hand, you may feel differently if the illness is one in which sudden death is possible. Under such circumstances, you may decide to put your dog down to avoid finding her dead later — or, worse, having your children find her.

✔ **Can I afford to continue?** Considering how your dog's condition is affecting you emotionally and financially is perfectly okay, too. If providing constant nursing care for your terminally ill senior has proved to be more emotionally draining than you can handle, the time may be right to consider euthanasia. The same may be true if your dog's prognosis is poor and treating her condition is depleting your bank account.

✔ **How does the rest of your family feel?** If you and your dog are part of a larger household, understand that you can't make the decision to euthanize her all by yourself. The adults and near-adults (in other words, teens) in the family need to have their say, too. If the members of your family significantly disagree about whether the time is right to let the dog go, re-evaluate the criteria that led to your individual decision and be open to the possibility that those who want to wait have points that are worth considering. Having the entire family visit the vet to discuss your senior's condition may also be a good idea. Such a discussion may help your family reach a consensus.

✔ **What's going to happen?** If your dog is under a vet's care, then he's undoubtedly told you how your dog's disease will progress and what you can expect to see as time goes on. If you know that your senior will begin to suffer as the condition progresses, you may decide that now's the time to let her go, before she must endure any pain.

✔ **What does your vet say?** Your vet won't tell you when to euthanize your senior, but he can tell you when a natural death may be near. He can also explain how your dog may indicate that she's in discomfort or pain and other signs that it's time to say goodbye. And if you're still not sure, asking your vet what he'd do if the dog were his may help you decide what's best for your senior companion.

Getting through the Process

Once you and your family have decided that now's the time to say goodbye to your dog, you need to turn your attention to the short-term needs of all concerned. Your objective is to shepherd everyone, including yourself, through this difficult time with as little stress and as much dignity as possible. In Chapter 13, I describe arrangements that you can make with your vet before the procedure to ease your dog's passing. Here's some information to help you understand exactly what occurs when your dog is euthanized, and some ideas to help all concerned before and during the procedure.

Understanding what happens during euthanasia

If you're prepared for what may happen when your dog is put to sleep, the process can be less stressful for all concerned. Your vet may have her own procedures but here's a general description of what happens when a dog is euthanized at a veterinary clinic or in your home.

Euthanizing your senior at a veterinary clinic

At a veterinary clinic, the vet or a technician prepares an intravenous (IV) catheter and places it in one of your dog's veins. The IV is used to pump the euthanasia solution into your dog. The placement of the IV usually occurs in a room away from where you're waiting. After the IV is placed, your dog is brought back to you. He may be placed on an examination table, in your lap, or on the lap of a family member; your preference usually dictates where he will be.

If your dog wasn't given a tranquilizer earlier to calm him down, your vet may pipe a sedative through the IV first, which causes your dog to go to sleep. At that point, the vet administers the euthanasia solution.

If your dog is on your lap during the procedure, you should place a towel underneath him before the procedure begins because he may become incontinent as the euthanasia drug takes affect.

At this point, your vet asks you whether you're ready for the procedure to start. When you agree, your vet activates the IV. The euthanasia solution, which usually is an overdose of anesthetic, begins to flow into your dog's vein. While this happens, you can pet your dog, look at your dog, and speak soothing words to him.

Within a minute or two, your dog appears to go to sleep. He may slump over or — as my senior dog, Molly, did — slowly place his head down on the table or on his paws. His eyes will not close. Your vet will check for a heartbeat, find none, and confirm that your dog is gone.

The vet probably will ask whether you'd like to stay with your senior's body for a few minutes. There's no right or wrong choice here; do whatever feels right for you. If the vet doesn't offer you this option and you want to stay with the body, ask whether you can remain for a few minutes.

Euthanizing your senior at home

A euthanasia at home may not involve an IV. Instead, the vet may inject the euthanasia liquid through a syringe into your dog's vein. The liquid takes effect quickly, and your dog passes away just as peacefully as he would have if an IV had been used.

No matter where your dog is euthanized, he may twitch or appear to take one or two final gasping breaths after his heartbeat stops. These movements are reflex actions that often occur after an animal dies; *they don't indicate that your dog is still alive.*

Helping your dog

In the days and hours before your senior begins his final journey, he needs your love and understanding more than he ever has before. By giving him that consideration, you not only ease his passage, but you also create sweet memories that can counter some of the pain you'll feel when he's gone. Here are some suggestions to help your dog — and, in the process, yourself — during this difficult time.

- **Give him your time.** That report deadline or conference call isn't nearly as important as giving the gift of your presence to your senior. If you can take vacation time now, do it. I promise that you won't regret spending a last day or two with your canine companion.

- **Indulge him to the max.** Give your senior whatever pleasures he still enjoys. The night before my parents euthanized their Dachshund, Lola, they brought her into bed with them (a privilege that had been denied up 'til then) and gave her some ice cream, which she dearly loved. If your dog has a favorite people food, let him have some; if the two of you have a special place you like to go, take him there if you can.

- **Live in the moment.** Try not to let your grief get in the way of this special time you spend with your dog. If something funny happens, let yourself laugh. Just before I took Molly, my geriatric mixed poodle, to the vet to be euthanized, she heard the doorbell ring and bolted out of her bed to run to the door and bark fiercely at the perceived intruder. I had to laugh at (but also appreciate) Molly's work ethic, especially because she was clearly in a very weakened condition.

✔ **Gather the pack together.** Before you have your dog euthanized, try to gather your other family members together to spend some last collective time with him. Talk about the happy and funny times that you've each shared with him and that you've shared as a family. This group hug for your canine companion not only helps him feel the love of his entire family — but the humans also feel better.

✔ **Visit him.** If your senior is staying at an animal clinic, go see him — and bring the other family members with you. While my Sheltie, Cory, awaited exploratory surgery at an emergency veterinary clinic, my husband, daughter, and I visited him at least once a day, including immediately before his surgery. Visiting helped us feel much better about not being able to be present when he was euthanized during surgery.

✔ **Try to control your emotions.** When you're around your senior, rein in your urge to cry or show sadness. Dogs are very perceptive; if you're upset, your senior is likely to become upset, too. You'll have plenty of time to mourn later; if you need to grieve now, try to do so in a place where your senior can't see or hear you.

Helping yourself

Don't let anyone tell you that losing a senior dog is less painful than losing a human family member. In both cases, you've had love between the two of you and a bond that's been created. Death breaks that bond, and the break can traumatize those who are left behind. Like any grieving person, you need to take special care of yourself before, during, and after your dog's euthanasia. Here's how:

✔ **Take time off.** I don't know anyone who can focus on work when faced with the loss of a long-time companion of any species, but some people try — or at least go through the motions. But you don't need to be one of those people. Do yourself and your colleagues a favor: Take a day or two off work and give yourself the time and space you need to grapple with your grief.

✔ **Don't drive alone to the vet's.** If your dog is being euthanized at the veterinary clinic, don't try to drive yourself and him there. If you live alone, ask a friend to drive the two of you; otherwise, have another family member come with you and your senior.

✔ **Have some company.** If your dog is being euthanized at home, have another person with you before, during, and immediately after the procedure. Other members of your household may also want to be present; if so, schedule the procedure for a

time when they can be there. Grief is less overwhelming when
you share it with someone.

✔ **Get a memento.** Plan to keep some item of your dog's: her
collar, leash, a favorite toy, or even a clipping from her coat.
I saved clippings from the coats of both my dearly departed
seniors. In the days and weeks that immediately followed
their deaths, I looked at those clippings often and felt that my
dogs were still with me.

Dealing with other people

Alas, not every human being loves dogs or appreciates why living
with a dog is such a special experience. Some people may have difficulty understanding why you're so upset over the impending death
of your senior. You may hear insensitive comments from these folks
and wonder how to deal with them without going ballistic.

My first impulse is to tell you to ignore the idiots who say such
things to you — but that tactic's not always feasible (for example,
when your boss or your mother-in-law is the idiot). Here are some
other steps you can take when someone makes one of the following thoughtless or cruel comments about how you're dealing with
the death of your senior:

✔ **"It's just a dog."** The word 'just', as used here, is so inappropriate. Your dog is a member of your family. By trying to give
her good care up to the very end and by grieving over her
impending death, you're treating her with the love and respect
that you'd give any family member. When other people say
that you should feel otherwise or that a dog's death is no big
deal, *they* deserve *your* sympathy. After all, although you're
in pain now, you've also had the good fortune of loving and
being loved by a canine companion — an experience that
they're not open to. And you can say truthfully, "He was a
member of my family, and I loved him."

✔ **"You can always get another dog."** A variation of this supremely
insensitive comment is "When are you going to get another
dog?" No individual, canine or otherwise, can truly be replaced.
Someday you may have another dog — or you may not. The
choice is yours. Meanwhile, though, you focus on honoring
your current senior dog — exactly as you should be. If the
person who makes the comment is persistent, you can always
say, "I'm really not ready to deal with that right now."

✔ **"Aren't people more important than dogs?"** This comment is
especially galling, not to mention a total *non sequitur.* Feeling
sad over the death of a beloved dog doesn't mean that you

don't feel (or haven't felt) just as sad over the death of a beloved person. The love, not the species, is what's important here. You can respond to this comment by saying, "Fido was a member of my family, and I feel sad when anyone in my family dies."

✔ **"He lived a long life, so you really shouldn't be upset."** So what? Maybe your dog lived a long time — but people who have the privilege of loving dogs know that no matter how long their canine companions live, they never live long enough. Outliving your pooch is the most painful aspect of living with one. But people take on that pain because they want to know the joy of sharing their lives with a dog — and that joy and satisfaction is well worth the pain. When confronted with this comment, your best course of action is to say, "I tried to give him a good life, and he was a great dog."

For much more about coming to terms with your dog's death, see Chapter 15.

Dealing with the Unexpected

As hard as you may try to prepare for your senior dog's passing, his actual death may catch you by surprise — and I speak from experience. When exploratory surgery revealed that Cory, our 7-year-old Shetland Sheepdog, had inoperable cancer, my husband and I had to decide what to do right away. Because the prognosis was very grim, we chose to have him euthanized immediately while he was still under anesthesia. We knew that choice was the kindest thing we could do for him. But the unexpected outcome of the surgery devastated me, my husband, and our daughter.

Here are ways you can ease the pain of dealing with a senior dog's unexpected death and its aftermath:

✔ **Talk, talk, talk.** Talk with understanding friends, a pet-loss hot line (see Chapter 15), a grief counselor, and other family members about your senior's unexpected death. These discussions help you clarify why you're grieving and enable you to work through your pain more quickly.

✔ **Listen, listen, listen.** The other members of your family are grieving, too, and need someone to talk to. Listening to what they say and giving them whatever comfort you can helps ease their pain and your own.

✔ **Don't rush post-death decisions.** The shock of a pet's sudden death adds to the stress of making decisions about body disposal and related matters. Experts caution against making hasty choices about after-care. Most vets can keep the pet's body for a few days so you have time to think through your options, which are outlined in Chapter 13.

✔ **Get comfort online.** Many online resources are available for bereaved pet owners. Among them are the Humane Society of the United States Web site on "Coping with the Death of Your Pet" (www.hsus.org/ace/11779) and the Association for Pet Loss and Bereavement Web site (www.aplb.org). For other sites, see Chapter 15.

✔ **Develop perspective.** Remembering that dogs almost always die before their people do is important. For that reason, every day you've spent with your senior is truly a gift that you can be grateful for. Viewing your time together in that way can help you heal from your loss.

What to Do When Your Dog Dies Naturally

Death is a natural process. Owners can end the suffering their senior dogs might experience through euthanasia, but as often as not, Mother Nature ends that suffering herself.

Even when your senior shows no evidence of any significant health problems, you may awaken one morning to find your four-legged friend appearing to slumber peacefully — until you realize that her chest isn't moving and her heart isn't beating. You may lift up her lip and see that her normally pink gums are white. The evidence is clear: Your old friend died in her sleep.

You may be shocked, particularly if your senior didn't seem to have any health problems. But if you were agonizing over whether to euthanize your dog, you may feel relieved that nature decided for you. Now, though, you need to take action. Here's what to do:

1. **Start by checking to see whether your dog voided her bowels or bladder.** You'll probably find that she has. Clean up as best you can, and place your friend on a clean sheet, blanket, or towel.

2. **Next, call your vet.** Your vet will probably ask you how you want your dog's body taken care of: group cremation, individual cremation, or left intact for burial (see Chapter 13 for information on each of these options). Depending on which option you choose, you can bring your dog's body to your vet's office, have a pet cemetery handle the transportation and after-care, or keep the body for burial at home.

3. **Remember the life you shared with your dog.** Before you remove your dog's body from your home, take some time to sit by her and remember the life you led together. Give other family members the opportunity to do the same, including your other dogs and cats. Without that opportunity, the remaining animals may search relentlessly for your departed senior dog — or, at the very least, wonder where she is. Dogs seem to understand the finality of death and that their packmate isn't coming back if they can see the deceased individual. Once they see her body, they're much more likely to accept what's happened and move on.

If your other pets don't get to view your senior's body, check out Chapter 15's tips for helping grieving dogs and cats.

Senior Super Dogs: A matter of Chance

He loved playing basketball with his kids, and the wrestling matches with his tail rivaled those of the WWE Smackdown. His ability to jump up to any height of a bouncing ball could have won him a starting slot on a volleyball team. And his majestic good looks could have landed him in countless dog-food commercials — if his people had tried to put him in one.

Chance (right) and Cynnamin, courtesy of Michael and Kim Smith

But for Michael and Kim Smith of Greensboro, Maryland, all that mattered was finding a good family dog to raise along with their three children. They found that dog in Chance, the Golden Retriever who joined the Smith household when he was 2 months old. For the next seven-plus years, Chance was an integral part of the Smith household: part entertainer, part playmate, and part caretaker.

Chance had just begun to cross the threshold between middle age and seniorhood when one morning, he failed to give Kim his customary paws-on-the-shoulder hug Michael recalls, "Kim tried to get a hug, but he didn't make it all the way up to her. . . . Kim tried again later, but he wouldn't move. We knew then that something was very wrong." That something turned out to be a *fibrocartilaginous embolism* (FCE). Essentially, FCE is to the spine what a stroke is to the brain.

After five days in the Annapolis Emergency Clinic, Chance came home. However, he couldn't use his hind legs that propelled his jumps or the tail that he used to wrestle with. Chance also lost bowel and bladder control.

But the Smiths adapted, even though Chance needed constant care. They had to rotate him every few hours, empty his bladder several times a day, and keep him clean. He needed to be exercised, too, to prevent muscle atrophy in his front legs. The Smiths met that challenge by using a sling and later a dog cart. Chance also required a little extra attention to keep him from getting depressed.

Unfortunately, Chance's problems had only just begun. In early January 2004, he became lethargic, stopped eating and drinking, and started vomiting. A chest X-ray revealed bronchitis, and Chance's vet prescribed antibiotics. But Chance's health continued to deteriorate.

The Smiths brought Chance back to the Annapolis emergency clinic. Tests revealed nothing, and after three days, the vet admitted to being stumped — although he mentioned that Chance may have a cancerous tumor that could be detected with additional testing. Michael authorized the test, and then visited his dog.

"During my visit he didn't even know I was there," Michael says. "He couldn't lift his head or open his eyes, and his breathing was very labored."

Michael and Kim discussed Chance's situation. "Kim could barely hold it together and asked me what difference this test would make," Michael remembers. "Even if they found a tumor and removed it, they didn't know whether he would improve."

Chance also had a faulty heart valve. That condition, along with his FCE and his current problem, made Michael and Kim wonder whether he could even survive surgery to remove a tumor, let alone recover.

"We went straight to the vet and made an appointment to talk to him," Michael continues. After talking with their vet, they decided to forego the test for the tumor and to euthanize Chance.

Then, Michael and Kim went to see their dog. Kim held Chance's head in her lap, and Michael sat on the floor behind the dog to pet him as their vet injected the drug. "He passed quietly in our presence," Michael says. "He never made any sounds or lost control of any body functions, as we were warned he might do. They allowed us to spend as much time as we wanted to with him."

Losing Chance has been tough for the Smiths. "We continue to grieve every day — some more than others," Michael says.

When asked what advice he would give other dog owners, Michael responds, "You have to know what is right for you. Many people thought we were crazy spending so much time and money on [Chance's] care. Chance was a member of our family, and we dedicated ourselves to helping him get better. When the time came to make that decision, we felt it in our hearts. We knew that we were comfortable with the decision and that it was the right time and the right thing to do for Chance and for us."

Chapter 15

Coping with Your Loss

● ●

In This Chapter

▶ Understanding your grief

▶ Seeking support

▶ Helping children and pets mourn

▶ Honoring your senior

▶ Deciding whether to get a new dog

● ●

*T*he death of your dog — no matter how old he was, how long he was with you, or whether his death was sudden or expected — is probably one of the most heart-rending, stressful events you'll experience. Unfortunately, pet loss isn't officially recognized as a stressful event in some professional quarters.

For example, the Holmes-Rahe Social Readjustment Ratings Scale, which assigns rankings to common stressful events, doesn't include pet loss on its list of stressful events. But dog owners know better. Losing a canine companion certainly qualifies as the scale's "death of a close family member" or, at the very least, to the "death of a close friend." Such losses bring pain to those left behind and generate a grieving process that can take weeks, months, or even years to complete.

In this chapter, I help you understand how you're likely to grieve the loss of your senior. I also discuss how to cope with that grief and how you can help other members of your family — human and non-human — deal with their sorrow. Additionally, I suggest ways you can memorialize your beloved senior and how to deal with the question of whether to get a new dog.

Grief Is a Process

Many experts have tried to describe how people grieve a loss, but the best-known explanation probably comes from Elisabeth Kubler-Ross, author of *On Death and Dying*. Although Kubler-Ross framed the process in terms of how a dying person comes to terms with his fate, you can apply her explanation to your effort to come to terms with your senior's death. The five stages of grief Kubler-Ross describes include

- **Denial:** In this stage, you simply can't believe that your senior is gone. You keep thinking that you hear his footsteps in the kitchen or you come home from an errand and expect to see him greet you at the door, just as he always has. Shock and numbness also can be part of this stage.

- **Anger:** After the numbness and shock over your senior's death wears off, you may find yourself feeling furious and resentful. You may direct such anger against your departed senior for having left you or against the fates (or whatever higher power you believe in) for taking your four-legged friend from you. You may also ask yourself, over and over, if you could have done anything else that would have spared your senior's life.

- **Bargaining:** A great example of this stage is in the movie *The House of Sand and Fog*. In the movie, the Iranian colonel portrayed by actor Ben Kingsley becomes distraught after he sees police officers shoot his teenage son. While emergency-room doctors attempt to save the boy's life, Kingsley's character enters the hospital chapel, where he prays and makes all kinds of promises to his God, if only the boy's life is spared. You may try striking a similar deal with fate before your senior dies — or after, when you think that you'll do just about anything to bring your dog back.

- **Depression:** In this stage, you realize that nothing you offer to do can bring your senior back. He's truly, irrevocably gone, and when you recognize that fact, you may fall into a significant funk. You may feel numb again, if only to keep from feeling the pain that comes from realizing that your senior is no longer here.

- **Acceptance:** Time passes, and so — really — do your feelings of desolation, pain, and sadness. Everyday life begins to replace grief at some point. You feel your sadness, anger, and grief begin to recede, and you're able to accept the reality of your loss. Your sadness over your senior's death fades, and memories of happy times replace those feelings.

Although the stages of grief apply to most people, realize that every person's grieving process is individual. Some people may skip one stage or go through the stages in a different order. Still others may shuttle back and forth between stages as they work through their feelings. And finally, as was the colonel's case in *The House of Sand and Fog*, one or more stages may occur before the death does in a kind of anticipatory grief.

Getting Help and Support

No one should deal with the loss of a loved one alone, whether that loved one is human or canine. Mourning your senior dog's death feels like less of a burden when you can share that burden with others. Some of those who you share your grief with may be people you know; others may be strangers at the other end of telephone line or sitting with you in a room. In the end, though, by talking with others about how you feel, you're helping to heal your wounded heart.

From friends and family

Your friends and family, especially if they're dog lovers or if they knew and loved your senior, can be sources of great comfort to you. They can share their memories of your dog, and they can empathize with your pain and give you the understanding that you need.

Save most of your outpourings for people who love dogs, or at least pets of some sort. Dog and pet lovers will understand your devastation when others may not. If you encounter such misunderstandings, though, use the comebacks I give you in Chapter 14 to help.

From pet-loss hot lines

Our culture has begun to recognize how important pets are to people, and that recognition has led to greater understanding of how devastating a pet's death can be. That understanding has fueled the growth of pet-loss hot lines and support groups (for more on support groups, see the next section "From grief counselors and support groups").

Bereaved pet owners can call hot lines to talk to either professional counselors or volunteers who're trained to deal with someone who's lost a pet. Some hot lines are staffed 24/7; others are staffed only during certain days and/or hours. If you call a hot line that's outside your local area, long-distance charges apply, although a few hot lines are toll-free.

You can start looking for a pet-loss hot line at the veterinary college that's closest to you. Many vet students staff and manage these kinds of services. Among the vet schools that offer such services are

✔ **Michigan State University:** 517-432-2696

✔ **Tufts University:** 508-739-7966

✔ **University of California Davis:** 916-752-4200

✔ **University of Florida:** 352-392-4700, extension 4080

For a more extensive list of hot lines, go to the Association for Pet Loss and Bereavement (APLB) Web site at www.aplb.org.

From grief counselors and support groups

Many professional counselors have specialties in dealing with the grief that comes from losing a pet. Some counselors are psychologists, others are licensed clinical social workers (also known as LCSWs). Counseling services usually are available on a one-on-one basis or in a support group.

To find a counselor for one-on-one therapy, you can search in a couple of ways:

✔ **Search an online database.** Several Web sites offer searchable databases, including the Association for Pet Loss and Bereavement (www.aplb.org) and Moira Anderson Allen's Pet Loss Support Pages (www.pet-loss.net).

✔ **Search the Internet.** You can also find a counselor by searching the Internet. Type the following search terms into your search engine: "pet loss counselors" plus the name of your state. Your search should cough up at least a few listings.

If you'd prefer talking with a group of sympathetic listeners (and, of course, do some listening yourself), a pet-loss support group may be right for you. You'll have a chance to talk about your own feelings regarding the death of your dog and get some sympathy from people who truly understand what you're going through. Generally, experienced counselors, such as psychologists or licensed clinical social workers, lead these groups.

Many animal shelters offer pet-loss support groups that meet on a weekly or biweekly basis. Contact your local animal shelter to see whether a support group meets there. You can also locate support groups on both the APLB and Moira Allen's Web sites, which contain online databases that list support groups by state.

If you'd rather not get support face-to-face, you can go online to a pet-loss support group. You can participate in a group via e-mail or the Internet. One of the largest online support groups is Rainbow Bridge, which to date, has more than 500 subscribers. To join this group, send a message to `rainbowbridge-subscribe@ yahoogroups.com`. To find out more, log on to the group's Web page at `http://health.groups.yahoo.com/group/ rainbowbridge`.

From your doctor

If you don't feel as though you're working through your grief at all, your doctor may be able to help. Such help may be as simple as a prescription that enables you to sleep for the first few nights after your senior's death or as complicated as treatment and a referral to a counselor if you exhibit symptoms of clinical depression.

Not every bereaved person suffers from clinical depression. However, according to the National Institutes of Mental Health (NIMH), a serious loss can trigger a depressive episode. See your doctor if you show some or all of the following symptoms for more than a few weeks, or sooner if those symptoms interfere with your ability to function:

- Persistent sad, anxious, or "empty" mood
- Feelings of hopelessness and pessimism
- Feelings of guilt, worthlessness, or helplessness
- Loss of interest or pleasure in hobbies and activities that were once enjoyable, including sex
- Decreased energy, fatigue, being "slowed down"
- Difficulty concentrating, remembering, making decisions
- Insomnia, early morning awakening, or oversleeping
- Appetite and/or weight loss, or overeating and weight gain
- Thoughts of death or suicide; suicide attempts
- Restlessness, irritability
- Persistent physical symptoms that do not respond to treatment, such as headaches, digestive disorders, and chronic pain

Depression is an illness, *not* a deficiency or a sign of personal failure. Please don't let shyness or shame keep you from seeing your doctor if you experience persistent symptoms of depression. Without treatment, you're suffering needlessly. Your doctor can help by prescribing medication and/or referring you to a counselor.

From yourself

You can be your own best source of support. As much as other people can help you deal with the death of your beloved senior, you need to help yourself by giving yourself good care. Good health habits — both mental and physical — can give you the strength you need to move through a period of grief. Here are some tips from mental health professionals:

- ✔ **Eat regularly.** Some people completely lose their appetites when they're grieving. Even if eating is the last thing you want to do, try to eat anyway. Tempt yourself by fixing some of your favorite dishes (or let someone else do it!).

- ✔ **Get regular exercise.** Consistent physical activity causes your body to produce endorphins — chemical substances that can lift your mood and help you feel better, at least for a little while. At the same time, you improve your physical health. You don't need to knock yourself out: 30 minutes of brisk walking 4 or 5 days a week will do the trick.

- ✔ **Avoid major changes.** This isn't the time to make significant changes in your life, such as getting a new job, moving to a new home, or ending a relationship. You're under enough stress already; don't add to the strain you're already experiencing.

- ✔ **Be careful with alcohol.** Excessive alcohol may suppress your feelings of unhappiness, but it also can create new problems that are tough to solve later on.

- ✔ **Keep going.** While you're grieving, you can take comfort in maintaining your usual routine and not looking too far ahead. "One day at a time" is the maxim recovering alcoholics use; this saying is equally appropriate when you're recovering from a significant loss.

- ✔ **Expect delayed reactions.** Weeks or months may pass after your senior's death, and you may be feeling okay — only to find yourself engulfed in tears when you encounter something or someone who triggers your memories and emotions. Finding a lost toy while cleaning out the basement or seeing a dog who looks just like your senior are just two examples of situations that can cause an emotional meltdown long after you think you've gotten past your senior's death. These reactions are normal, and they're to be expected.

- ✔ **Know it will end.** You may not believe it now, but eventually your grief will pass and you'll be more interested in looking to the future than in mourning the past.

Helping Others Cope

Chances are, you're not the only one who's sad over the death of your senior canine companion. Dogs have a way of eliciting love from almost anyone — human or canine — of any age. Consequently, other individuals in your life are probably grieving with the same intensity that you are. Here are some ideas on how to help them — and, in the process, help yourself.

Comforting other adults

The other adults in your family may feel just as bad as you do about your senior's death. Even if you were your senior's main caregiver, your spouse, adult child, or elderly parent undoubtedly loved your canine companion and feels her absence keenly. Here are ways that you can help the other adults in your family:

- **Be accessible.** Other adults in your family may need to share their grief with you. Don't be so caught up in your own sadness that you don't recognize that the people around you are in pain, too.

- **Remember the good times.** After the initial shock of your senior's death passes, make it a point to remind the other human members of your family about the funny, heroic, and otherwise positive things that your senior did. Funny memories are especially important because they'll probably trigger some laughter — and laughter is a balm for a wounded heart.

- **Honor your senior together.** Paying tribute to your senior dog, as outlined later in this chapter, may be even more meaningful if you make it a family affair.

- **Watch for signs of trouble.** Even if you're working through your grief process in a healthy manner, others in the family may not be. If you sense that someone else in your family is showing some or all the signs of depressive illness outlined in the "From your doctor" section earlier in this chapter, encourage him to seek medical help.

Comforting children

Losing your senior dog may be your child's first experience with death. And although this experience may be painful for your child, it also gives you an opportunity to show her how to deal appropriately with similar circumstances and feelings in the future.

If you heeded the advice I presented in Chapter 13, your child already understands that your senior died. Now you need to help your child deal with the grief that follows your senior's death. Here's what experts suggest, and what I discovered from my own experience as a parent:

- **Be understanding.** Young children (5 years of age and under) usually don't realize that death is permanent. They're likely to feel sad one moment and ask to play with a friend the next. This is normal behavior; don't let it bother you.

- **Answer questions.** School-aged children may ask some pretty direct questions about the actual death of the dog and what happened to the dog's body afterward. Answer as honestly as possible — without getting too graphic — and in a way that's appropriate for your child's age.

- **Show your feelings.** If you feel sad or teary over your dog's death, showing those emotions to your child is okay — in fact, it's vital. By showing how you feel, you're giving your child permission to show those feelings, too. In essence, you're acting as a role model.

- **Provide outlets.** Children may want to express their feelings about their dogs by drawing pictures, writing poems, or helping plan tributes. Providing the items needed for them to do these activities, participating with them in the activity (if your participation is needed or requested), and encouraging their efforts can help children process their grief in a healthy manner.

- **Be watchful.** Most children can deal with their pet's death if they get guidance from their parents — but if your child appears to have prolonged difficulty dealing with it, consulting your pediatrician and/or a mental health professional is a good idea. Signs of such difficulty include

  - Lethargy

  - Inability to concentrate

  - Lower grades in school

  - Changes in sleeping and eating patterns

  - Regressive in behavior (for example, bedwetting)

If these symptoms don't abate within a couple of weeks, a pro can help you get your child back on track.

Comforting other pets

If you have other animals in your household, they probably know that something — or, rather, someone — is missing. For dogs and cats, the sudden departure of a family member can trigger an emotional tailspin that has both physical and behavioral effects. A grieving animal may show one or more of the following symptoms:

- **Refusal to eat:** The dog or cat in mourning all too often shows his grief by losing interest in food. He may refuse to eat entirely or just cut way back on his dining.

- **Bathroom lapses:** The canine or feline mourner may decide that maintaining proper bathroom behavior — whether the bathroom is a litter box, newspapers, or the backyard — is just too much trouble. Potty accidents result.

- **Crying or wailing:** A cat who's grieving the loss of a companion may start meowing, crying, or wailing constantly.

- **Moping:** The grieving or depressed dog or cat may lose interest in normal activities. Instead, the animal may sleep more, walk at a snail's pace, and otherwise act lethargic.

In most cases, easing your pet's grief requires just a little help from you. Here are some ways you can help your canine or feline friend move beyond mourning and renew his interest in living:

- **Resume your routine.** A grieving dog or cat may be more upset by the change in routine that your deceased senior's absence may cause than by the absence itself. As soon as you can, return to the schedule or regimen that your pet is accustomed to.

- **Go gourmet.** If your feline or canine companion isn't eating much, try re-booting his appetite by enhancing what he eats. Microwave your pet's food for a minute or two to release aromas that can tempt the most finicky appetite or add a tasty treat or two to your pet's meal. Be sensitive to your dog's or cat's social dining needs, too: A little bit of hand-feeding or human company during mealtimes can reassure your pet.

- **Don't coddle.** Spending extra time petting, holding, cuddling, or otherwise consoling your grieving pet can be tempting, but by doing so, you may be reinforcing his lethargic behavior. If you take your mourning dog for a walk, he's much more likely to perk up. And you can rouse a grieving cat from his lethargy by offering him some toys to pounce on.

- **Let the pet comfort you.** Spending time with your dog or cat can help your pet feel better, but it can help you feel better, too. Interacting with a dog or cat can lower your blood pressure and heart rate, and help you relax at least a little bit while you're under such strain.

Although most dogs and cats can overcome their grief with just a little help from their human friends, others may need some professional help to get back on track. Some signs of grief may actually signal the onset of a serious illness. Either way, if your cat or dog shows any of the following symptoms, call your vet for guidance:

✔ Your dog or cat hasn't eaten anything for two days.

✔ Your cat (especially a male) hasn't urinated for several hours.

✔ Your cat begins missing the litter box or your dog develops housetraining amnesia.

✔ Your cat or dog has other symptoms such as lethargy, crying, and wailing that continue for more than two weeks.

Paying Tribute to Your Senior

Celebrating your senior's life and showing your appreciation for how she enhanced yours can be a tremendous help in coming to terms with her death. Here are some ways you can pay tribute to your late, great canine companion and celebrate the bond you shared. They're even more therapeutic when other members in your family participate, too:

✔ **Get artsy.** Creating a picture, poem, or essay about your senior helps her and your time together live on, and also helps you express your feelings about her life and death.

✔ **Donate stuff.** Throwing out your senior's old toys, crate, dishes, bed, and food can be tempting because they're so painful to look at, but consider not giving in to that temptation. Animal shelters and rescue groups always need these items, and they usually lack the money to buy them. Knowing that another dog is benefiting from your senior's dog's stuff can ease your heart immeasurably.

✔ **Make a photo album.** A memory album devoted to print or digital photos of your senior can help rekindle happy memories of your senior and comfort you as you process your grief.

✔ **Write a check.** If you can afford to do so, send a check in your dog's memory to a rescue group, animal shelter, or veterinary research group. Your generosity will help other dogs _and_ be very therapeutic for you.

Should You Get a New Dog?

A few months ago, a friend told me that his aging Bernese Mountain Dog had just been diagnosed with lymphoma. He and his family decided not to pursue aggressive treatment, opting instead to keep the dog comfortable until the animal died. Meanwhile, my friend was already thinking about what kind of dog to get next.

Nearly two years ago, my parents lost their beloved 11-year-old Dachshund when accumulated ills prompted them to make the compassionate decision to euthanize her. They're also getting older and feel less able to give a dog the care he needs. As much as they love having a canine companion, their days of dog ownership are probably over.

A month after our adored senior Sheltie, Cory, died unexpectedly, my family and I placed a deposit on a new Golden Retriever puppy. Just 9 weeks after Cory's death, we welcomed a new dog into our home: Allie, our golden girl. Suddenly, I had less time to wallow in my grief over Cory's death; I was too busy cleaning up after Allie's potty accidents and teaching her not to use my arms as chew toys. My friend, my parents, and I all felt the emptiness that results when an aging dog dies. We all dealt with that emptiness differently — and that's okay. There's no single right or wrong time to welcome a new pet after an old one dies. In the end, the right time is as individual as the individuals involved. Still, here are some general principles to keep in mind as you decide if and when to begin life with a new four-footed friend:

- ✔ **Confront what's happened.** Most experts counsel against getting a new dog if you haven't at least begun to work through and understand your grief over the dog who's died. Your grieving doesn't have to be complete, but you do need to be at the point where you feel capable of making an intelligent decision about selecting a new dog.

- ✔ **Seek change.** To be fair to all concerned, try to adopt an animal who looks at least somewhat different from your departed senior. By choosing a dog whose looks differ significantly from those of your late, great senior, you're better able to appreciate the new dog's unique qualities instead of comparing him to the dog who's no longer here.

- ✔ **Trust your instincts.** If you meet a wonderful dog but don't feel ready to welcome a new canine companion, trust your gut and pass him by. Every dog deserves an owner who's ready to give him the same unconditional love that he will offer his human. When you meet the right dog, you'll know — and a wonderful new adventure can begin.

Senior Super Dogs: Presley lives on

Unlike her male namesake, she didn't swivel her hips. She didn't wear sequined jumpsuits, nor did she sport a Brylcreemed pompadour. Playing a guitar and singing about hound dogs were quite beyond her abilities. Still, when the Spikloser family of Reisterstown, Maryland, brought their puppy home, they named her Presley. "We named her after Elvis even though she was a girl," admits her 'dad', Ron Spikloser, VMD (Technical Editor on this book).

Presley was a peppy puppy: "a 9-pound poodle with a spirit as big as all get out," says Ron. As a puppy, she barked at everything and everyone, never biting but annoying the people who didn't know her. "But as soon as people were with her for a moment — not even minutes — they fell in love with her," Ron says. Fortunately, the Spiklosers had lots of time to love Presley — nearly 18 years.

Still, age eventually caught up with Presley. As she grew older, she had trouble with her eyesight and lost her hearing. She also suffered from arthritis, dementia, heart problems, urine leakage, and "uncountable tumors," Ron recalls. "But she never complained and was still trying to do her thing."

Eventually, Presley was overwhelmed by her ailments. "Her arthritis was getting worse, and none of the medicines were helping enough," Ron says. "The ice [from winter storms] magnified the problems and helped [me] overcome my denial." He euthanized Presley at home, surrounded by the rest of the family.

Although he's a vet, Ron's grief is much like other dog owners'. "I did a lot of grieving before we put her to sleep. I was sad, cried at times, and felt helpless. As a vet I thought I should be able to do something." He was also angry because he wanted her to die in her sleep, which rarely happens.

Now that Presley's gone, Ron and his family miss her and still experience periods of sadness. "But then I become grateful that we had her for 18 years and reflect back on the love we showed each other. As long as we talk about her and reflect on her stories, she will be alive in our hearts."

Courtesy of Ronald Spikloser, VMD

Part V
The Part of Tens

The 5th Wave   By Rich Tennant

In this part . . .

Caring for a senior dog can be considerably more demanding and difficult than caring for a pooch who's in the prime of his life. In addition, knowing that your senior may pass on sooner rather than later may cast a shadow over the time you spend with your aging friend. In Part V, I offer help to offset those challenges and dispel that shadow by reminding you about the many ways senior dogs enhance our lives and how we can enhance theirs.

Chapter 16

Ten Reasons to Appreciate Your Senior Dog

In This Chapter

▶ Remembering why senior dogs are great

▶ Appreciating your senior's special qualities

*Y*ou love your senior dog to distraction and treasure her as you would any other member of your family. But although you adore her and value her, be honest: Caring for her isn't always easy.

For one thing, you know that your days with her are probably numbered. You no longer have what feels like an infinite amount of time with which to bond with your precious pooch. Knowing that your time has reached its twilight can add nearly unbearable poignancy to your day-to-day interactions with her.

Then you face all the issues that seniorhood seems to bring along with it. Almost certainly, your dog has slowed down, or she will in the foreseeable future. In addition, she may not see or hear you as well as she used to, and she may need more trips to the outdoor potty if you want her bathroom manners to stay up to par. And, just like your elderly Uncle Albert, your aging four-legged friend probably needs to visit the doctor — or, more accurately, her veterinarian — more often than she needed to in her prime.

But for all the downers and disadvantages that are part of living with an older dog, you have at least as many reasons to savor this time in your pooch's life. In fact, many people enjoy canine seniorhood so much that they skip puppyhood and young adulthood and instead opt for adopting an aging canine from an animal shelter or rescue group. Here are ten reasons to appreciate any dog's golden years.

She Potties in All the Right Places

Yes, your canine companion needs to potty more often. But after you get her to her bathroom — whether indoors or outdoors — you know she'll do her business exactly where she's supposed to.

The senior dog is already housetrained, so you don't need to engage in the tedious business of watching the clock, taking Fifi out according to a rigid schedule, and keeping an eagle eye on her at all other times to ensure that she doesn't take a whiz or unload a deposit in the wrong place. You've been there, done that. For you and your older dog, taking care of bathroom business is a snap, even if you have to take her out more often than you used to.

His Demolition Days Are Done

Just typing that heading causes me to envy you. Why? Because although I'm crazy about Allie, my 1-year-old Golden Retriever, she poses a grave danger to my house — and sometimes to herself. That's because my golden girl likes to check out anything that isn't nailed to the floor or a wall. Among the items she regularly sniffs, licks, and chews in an apparent effort to find out more about her world are toilet paper, paper towels, elastic hair scrunchies that my daughter drops on the floor, wooden spoons, and knives. Oh, and I almost forgot: matches. Yes, Allie plays with matches — although, thankfully, she's shown no interest in trying to light them.

But you, the fortunate owner of a settled senior, probably don't have to deal with Demolition Dog behavior anymore. The only sign that your dog even notices your floor pillows is the dent that's left when he gets up from a nap on one of them. He's long past the stage that Allie's in, where the stuffing of said pillows would be strewn all over the floor if I didn't watch her carefully. No holes puncture your carpet as a result of your four-legged friend's interest in archaeology (with Allie, we've already had to replace the carpet on our stairs because she gouged a 6-foot-square hole in it).

Perhaps best of all, you don't have to watch your well-behaved friend at all times to ensure that he doesn't get into trouble. You can leave the house and know that when you get back it won't look as though a tornado barreled through it. For you and your aging pooch, dog-proofing is part of the distant past.

Meanwhile, I'll look forward to Allie's seniorhood as a time when . . . oops, gotta go. I hear her unraveling the toilet paper again. . . .

What You See Is What You Get

The senior pooch is the perfect example of a WYSIWYG dog: What you see is what you get — and what you'll keep getting. The only way her looks are likely to change is if she develops the silvery muzzle or white face that reflects a long, well-lived life. And, for the most part, her behavior doesn't change much either. She thrives on predictability every day. In return for the consistency you offer her, she offers the same to you.

Puppies, on the other hand, are another ball of wax — or, rather, fluff. Some of those little fluff balls may stay little, while others may morph into canine versions of Chewbacca, the Star Wars wookie. And don't think that by getting a purebred, you know what you're getting. Even when you know your puppy's parentage and have a five-generation pedigree to show, you can't be totally sure how much your puppy will grow or what he'll look like. Again, my golden Allie serves as an example. Although her parents are both champion show dogs, Allie's grown bigger than the breed standard (kind of like the written blueprint) for Golden Retrievers. And even basic elements such as coat colors are up for grabs when dogs haven't fully matured. Allie has a creamy blonde coat, but one of her littermates is as red as an Irish Setter — even though the two looked almost identical as puppies.

Puppies are full of surprises, whether you like surprises or not. If you're a person who craves consistency, your best four-legged friend is more likely to be a consistency-loving senior.

She Has Good Manners

Chances are, your senior dog is a mannerly creature. She doesn't jump up on you to get your attention. When you pet her, she doesn't get all wiggly; she sits politely. If visitors arrive, she's not likely to make a fuss and start barking to signal a canine-style "Intruder alert!" Heck, she may not even hear the doorbell ring.

And if you have a large dog, do you remember the days when your canine Amazon would plunk her paws atop the kitchen counter in order to score some unauthorized goodies? This practice, which many dog people have dubbed *counter-surfing,* is usually history for those who own older dogs. Maybe seniors don't have the stamina to counter-surf. Or maybe they just know better.

Either way, such restraint is one more reason why owners of puppies and young adult dogs may envy those who live with senior dogs. As much as the owners of juvenile canines love their dogs' youthful exuberance, they look forward to the day when their pooches will exercise at least a little restraint. You whose dogs have already achieved that milestone should savor this time accordingly.

Adopting Him Doesn't Break the Bank

If you want to add a senior dog to your pack but hesitate because you remember how much money you spent to buy or adopt a puppy, take heart. Seniors are cheaper. As an example, one rescue group in my area (northern Virginia) requests a donation of $300 to adopt a puppy up to 1 year of age. Adults 1 to 9 years of age fetch a $200 donation. For seniors, the requested donation is just $100. By contrast, a puppy from a northern Virginia breeder of this same breed fetches at least $1,000.

Does this mean seniors are worth less money than puppies are? Not at all! Rescue groups simply recognize that relatively few people have discovered the joys of adopting an older dog. You can help your bottom line by becoming one of those few.

She Sticks Around

I don't let my 1-year-old dog off the leash unless she's in an enclosed area (and if you have a 1-year-old dog, you shouldn't, either). Puppies and young adults not only have considerable wanderlust, but also run too fast for humans to catch. The unhappy result is a lost dog who's at significant risk for being hurt or even killed.

A senior dog, on the other hand, has pretty much tapped out her Inner Wanderer and is happy to dream about her youthful travels while sleeping at your feet and/or near a fireplace. The open road no longer holds much interest for her; she's seen all there is to see and done all there is to do. This is a lady whose experience has taught her the wisdom of appreciating creature comforts, not to mention the person (for example, you) who provides them.

He's Oh-So-Mellow

Puppies and young adult dogs are a hoot. Their counter-surfing, dumpster-diving, breakneck racing and other antics provide wonderful entertainment for their people. Their curiosity and reactions to new experiences help many a human recover his or her own joie-de-vivre and ability to live in the present. Unfortunately, though, the same behaviors that light up our world also have a negative effect: They exhaust us.

Diverting a young canine from getting into the trash, chewing on the electrical cords, or shredding today's newspaper is debilitating. Dealing with a pup's perpetual exuberance is a full-time job. People with puppies wonder when they get their own lives back.

The answer is: when your dog is a senior. The older dog has already indulged in the mischief that intrigues the younger pooch. The world holds few mysteries for this canine man-of-the-world (or woman-of-the-world). He's happy just to spend time with you.

She Knows When to Mind Her Own Business

Older dogs tend to be Velcro dogs — but that doesn't mean that they'll keep you from doing whatever else you have to do. They don't act up; they simply make sure that they are where you are.

For example, if you're sitting in your home-based office, banging away on your computer keyboard so that you can make a deadline for a book you're writing, your senior canine office-mate will be perfectly happy just to snooze behind your chair or under your desk. She won't go routing through your trash, accidentally shut down your computer, attack an incoming fax in a misguided attempt to defend you, or shove toys into your hip in an effort to get you to bag your deadline and come play. Moreover, you won't need to spend an hour in what may be a futile effort to get her to settle down so that you can get your work done.

The senior dog minds her business while you mind yours. Whether it's meeting a deadline, getting the laundry done, or just watching your favorite TV show, the senior Fidette is more than happy to let you do your thing — as long as she's there while you do it.

He Listens

The adolescent or young adult dog frequently is guilty of what savvy owners call "selective deafness." All too often, when you tell him to sit, come (especially when you ask him to come!), lie down, get off the couch, or drop the sock he swiped from the laundry room, his only response is to stare at you blankly. If you didn't know otherwise, you'd swear he didn't know what you were talking about. Of course, words like "cookie," "din-dins," or "walk" result in your canine companion materializing from nowhere right at your feet.

Such selective deafness is typical behavior from a dog who ranges from 6 months to 2 years of age. These canine teenagers are exhibiting the same sort of rebellion — in their own way, of course — that human adolescents show when someone tells them to do something that they don't want to do.

A senior dog doesn't need to rebel. Her adolescent high-jinks are part of another era. The only deafness your aging canine companion may show is the real kind — and if you've read Chapter 7, you already know how to deal with that.

She Worships Her People

Have you noticed how puppies and young adult dogs are too busy to really be affectionate? Oh sure, they give you the occasional lick on the hand. Their antics entertain you for hours. Their misbehavior keeps you alert all day long. But the soulful glance, the head in the lap, the gluing herself to your side, and other signs of canine adoration come much later.

The senior dog — especially if you've adopted her from a shelter or rescue group — knows how good her life is with you. She savors a tummy rub, a gentle massage, an extra goodie slipped into her dinner, and any opportunity to share the couch with you. She takes nothing for granted.

Your older dog, not your younger pooch, rewards the smallest gesture of kindness with a meltingly loving look that comes not just from her eyes but also from her soul. Whether she's savoring the quiet joy of a long-time bond with you or realizing that life is a lot better than it was before you adopted her, the older dog worships the ground you walk on. And she's not afraid to show it.

Chapter 17

Ten Ways to Lengthen Your Senior Dog's Life

As much as you want your dog to live forever — or even as long as you do — the sad truth is that your canine companion is neither immortal nor even able to match the average human being's life span. These facts of canine life and death add a poignant edge to the time that you share with your older four-legged friend.

However, you don't have to wallow in your sadness over the inevitable prospect of saying goodbye to your senior dog sooner rather than later. In fact, you can maximize your dog's chances of living a longer, higher-quality life in plenty of ways. In this chapter, I give you a list of ten ways to help add months or even years of happy, healthy living to your senior dog's life span.

Keep 'Em Fit

Dogs benefit just as much from being physically and mentally sharp as humans do — and that's just as true of senior pooches and people as it is for dogs and humans in their prime. Regular exercise helps the senior canine get fit and stay that way. Physical fitness helps keep the older dog's heart and lungs in good working order; helps him hold the line against life-sapping obesity; enables him to forestall some of the creakiness that old age inevitably bestows upon bones, muscles, and ligaments; helps prevent the boredom that spurs all too many canines to become Destructo Dogs; and gives the aging canine a sense of purpose. In other words, regular exercise not only keeps your dog healthy, it also keeps him happy — and helps keep you happy, too.

Physical fitness for the aging pooch doesn't mean that your graying Fido must tear up an agility course or that your mature Fidette has to fetch a gazillion tennis balls in one exercise session. A couple of moderately paced walks of 20 minutes or so every day can do a lot to keep your older dog's body in good condition. Such walks can help his mind, too. The stimulus of being in an ever-changing outdoor environment can be a source of real pleasure to him. And, perhaps most importantly, daily constitutionals can soothe your senior dog's spirit because those walks give him a chance to be with the individual who matters more to him than anyone else — you.

Of course, walks aren't the only exercise available to the aging canine. Chapter 3 describes a variety of pursuits that work out the body (jogging, swimming, yoga, and canine sports) and the mind (fetching and hide-and-seek). Try any or all of these pursuits with your senior dog after you get a thumbs-up from his vet. You may well find that staying on the move gives your dog a new lease on life.

Keep 'Em Lean

Fat people usually live shorter lives than thin people do. Between the strain that excess weight imposes on the heart, lungs, bones, joints, and ligaments, and the increased risk of life-threatening diseases that too many pounds trigger, no person in his right mind would deliberately allow himself to pork out.

Fortunately, people have considerable control over the sizes of their physiques. People decide how much they're going to eat and how much they're going to exercise. Unfortunately, though, our canine companions don't have that kind of control. They only get to exercise when their owners play games with them, go for walks with them, or take them to the dog park. They also have to eat whatever's put in front of them — and if someone puts too much in front of them, the results can be disastrous.

Veterinarians report that as many as half their patients — canine and otherwise — are overweight. And, as a study from Nestle Purina Pet Care shows, too much food may cause a dog to show signs of aging earlier than she would have with a normal diet and can shave at least two years off her life.

Your canine eager eater isn't capable of deciding that you've put too much food in her dish and walk away from her dining area, especially if you give her grub that she really likes. She can't determine that only a portion of what you've served her fulfills her caloric requirements and tell you to chuck the excess. She depends on you to figure out how much food she needs to stay trim, and she needs you to serve only that amount. She counts on you — whether she knows it or not — to refrain from slipping her too many calorie-laden goodies that can cause her to pork out.

The bottom line here is that the dog with the smaller bottom lives longer than the pooch with the tubby tush. By keeping your four-legged friend's weight where it should be (your vet can help you determine just what weight level you should aim for), you up her chances of living a life that's free of many conditions that can shorten both the quality and quantity of that life. The treat you refuse to give your senior dog today can mean one more tomorrow that she otherwise wouldn't have had.

Brush Those Chompers

Wielding a toothbrush on your senior dog's teeth every day does a lot more than help him avoid having doggy breath. A daily brushing with a soft brush and toothpaste designed especially for dogs can help control and even eliminate the plaque and tartar that cause gum disease. This disease, which starts off as simple gingivitis but progresses to periodontitis if you don't intervene, can result in the eventual loss of your dog's teeth — and cause considerable pain in the meantime.

Even worse is the fact that periodontitis causes infections in the gums that the bloodstream may transport to other areas in the dog's body. Those areas include vital organs, such as the heart and lungs. Infections in these organs can be fatal.

Taking five minutes every day to brush your pooch's pearlies is a small investment with a big payoff: fresh breath, healthy teeth and gums, and the elimination of life-threatening infections. Chapter 5 tells you exactly how to keep your canine's canines (not to mention his other teeth) in mint condition.

Use Your Hands

Hands-on care for your senior dog can benefit both her and you. Studies show that petting a pooch lowers a person's blood pressure and slows her breathing rate and heartbeat. High levels of all three of these vital signs can signal stress. Stress has been shown to shorten a person's life — so by petting your dog, you may boost your own longevity.

Petting your pooch can boost her longevity, too. For one thing, a regular petting fest can help you feel for lumps and bumps when they develop early, and you can have your vet check them out right away. Hands-on love fests also can help you uncover flaky skin or rashes that indicate that your dog's not in tip-top shape. A flinch or wincing response to your touch tells you that your four-legged friend feels pain when touched in that spot, which should prompt you and your vet to investigate further. And, as mentioned in Chapter 3, being pet may help lower a dog's blood pressure and other stress indicators.

Certain kinds of touch, such as massage, acupressure, and Tellington T-Touch, can have even more therapeutic value than regular petting does (see Chapter 3 for more on these therapies). Massage can help reduce your dog's post-workout aches and pains. Acupressure adherents believe that this version of the traditional Chinese medical practice of acupuncture — without the scary needles — can help uncover and even heal certain physical conditions and problems. Tellington T-Touch may help a dog or other animal to overcome a wide range of physical and behavioral ills.

Just as important as the physical benefits to you and your senior dog is the fact that regular touch — whether it's just plain petting or a more sophisticated therapy — can build and maintain the bond between the two of you. Taking a few minutes to literally stay in touch helps you both make the most of this time in your canine companion's life and in your time together.

Limit Changes

As people age, many become more uncomfortable with change than they used to be. Older people don't want things to be any different from the way they've always been — and if they're forced to change, they stress out (at least a little).

Age probably affects your dog the same way. Like you, he takes comfort in consistency. Being able to count on eating in the same place today as he did yesterday or going to the same potty place now as he did this morning gives him feelings of comfort and safety. Routine is to your senior like a blankie is to a human toddler. Both help ensure security to the individual who may not otherwise feel all that secure about his world.

Of course, you can't avoid some changes — either in your life or your dog's. Still, compensating for unavoidable changes by limiting avoidable ones can help your senior pooch cope. For example, if your senior dog becomes blind due to cataracts, glaucoma, or another ailment, now is not the time to rearrange the furniture in your home. His memory of how your crib was configured before he lost his eyesight helps him navigate through your home now that his vision is gone.

The same principle applies to changes in your life that affect your dog. Suppose your elderly parent who's been living with you and who also dotes on your senior dog must relocate to an assisted-living facility. Your dog's probably going to be at least a little grief-stricken at the loss of a beloved friend and may manifest that grief by eating less, moping, or searching the house for the departed family member.

To help your four-legged friend out of his funk, experts generally suggest keeping the rest of his life as unchanged as possible (and also keeping him busy). They even suggest gradually helping other family members spend more time with your senior dog than they have in the past and having your elderly parent spend less time with the animal. Taking such steps limits the impact that the change caused by your parent's departure has on the dog, and thus reduces his stress. Chapter 15 outlines other ways to help the dog who's grieving.

Watch for Changes

Despite a senior dog's general dislike of change, she's going to go through a lot of changes as she grows older. Some of these alterations are normal aspects of the aging process, such as gray hair on the muzzle, a thinner coat, and some impairment of sight and hearing.

But other changes may not be so normal — even though they may be more prevalent in old age than in youth. Many changes in a dog's physical appearance or behavior can reflect the presence of illness. For example, if your aging friend suddenly starts drinking more water, the cause of her thirst may be as simple as a hot day or as complicated as a serious disease, such as diabetes. A senior dog who develops a spongy lump under her skin may have a harmless fatty tumor, or a dangerous cancer. Only a laboratory test can determine the exact nature of the lump. Even seemingly harmless symptoms, such as less stamina when walking, may signal that something's seriously wrong. Chapter 9 outlines these and other symptoms of possible problems your senior may have.

When your dog reaches seniorhood, a baseline wellness exam by your vet can establish what's normal for your pooch and what isn't. (Chapter 5 explains in detail why this exam is important and what the vet will look for.) But because you're with your dog every day, you're in a better position than your vet to know immediately when her body or behavior changes. If you see any changes for the worse in your dog's physique or behavior — and especially if you see more than one such change — don't hesitate. Contact your veterinarian.

Adjust for Age

You need to help your canine companion make adjustments in his lifestyle for his age. The retriever who used to relish swimming in the ocean surf may now need to confine his aquatic maneuvers to a warm, slow-moving pond. The wiener dog who loved hopping up on the couch to share some space with you probably would appreciate being lifted onto your lap now. The Doberman who used to love sleeping on a hard floor probably would prefer to snooze in a nice soft bed now that he's reached senior status.

Other physical conditions, although not necessarily age-related, also require fine-tuning on your part so that you can help your dog deal. Chapter 7 explains that blind dogs need to have unchanging surroundings so that they can navigate through them and that deaf dogs need for their people to find new, soundless ways to communicate with them. Chapter 6 points out that your senior dog probably doesn't have the iron bladder of his youth, and that you need to respond to that change by getting him to his bathroom more often.

People need to be comfortable with their dogs' aging process. Wishing the years away can't reverse or even suspend the passage of time. Life goes on for both you and your four-legged friend. The trick to enjoying your dog's maturity is to accept where he is now in his age, have the good sense not to push him beyond his current limits, and to savor this special time that you have together.

Be Proactive

"An ounce of prevention is worth a pound of cure." I know that this quote is a trite truism, but, well . . . it's true. And if your dog has reached seniorhood, you have an especially compelling reason to take that truth to heart.

Your vet has a much easier time taking care of your aging canine if he has a chance to catch problems early, if not prevent them entirely. But because your vet doesn't see your older dog all that often, it's up to you — the owner who sees her every day — to be on the alert for signs of illness and to take a little extra time to catch possible problems that may be hiding from your view. In short, when it comes to safeguarding your senior dog's health, you need to be proactive.

The proactive owner's first line of defense is to take his dog for a baseline veterinary exam as soon as the dog reaches seniorhood. The baseline, or initial, exam establishes what's normal for your dog and provides the standard that your vet will compare every future exam and test with.

After the baseline exam is behind you, plan to take your old friend for wellness checkups every six months. Twice-yearly checkups give your vet additional opportunities to catch problems early and to monitor your dog's aging process.

At home, keep track of your dog's health exams and other procedures. Note when she had her last checkup and mark on your calendar when you need to call for the next wellness exam. Some owners find that using a doggy diary helps them remember unusual events or occurrences that they can report to the vet on subsequent visits. You can make this journal even more useful if you include copies of lab-test reports. Such reports, kept close at hand, can help you work with any vet to achieve and maintain optimal health for your four-legged friend.

For all dogs — but especially for senior dogs — prevention is paramount. Being proactive now can save you and your dog a lot of pain later on.

Trust Your Instincts

No one knows your dog better than you do. The people who help you care for him — your vet, your groomer, your pet-sitter, and others — can share knowledge and expertise that you can use to give your dog the best life possible. But they see your dog only every few weeks, so they can't possibly have the knowledge that comes from living with your dog day in, day out for years. Consequently, figuring out whether your dog is behaving normally is a dicey proposition for any of these pros.

But you should be able to make such determinations a lot more easily. You've invested time and love in your aging canine companion, and that investment has resulted in a knowledge and understanding of your dog that no one else has. Nobody else is in a better position to know when something's amiss with your four-legged friend and when everything is just fine.

So if your dog behaves in a way that differs from his usual demeanor or shows other signs of not feeling up to par, act on your knowledge. Report any such changes to your vet and work with her to determine what strategy you should use. Above all, don't ever be afraid to contact your vet because you think that you're making a fuss over nothing or that she'll tell you that nothing is going on. An owner's instincts are the best tools a vet has for discovering problems early — and the earlier you find those problems, the more likely you are to resolve them. If you think something's amiss with your dog, trust your intuition. Depending on what you're observing, call your vet — or at least watch your dog with even greater care than usual (see Chapter 9).

Lay On the Love

At this time in your dog's life, there's no such thing as giving her too much love. If you've cared for your senior dog for most her life, now's the time to let her know how much you appreciate the devotion and affection that she's given you all these years. If you've adopted your senior dog fairly recently, you want to let her know that here, in your home, she can feel safe and loved for the rest of her life.

Go on: Get down on the floor and coo baby talk into your four-legged friend's ears. Consider lightening up on some of your no-getting-up-on-the-bed-and-couch rules. Pet her at every opportunity and treat her to a massage when you have more time. And speaking of treats, lighten up and slip her one every now and then (if her physique and health permit it).

You don't need to confine loving gestures to indoors, either. Take your dog to her favorite places: the woods, the beach, the mountains, the kids' soccer games, an outdoor bar or restaurant that allows dogs to dine with their people. Take her traveling with you, if you can. Let her supervise when you're out in your garden, and let her eat on the patio when you and your family do.

Knowing that someone loves you helps anyone live a higher-quality life. That fact holds just as true for your dog as it does for you. You'll never regret making all this extra effort to please your senior dog — not now, and certainly not in the future, when your four-legged friend is no longer with you. Doing all you can to make your dog's golden years the best they can possibly be and going out of your way to show her how much you cherish her are gifts that brighten the remainder of her life and create memories that brighten the rest of yours.

Index

FOR DUMMIES®

A world of resources to help you grow

TRAVEL

0-7645-5453-0   **0-7645-5438-7**   **0-7645-5444-1**

Also available:

America's National Parks For Dummies
(0-7645-6204-5)

Caribbean For Dummies
(0-7645-5445-X)

Cruise Vacations For Dummies 2003
(0-7645-5459-X)

Europe For Dummies
(0-7645-5456-5)

Ireland For Dummies
(0-7645-6199-5)

France For Dummies
(0-7645-6292-4)

Las Vegas For Dummies
(0-7645-5448-4)

London For Dummies
(0-7645-5416-6)

Mexico's Beach Resorts For Dummies
(0-7645-6262-2)

Paris For Dummies
(0-7645-5494-8)

RV Vacations For Dummies
(0-7645-5443-3)

EDUCATION & TEST PREPARATION

0-7645-5194-9   **0-7645-5325-9**   **0-7645-5249-X**

Also available:

The ACT For Dummies
(0-7645-5210-4)

Chemistry For Dummies
(0-7645-5430-1)

English Grammar For Dummies
(0-7645-5322-4)

French For Dummies
(0-7645-5193-0)

GMAT For Dummies
(0-7645-5251-1)

Inglés Para Dummies
(0-7645-5427-1)

Italian For Dummies
(0-7645-5196-5)

Research Papers For Dummies
(0-7645-5426-3)

SAT I For Dummies
(0-7645-5472-7)

U.S. History For Dummie
(0-7645-5249-X)

World History For Dummies
(0-7645-5242-2)

HEALTH, SELF-HELP & SPIRITUALITY

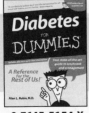 

0-7645-5154-X   **0-7645-5302-X**   **0-7645-5418-2**

Also available:

The Bible For Dummies
(0-7645-5296-1)

Controlling Cholesterol For Dummies
(0-7645-5440-9)

Dating For Dummies
(0-7645-5072-1)

Dieting For Dummies
(0-7645-5126-4)

High Blood Pressure For Dummies
(0-7645-5424-7)

Judaism For Dummies
(0-7645-5299-6)

Menopause For Dummie
(0-7645-5458-1)

Nutrition For Dummies
(0-7645-5180-9)

Potty Training For Dummies
(0-7645-5417-4)

Pregnancy For Dummie
(0-7645-5074-8)

Rekindling Romance Fo
Dummies
(0-7645-5303-8)

Religion For Dummies
(0-7645-5264-3)

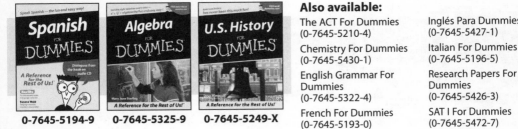

Available wherever books are sold. Go to www.dummies.com or call 1-877-762-2974 to order direct

FOR DUMMIES®

A world of resources to help you grow

FOR DUMMIES®

Helping you expand your horizons and realize your potential

GRAPHICS & WEB SITE DEVELOPMENT

0-7645-1651-5   **0-7645-1643-4**   **0-7645-0895-4**

Also available:

Adobe Acrobat 5 PDF For Dummies
(0-7645-1652-3)

ASP.NET For Dummies
(0-7645-0866-0)

ColdFusion MX for Dummies
(0-7645-1672-8)

Dreamweaver MX For Dummies
(0-7645-1630-2)

FrontPage 2002 For Dummies
(0-7645-0821-0)

HTML 4 For Dummies
(0-7645-0723-0)

Illustrator 10 For Dummies
(0-7645-3636-2)

PowerPoint 2002 For Dummies
(0-7645-0817-2)

Web Design For Dummies
(0-7645-0823-7)

PROGRAMMING & DATABASES

0-7645-0746-X   **0-7645-1626-4**   **0-7645-1657-4**

Also available:

Access 2002 For Dummies
(0-7645-0818-0)

Beginning Programming For Dummies
(0-7645-0835-0)

Crystal Reports 9 For Dummies
(0-7645-1641-8)

Java & XML For Dummies
(0-7645-1658-2)

Java 2 For Dummies
(0-7645-0765-6)

JavaScript For Dummies
(0-7645-0633-1)

Oracle9i For Dummies
(0-7645-0880-6)

Perl For Dummies
(0-7645-0776-1)

PHP and MySQL For Dummies
(0-7645-1650-7)

SQL For Dummies
(0-7645-0737-0)

Visual Basic .NET For Dummies
(0-7645-0867-9)

LINUX, NETWORKING & CERTIFICATION

0-7645-1545-4   **0-7645-1760-0**   **0-7645-0772-9**

Also available:

A+ Certification For Dummies
(0-7645-0812-1)

CCNP All-in-One Certification For Dummies
(0-7645-1648-5)

Cisco Networking For Dummies
(0-7645-1668-X)

CISSP For Dummies
(0-7645-1670-1)

CIW Foundations For Dummies
(0-7645-1635-3)

Firewalls For Dummies
(0-7645-0884-9)

Home Networking For Dummies
(0-7645-0857-1)

Red Hat Linux All-in-One Desk Reference For Dummies
(0-7645-2442-9)

UNIX For Dummies
(0-7645-0419-3)

Available wherever books are sold.
Go to www.dummies.com or call 1-877-762-2974 to order direct

WILEY